*Modern Hawaiian Gamefishing*

# Modern Hawaiian Gamefishing

JIM RIZZUTO

*A Kolowalu Book*
THE UNIVERSITY PRESS OF HAWAII Ⓧ
Honolulu

Manufactured in the United States of America

*Line drawings by Judy Hancock*

**Library of Congress Cataloging in Publication Data**

Rizzuto, Jim, 1939–
    Modern Hawaiian gamefishing.

    (A Kolowalu book)
    Bibliography:    p.
    Includes index.
    1.   Fishing—Hawaii.    I.   Title.
SH679.H3R59                 799.1'2'09969              76-58414
ISBN 0-8248-0481-3

In Memory of Peter Budge

# Contents

# *Preface*

THE HOOK AND LINE fishing methods used in Hawai'i are so different from those employed in other parts of the world that standard reference books on salt water fishing are of little value to the serious island angler. It is easy to see why this difference exists. The fish have different habits, and often even different identities. The environment presents obstacles and advantages found in few other places. The fishermen themselves have evolved from a different cultural heritage.

Since the days of the first Hawaiian fisherman, who plied his trade sometime before A.D. 750, an extensive treasury of island fishing lore has developed, extending to the techniques of the modern angler with his sophisticated space-age equipment. No comprehensive analysis of all of these diverse hook and line methods has yet been compiled. This book is intended to fill the gap. It is written in the words and deeds of hundreds of expert fishermen for whom angling is both a sport and a way of life.

Several contemporary sports fishermen deserve special mention for their unique contributions to this book.

Ken Ozaki first introduced me to the sport of whipping with light spinning tackle and has remained my tutor for fifteen years of stalking the inshore waters of O'ahu, Moloka'i, and Hawai'i.

Zander Budge steered me to my first offshore game fish and has unselfishly shared his skills, his knowledge, his equipment, and the companionship of his princely personality.

Freddy Rice has always dreamed of a book about marlin fishing—the Kona way. Toward this end he kept hundreds of pages of notes on techniques and theories of fishing, as well as personal reminiscences of frequent encounters with billfish and tuna. When he heard of my efforts to produce this book, he volunteered his notes without hesitation. It is a far better work for his contributions.

Peter Hoogs is an innovative fisherman constantly searching for better ways to catch fish. More than merely hooking and landing them, he has used his special talents as a cameraman to capture the exclusive world of big game fishing. His discoveries and his pictures illustrate many of the peculiarities of marine angling.

Bart Miller would not, and could not, take sole credit for originating the fishing methods he describes in the chapter "Bart and Bait." An account of the techniques Bart discusses might have been given by any of a hundred of Hawai'i's professional fishing skippers. But none could have done it with the same mixture of passion and authority. Bart's narrative took place at the 1973 symposium of the Hawaiian International Billfish Tournament.

And, of course, Bette Fay. These words are being written just as the report has come of Bette's death. Her efforts over more than a decade have resulted in a continuous record of the daily statistics of Kona fishing, diligently gathered and published in her weekly column in *West Hawaii Today*.

Special thanks go to Leighton Taylor, director of the Waikiki Aquarium, for his help in checking the scientific names of the fishes, and to editor Norma Gorst for untangling the loose coils of my lines to prevent verbal backlashes. Authorities for spellings, with diacritical marks, of the Hawaiian words are the Pukui-Elbert *Hawaiian Dictionary* and *Place Names of Hawaii* by Pukui, Elbert, and Mookini.

All of the line drawings—for the text figures and the vignettes that help introduce each chapter—are the work of artist Judy Hancock.

Several parts of the book have been adapted from articles I've written for magazines. My thanks go to Frank Woolner, editor of *The Salt Water Sportsman,* for permission to use parts of "Go

Light for Aku,'' November 1970 (chapter 5), "Small Boats and Big Fish,'' March 1972 (chapter 7), "Hawaii's Mighty Midget,'' July 1972 (also chapter 5), "Rig for Fast Running,'' March 1973 (chapter 4), and "Down Deep in Hawaii,'' December 1974 (chapter 9); and to Jack Samson, editor of *Field & Stream,* for the rights to "Plug in for Big Game Fish,'' April 1973 (chapter 1).

Where should a book on Hawaiian fishing begin? Each of us would answer the question differently, depending on whether we prowl the shallows in *tabi*-ed feet, or churn blue water in the constant chase for the biggest fish in the ocean. Begin this book anywhere. Each chapter is written to tell its own story; none needs any other.

To be sure, there is an order to the sequence of information presented here, but that order has been only gently imposed on a subject for which diversity is a major feature. We've started offshore in boats, luring and baiting the marlin, tuna, and sharks. Our focus is always on those aspects of Hawai'i's fishing you will never learn from any general reference book on big game fishing. We've moved from the heavyweights to the middleweights (mahimahi, ono, and ulua) to the lightweights (aku and kawakawa).

Before deserting boat fishing, we've explored how to fight a fish from a powered craft, how to outfit a boat for fishing, where to look for fish, and how to probe the bottom for the deep-living and delicious fish.

Once on solid ground, we've turned our attention to the basic inshore methods. An appendix of recipes for preparing fish should give you something to chew on, while some personal reflections on some of the more intriguing aspects of Hawai'i's fishing should give you something to chew on mentally.

*Modern Hawaiian Gamefishing*

# 1
# *Breaking the Rules in Hawai'i*
## BIG GAME ON LURES, THE HAWAIIAN WAY

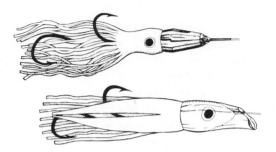

THE MORE YOU KNOW about big game fishing in the rest of the world, the more you will be surprised by the methods Hawai'i's anglers use to establish more billfish and tuna records than any other band of fishermen in any other marine locale. We break all of the rules of big game fishing by trolling at high speeds with artificial lures designed to enrage big fish rather than to feed them.

Everywhere else in the blue-water world, expert anglers cautiously entice finning billfish with the promise of a juicy meal of bonito, flyingfish, or maybe even deboned eel. Hawai'i's billfish don't fin; they must be found some other way. Three-fourths of Hawai'i's offshore catches are made by provoking the fish into belting something that bears only a superficial resemblance to anything they've ever eaten before or will ever try to eat again.

The three world-record marlin caught during the first two days of the 1973 Hawaiian International Billfish Tournament (HIBT), like nearly all of the other marlin and tuna caught in every Hawaiian fishing contest, smacked plastic trolling plugs. The largest marlin ever landed on sporting tackle, a 1,805-pound Pacific blue bigger than an entire baseball team, committed suicide by trying to murder a 10-inch plug.

There is no reason why fishing with Hawaiian lures shouldn't be just as successful in the Bahamas, the Sea of Cortez, or anywhere else big billfish bash baits. Perhaps it's because our kind of lure fishing is so poorly understood that it is not a standard fishing method elsewhere. If a plug is used at all in the Atlantic, for example, it is generally run without a hook and referred to disparagingly as just a "teaser," a device intended merely to excite a trophy fish so that it'll attack a "real" bait.

Just running a plug at the same speed as you would a rigged bait is a mistake. You can't correctly skip a flyingfish at the 8 or 9 knots it takes to make a plug work at its frantic best. Your flyingfish would spend all of its time trying to put its tail into its mouth.

But why skip flyingfish anyway? I talked with veteran Kona charter skipper Jack Ross before a trip on which he was to host a California team that specifically wanted to use flyers. Jack was unhappy.

"I've skipped a couple of hundred pounds of those *mālolo* in my life and never caught a marlin on the stuff. These fellows even air-shipped their mālolo in frozen from California when we told them we couldn't get any. This is going to be one of those days."

Later that day, after hearing Jack report over the CB radio that his team had just boated a marlin, I couldn't resist asking if he had a new opinion of flyingfish.

"Hell, no," he countered. "That fish hit a white plug with a bloodshot eye. These guys got tired of listening to what everybody else was catching and decided to quit fooling around."

Why should a lure work when bait doesn't? The typical angler's idea of a plug is a realistic replica of some common bait fish designed to act in as natural a way as possible. Not so with a Hawaiian marlin lure.

Our marlin plugs do not "imitate" anything. A properly working plug neither looks like, nor acts like, any living creature marlin feed on. If it did, they probably wouldn't strike at it. The amount of food value represented by a swimming creature with a total length of 10 inches just could not interest an 1,805-pound marlin enough to work his huge bulk up to chasing speed.

That is not to suggest a marlin wouldn't eat a tiny tidbit that could be gulped in passing. Peter Hoogs of the boat *Pamela* has observed marlin leisurely picking their way through a school of helpless pufferfish drifting at the surface with distended air sacs that rendered them completely unable to escape. But the eating of these small puffers required very little wasted energy on the marlin's part.

The fact that a marlin is quite willing to hang on to an object that bears no resemblance to anything edible is well documented. The crew of the Kona boat *Kakina* knows how crazy these volatile creatures are. An angler on board was putting a new line on a reel by cranking the line off the manufacturer's spool as it was being dragged in the water astern to maintain constant tension. A marlin grabbed the whirling, gurgling spool and hung on for seven jumps. He could have let it go anytime—there were no hooks attached. That spool could not possibly have either looked like, or acted like, anything the marlin had ever eaten. And certainly it could not have tasted like anything edible unless the company that makes the glue for the labels has an undiscovered secret weapon.

How long did it take that fish to figure out that the spool was not something to eat? Certainly not seven jumps' worth. Well then, what did he think he was doing with it? He knew he wasn't eating it and he wasn't jumping to get rid of it, because *it* wasn't hanging on to *him*. That was a curious fish exploring something brand new on his horizon.

Marlin have been known to take a plug, hang on, let go, then come back and repeat the process until they finally get hooked. Zander Budge on his boat *Spooky Luki* had a 600-pound marlin solidly strike one of the short flatlines and then race back to grab two other lines in spite of the fact that he was solidly hooked, eventually by all three lures. Either marlin have no taste buds at all, or they don't really expect the thrashing lures to be edible in the first place.

Their curiosity can be amazingly frustrating. Francis Ruddles, skipper of the *Vici*, was hosting football great Darryl Lamonica on a billfish expedition when they noticed a long, dark shape trailing the yellow flare-nosed jumper Francis tows 20 feet behind the transom just outside the prop wash. The marlin held his position for a mile while carefully inspecting the hopping, diving oddity. Finally, the big billfish lighted up his feeding colors and crashed the bait, adding himself to the football player's trophy collection.

Add to all this the fact that plugs seem to take bigger fish than live baits do, and the mystery of their attraction deepens. Many successful Hawaiian skippers tow live bonito or yellowfin tuna baits to entice marlin. The typical catch on live bait is rarely over 300 pounds. The bigger fish are usually caught on nothing but plunging, splashing plugs.

Hunger is not the answer. Every skipper can tell you a story of a supremely well fed marlin that became a maniac when he spotted a lure. That 1,805-pound monster marlin had his belly full of undigested prime *sashimi* in the form of a 150-pound yellowfin tuna. The evidence against hunger includes not only the biggest marlin ever caught, but also the smallest. When Charley Spinney of the fishing boat *Hawaiian* reeled in his lines at the end of an August trolling trip he noticed an odd creature tangled in the filaments of the skirt on one of his lures. It was a 4½-inch marlin, perfectly formed, which had obviously tried to attack a lure more than twice as big as itself. The striking instinct starts early.

OK, so why do they work? To understand, you have to know what a trolling plug looks like and how it acts in the water. These plastic tempters average between 8 and 10 inches long but may run as big as 16. From one-fourth to one-half of the total length is a solid plastic head with a central hole big enough to take a 500-

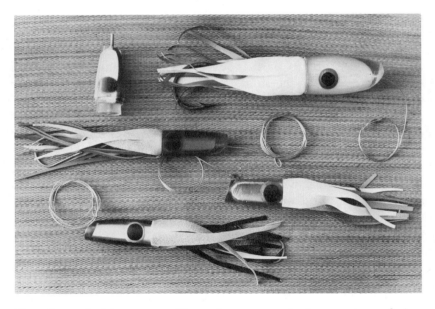

Hawaiian-style big-game trolling plugs are made in a variety of sizes, shapes, colors, and actions. The head in the upper left corner shows the lure as it comes from the mold, before polishing and without a skirt.

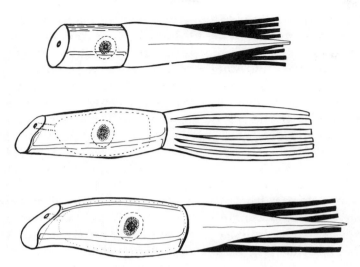

The action of the Hawaiian big-game plug is determined by the angle of the front face, the position of the leader hole, and the convexity of the sides. The three basic shapes are the straight runner, or "Henry Chee" lure *(top)*, the Konahead or "K. O. Dean" lure *(middle)*, and the flare lip *(bottom)*, in order from least to most active.

pound-test cable leader. The front end of the plug is cut at an angle and may be either perfectly flat or channeled.

The shape of the front end determines the action, and each angler has his own pet theories about just what silhouette is best. One of the most effective lures for the past two decades has been the simplest, the "straight runner" pioneered by Henry Chee on the *Malia*. With straight sides, a dead center leader hole, and an attack angle of about 15 degrees from the perpendicular, the lure relies somewhat on the action of an outrigger, which adds markedly to its effectiveness. Chee's son Butch still proves its power over marlin with such excellent catches as the stunning trio hooked on the first day of the 1973 billfish tournament. One of these, a 669 pounder, became the women's all-tackle record, thanks to the durability of diminutive anglerette Doris Jones.

Attached to the typical head are two skirts. The inner skirt is plastic or rubber (red inner tube rubber is a Kona favorite) cut into strips. The overskirt is a pair of triangular panels cut from silverflake plastic auto seat cover material. Skirts vary little from lure to lure. Their main function is to hide the hooks. All of the lure maker's art is concentrated on fashioning the head.

Actions vary markedly from the straight runners to the frantic jumpers, but the one thing all lures have in common when they are working correctly is the jet stream of bubbles. Plugs plunge along just under the surface making quick trips above water to gulp more air, which they drag under with them to form a continuous trail of bubbles. This jet stream is the difference between a plug and a feather jig of the same size. The leadhead doesn't make one and draws few marlin strikes. As a matter of fact, no natural food acting in a normal behavior pattern makes the bubble trail. Actively feeding tuna don't even churn one up when they are leaping in and out of the water. Flyingfish make only the shortest of bursts, barely detectable, while taking off and then no more, even when landing. A plug's jet trail is different. This stream of foamy bubbles is an entirely new experience for the marlin. Mr. and Mrs. Marlin seem always willing to try something new.

Hawaiian plugs come in all colors technology can dream up, sometimes all in the same lure. A long-standing favorite is the "rainbow" plug made with streaks of red, yellow, and blue molded around a pair of mirrors that flash out through the clear plastic. Pale purple and light blue plugs, with mirrors of course, are top producers in tournament competition where results can be measured, since the lure that caught the fish is inspected in public by judges to make sure all aspects satisfy International Game Fish Association (IGFA) regulations. Of all kinds, the lures with pearl strips inside seem to be leading the pack in recent years, but it's probably not possible to make a lure in a color that won't catch fish—even black, which was anathema to the ancient Hawaiians. Some modern anglers swear by the "pepperhead," which is cast around a black insert that has been splashed with silver freckles.

But does color really mean anything? Ask a group of old-time fishermen and you'll get twice as many opinions as there are anglers. That's because fishermen are apt to change their minds in mid-sentence. "Color doesn't mean a damn thing, but I do have a blue lure that outfishes everything else I own."

Charley Spinney departs from the theories of his Hawaiian ancestors by claiming, "Color is for the fishermen, not the fish." The ancients were very careful to match their pearl-shell lures to the light conditions. Their modern counterparts use systems based on hue—bright lures for bright days, dark lures for dull days. One skipper swears that color preference changes with the season and relies heavily on yellow in the spring. The only plug marlin hit on any Kona boat for three days one summer was bright orange. It takes a lot of courage to put out such an unnatural looking thing and expect a noble fish to try to eat it. Unless, of course, you don't think plugs are supposed to imitate anything real.

The typical fisherman runs a pattern of from two to six plugs, using those which have proved successful in the past for his boat along with a few new lures to test against his old standards, in preparation for the day when he loses one. When he does lose one, the CB radio crackles for hours with the heartfelt commiseration of his colleagues. For some reason that maybe even the fish don't understand, one plug will get hot for days, and then, suddenly, all strikes will switch to an entirely different one. It doesn't reflect any change in diet because stomach contents don't seem to vary much from season to season.

Perhaps the major reason anglers like plugs is their efficiency. There is no mess and no time lost getting and rigging baits. You might have to change a skirt now and then when a fish gets too rough with it, but tying on new skirts just makes you feel a bit more useful. The most important advantage is that you can troll at a rate that explores a lot of water fast—8 knots is average and fish can be caught while lures are bouncing along at 12. Sheer mathematics gives the nod to a fishing method that allows you to cover more water in less time, as long as the attractive characteristics of the lure aren't decreased.

Perhaps it is superstition rather than logic, but many experienced anglers want their lures to have eyes. The bigger the orb, the better. The fact that an eye is not a necessity has been proven time and again by all of the billfish and tuna that have been taken on "blind lures."

One outstanding example of this is the 193-pound yellowfin tuna landed by Bernice Spalding during the 1972 HIBT. If you are familiar with the record books, you'll know that at that time this fish was only 12 ounces under the IGFA mark for the 80-pound-class tackle Miss Spalding was using. The record has since been broken repeatedly. It was four hours before the fish was weighed and probably bested the record when first boated. The tuna hit an eyeless pearlhead plug with an overskirt of *mahimahi* (dolphin fish) skin.

Even the placement of the eye is controversial. An experienced Kona fisherman like skipper Zander Budge, who once held the

IGFA 80-pound-test record for Pacific blue marlin, will tell you to "get that eye as far back on the lure as you can, and never mind if it looks backward." It may sound like witchcraft, but Zander insists that a marlin will grab the lure by the eyes, and that means you'll get more hookups with the eyes back near the hooks.

Smart lure makers can double the price of a lure just by putting those eyes in, and the cost of even a blind plug staggers most newcomers to the sport. There is no misplaced decimal—the typical price is twelve to fifteen dollars, with some going as high as thirty!

The materials aren't expensive, probably less than a dollar a lure; it's the labor. Plugs are cast in rubber molds with liquid resin, and, if they came out of the mold with the right surface finish, they would cost about one-third the current price. A chemical reaction between the rubber of the mold and the plastic resin keeps the surface from hardening completely. A gummy film covers the lure, and this must be either scraped off by hand with a sharp knife or rubbed off with acetone. Several grades of wet sandpaper smooth the lure further, and a final polish with rubbing compound brings up a hard, glossy surface. The entire process may require as much as an hour of hand labor and a half-day of setting time, during which the mold cannot be used for more than one

A marlin always strikes an artificial lure in the heat of excitement, often racing across the surface to intercept it. This 200-pound fish has not yet caught the lure and is still chasing it.

lure. For those of you who want to try your creative talents, complete instructions are included in chapter 14.

The finished plug will take not only marlin and tuna, but also dolphin, wahoo, amberjack, rainbow runner, and many other small and medium-sized game fish. For these latter species, the provocative aspects of the lure's action may be of less importance because the size of the plug fits well within the meaningful food range. Dolphin and wahoo, for example, seem to have no preference for plugs over feather jigs, which don't make bubbles. These middleweights seem to grab whatever is closest, or has a color that appeals to them at the moment. There is little doubt that they see a plug as a good meal rather than a curious invader.

One constant feature of plugs is the attachment of the hooks. Unlike a bass plug, the hooks are not hung from the lure itself but are fastened to the leader which slides freely through the center of the lure. When a fish is hooked, the artificial bait slides away from the hook and up the leader. This is an advantage for the angler, since plugs which hang directly from their hooks can be hurled by a jumping fish the way an Olympic weight man tosses his hammer.

Many skippers rig the lure so that it slides the full length of the 15- to 30-foot leader, while others say that this is a good way to lose fish. If a second fish spots the lure where it rests against the swivel connection between line and leader, he'll sometimes grab the plastic bait and cut the line. If you fish long enough in waters where voracious, sharp-toothed fish like wahoo are common, it will happen to you eventually.

Even tuna will do it. On an early autumn day, Jon McCreary, on the Honolulu boat *Diamond S,* was trolling off Barbers Point, O'ahu, when he was attracted by the action of a few birds. He got to them as they began working over a tuna school that had surfaced to rip up a bunch of bait fish. All five lines screamed at once. But the pandemonium was short-lived; the action stopped immediately without a single fish staying on long enough for an angler to start fighting it. The big yellowfins had pulled the lines back into the school where the fins and teeth of the others had cut through the braided Dacron above the wire.

I am not suggesting that such action is a kind of reasoned rescue mission, but it is not unusual to lose as many as a dozen lures during an afternoon bout with a school of big yellowfins. You can lessen this cutoff problem by making your leaders in two pieces with a swivel in the middle. This way, no matter where the plug goes there will be cable on both sides.

Hooks used for billfish need special attention. Captain George Parker, a Kona fisherman with three decades of chartering experience, describes plug fishing as a "snagging operation" because so many billfish are hooked outside the mouth and even up on the dorsal hump. The majority of foul hookups are on the bill, however, and George has developed a special tactic designed to increase the chances of landing a bill-hung fish. Since the bill slides into the bend of the hook while the fish is running straight away from the boat, such hookups come apart when the angler finally gets the fish turned around because the bill slides back out of the bend. George sharpens the barb as well as the point of the hook until both can pierce leather. Line pressure on the first run jams the barb into the bill for a solid anchor as long as the angler keeps the tension on.

Setting the reel drag right is more important with plugs than with any other kind of trolling rig. A too-light setting won't ram the hook point into the tough marlin maw since a marlin has bone every place you and I have lips. A too-heavy setting presents other dangers in addition to the increased chance of line damage and break-off. For one thing, the marlin can't turn away from the boat in the instant after the strike, but you want him to turn so that the hooks will slide into the corner of his mouth and grab a piece of bone they can hang on to forever.

A plug-hooked billfish gives a much more exciting fight than one taken on a swallowed natural bait since the metal fangs aren't piercing a vital region. The hooks barely hurt the marlin at all, whereas a belly-hooked marlin can be stunned enough to give no fight whatsoever. Every day of a marlin's life he chomps down on something with spines and teeth just as sharp as your hooks and his mouth is built to take it.

No, it is not the hooks but the fight that kills the marlin. Experiments in cooperation with the National Marine Fisheries Service (NMFS) suggest that three of four marlin tagged and released in Hawai'i have died within a half hour or so. These were sonic tags and the marlin appeared to die as they were tracked with electronic equipment.

Not all of the evidence is discouraging, however. Marlin do live to fight again, despite the trauma of intense battles for survival. One such was a marlin caught during the 1976 HIBT. The fish displayed over 100 square inches of scar tissue. The pattern of the wounds indicated that they had been made by the propellor of a boat, probably when the fish was pulled to gaff at the end of a previous fight. The fish escaped in the melee and recovered from the wounds and the oxygen depletion of the battle. When recaptured, the fish fought at full strength. Though glazed over with a thin layer of new flesh, the wounds were still red. Scientists who observed the injuries speculated that they were no more than three weeks old.

Captain Parker is working with a new type of "hookless" lure of a construction that seems to defy common sense. Its main positive characteristic, which may offset the fact that it is illegal in the eyes of the IGFA, which outlaws "entangling devices," is that it may eventually make possible the release of billfish with only a fraction of the mortality rate. Instead of hooks, this lure has a skirt made of thin filaments of nylon that catch in the rough "teeth" covering all marlin bills. Parker has landed well over a hundred fish on this lure, even though the connection may seem tenuous to someone who has never tried to pull one away from a marlin. Actually, the ratio of catches to strikes is increased in favor of the angler and the fish is then more easily led to the boat by the leverage on his bill; he's led around like a bull by the nose. In this way the marlin does not use up so much of the oxygen reserve stored away in the deep red meat along his lateral line that he cannot recover.

As Parker's experiments with hookless plugs show, George is a real student of the trolling lure. His experience goes back to before the days of plastic resins when marlin plugs were made out of broomsticks jammed into chromed plumbing pieces. Parker once caught a 1,002-pound blue marlin on a lure made from a chrome bath-towel holder. So when he talks about artificial baits, you listen.

His theory is that sound will toll in a marlin from a lot farther than sight will draw him. The marlin is first attracted by the throb of the boat motor and then by the popping and slapping sounds of the plug as it breaks water. The fish's curiosity is sharpened to the striking point by the erratic movement of this unusual little thing shooting out bubbles.

Freddy Rice embellishes the theory with thoughts on the psychology of a primitive creature more "volatile than anything else in the ocean." Freddy suspects that the marlin may actually become enraged by the sight of something brand new violating the sanctity of his watery backyard. The territorial imperative with fins—the lure serving as a trigger on a primitive reflex. Freddy ought to know; he and wife Sally have cornered their share of the record books, marlin chapter.

That a marlin will defend its territory with the motto "trespassers will be eaten" can be supported in many ways. A 585-pound black marlin caught by Bart Miller off Kona contained three bills from marlin estimated to weigh about 50 pounds each.

If sound is the answer, some plugs play prettier tunes than others. The Hawai'i Big Game Club team which won the 1972 HIBT caught every one of its fish, including not only marlin but the biggest yellowfin tuna of the contest, on the same plug, even though they trolled as many as five others during the five-day affair. The lure was nothing special; a straight-sided, flat-faced plastic hunk looking as if it had been molded in a beer can with two black plastic panels inside that had been covered with flakes of pearl shell. When they lost the lure because of a broken line they fished the final three days without a strike. Although they replaced their lost lure with others from the same manufacturer that appeared identical in every way, no substitute had the special magic of the lost one. The mistake that cost them their killer bait was to ease up so much on the drag after the strike that the spool overran and the whirling drum of line snarled and tangled.

Though some smart anglers do ease up on the drag as a marlin sprints away and the line tension increases, both from its drag in the water and the diminishing leverage on the decreasing line core, others prefer to set a moderate tension and leave the reel alone. A drag setting one-fourth of the rated line strength will usually do from strike to gaffing. This drag should be measured with a spring scale attached to the line after it has been fed through the guides and the rod is seated at the exact angle it will be fished.

If you are willing to baby-sit the rod, keeping constant attention from a vantage point no more than a step or two away from the outfit in its holder, you can set the striking drag at a heavy one-third of the rated line strength to sock the hooks in hard, maybe even accelerating the boat to give an additional pull before the fish recovers from his surprise long enough to get into high gear. Then reduce it to about one-fifth during the first few runs, while the fish has his full power. When he settles down you can jack it back to one-fourth to regain some line, then to one-third after the fish "breaks" from his exertion and lets himself be led to the boat for gaffing.

Trolling with artificial lures is a continuously evolving sport that is now in what Hawaiian anglers have begun to call the "jet" age.

"When I drag jets, nothing ever hits plastic, so I don't even bother with plugs anymore." That's a comment you hear more and more along the waterfront, especially from trollers with full fish boxes. Whether it is just the ballyhoo of a passing fad, or the death knell for the traditional molded plastic trolling plugs known worldwide as "Konaheads" and "Honolulus," will be decided by the count of big fish over the next few years, but even if the jet is really no better than the plug, it deserves the careful study of every determined fisherman.

Is it called a jet because it is fished at high speed (as fast as 16 knots), or because it bears some evolutionary resemblance to a water-jet shower nozzle? Who knows and who cares as long as the lure regularly takes marlin, mahimahi, 'ahi (yellowfin tuna), and ono (wahoo). There is weighty evidence that the jet is the best 'ahi lure ever designed. When the spring run of yellowfin tuna hit

Jets are chrome-plated metal lures ported by central air passages. Some models have angled fronts to provide an erratic action, but most are tapered to run straight, just below the surface.

Kona in 1975, in conjunction with the Kona Mauka Trollers annual battle, as many as eight tackle busters per boat per day were
dragging the gunnels down to the water level. These were fish
hovering around the 200-pound mark, and it was the rare 'ahi
that was caught on anything but a jet. To win the top prize in the
tuna division, the champion had to boat over 2,000 pounds of
gilt-edged sashimi. One boat, one crew, one ton of tuna!

Open the tackle box of a top tuna troller and you may be stunned
by the riot of colors and the gleam of jewelry. The jethead itself is a
polished, chrome-plated bauble, but many fishermen increase the
brilliance of the metal with patches of prism foil reflecting fiery colors that burn in the sunlight. The skirt is a billowing glow of artificial
color radiating from at least two vinyl "takos." These molded fake
squids are red, blue, yellow, white—or even chartreuse and puce,
depending on the proclivities of the buyer. At least two colors per
lure is standard.

Most angling experts ballast the jet with lead weights, either
strung out along the leader or poured into the cavities in the
head. The true high-speed men just fill the jet with molten lead
so that it will never pop up even at a speed that would water ski
an elephant. Many are satisfied merely with threading a large egg
sinker onto the leader behind the lure, hidden in the skirt. That's
the way Haku Baldwin's prize-winning jet was rigged in the 1974
billfish tournament, and her prize was an IGFA women's tuna
world record.

However you weight it, note that the lead generally chokes off
the holes and throttles the argument about whether these
"whistlers" really have any sonic effect on fish because of the
passage of water through the lure. Many fishermen weight half
their lures and leave the rest light. The heavy ones dig in and
never pop, the light ones skim the surface and stream bubbles.
The heavy ones grab tuna and the foaming churners entice marlin,
or so it seems.

The experts risk their bankrolls by rigging their jets on *suji*
(nylon monofilament) leaders. A completely equipped jet lure,
with decorations and rigging, drains the bank account at the rate
of twenty bucks a rig. Trusting it to a clear nylon leader takes guts
in waters where ono can whomp the lure off with one bite. The
risk is worth it, because suji outfishes cable for both tuna and
marlin, and ono generally stay closer to shore where they can do
no damage. The trick is not to put your lines out until you've

crossed the 50-fathom line, and then you'll rarely encounter an ono.

By the way, an ono *can* be caught on a suji leader—in fact, many fishermen turn the trick regularly. At the very least, the ono will chop off those four-dollar takos, but he will also cut through the suji a discouragingly high percentage of the time, especially when he is "headhunting." In the latter case, he may grab the lure at its front end and take a clear shot at the leader as much as 6 inches in front of the lure.

There is one more trick to using nylon leaders, and that is to protect the leader from the lure itself. The edges of the metal leader hole will chew on the nylon as the lure works back and forth, lazily turning through the water. A 6-inch plastic sleeve threaded on the leader will act as a buffer. If you can find no other tubing that will work, use an empty ink tube from a discarded ball-point pen. Clean the last bit of ink out of the tube by poking a piece of leader through it and squirt in some aerosol lubricant like WD-40, which is a great ink solvent. The 300-pound-test nylon leader should just fit inside the tube, and the tube should still fit the leader hole.

Arming the jet is a matter of argument. Some anglers crimp on a pair of hooks in tandem. Unfortunately, the rear hook comes so close to the end of the skirt with a double-hook arrangement that the supple plastic tangles in the hook, knotting the strands of colorful vinyl around the bend. A single hook is all that is needed for 'ahi fishing, however, since the tuna completely engulfs the lure on the strike and jams the point into a firm anchoring spot. It's the marlin fishermen who prefer the double-hooking rig.

Plugs and jets—no fuss, no mess, no bother, but are they always the best answer? There are times when a man who fully understands live or fresh bait can outfish the lure specialist. Such a man is Bart Miller, one of Hawai'i's most successful charter fishermen.

## 2
# Bart and Bait

### HAWAI'I'S MOST SUCCESSFUL SKIPPER TALKS
### ABOUT BAIT FOR BIG FISH

THE YEAR BART MILLER rewrote the record books by catching 111 marlin, he did it almost entirely with natural baits. Only 6 were caught on lures. No other Hawaiian skipper had ever boated more than a hundred billfish in one year, yet 1972 was the second time Bart had hit the century mark; he had caught an even 100 marlin in 1968.

Bart took sixty marlin on live bait, but even more unusual were the thirty-seven he took on rigged dead baits, a surprising departure from typical Hawaiian methods. To reach such a goal, which some skippers actually thought was unattainable, Bart had to fish 215 days whether he had a paying charter or not, but it also meant that he had to be an expert on three widely differing techniques (lures, live baits, and fresh dead baits) and especially on knowing when to choose the best one as the conditions varied.

No two of the methods can be employed at the same time by an angler who thinks that he might cover his bets by trying everything at once. "There is a rhythm to fishing and fish movements and you must correctly read that rhythm to know the best way to fish," according to Bart. "Lure fishing is like a rodeo; things are happening very fast. It's the best way to fish when bait and billfish are moving rapidly over great distances. You might be on a bank watching the birds race back and forth. One minute there are a thousand fish around you and three minutes later they are gone and you can see them working hundreds of yards away.

"You must keep up with the pace and movement of the fish. If they are moving at 8 or more knots, you've got to go to lures to stay with them; you won't catch fish with such a slow technique as live bait that must be worked at less than 3 knots."

When the fish settle down to a speed of around 6 knots, Bart prefers to switch to one of the dead bait rigs he has perfected for trolling at this speed. Live bait is the best answer for the slower rhythms characterized by stable concentrations of bait fish.

"Obviously, I lean toward natural baits. I favor natural things. Right or wrong, I like working with fish. It is my nature and it is the way I've been trained. I like the feeling of the strike; the slowness of it all, especially getting the quarry up on the surface and watching him charge the bait."

But there is more to Bart's preference than emotion. "Lure fishing is so fast that there are plenty of chances for mistakes and missed fish. That's why it is my *last* choice of a method. The year we boated the 111 marlin, I didn't hook my first one on lures until September. And that was only after a disappointing month when the currents weren't right for bait fishing and the other boats were catching many more fish on lures than I was on bait."

To fish live bait well you must know your spots. It is so slow paced that you can't explore new territory well. Bart feels that seven out of ten of his strikes occur in the spots he has painstakingly learned over the many years he's fished the Kona Coast. How does a fisherman discover such glory holes?

"You shouldn't look at the water and see just water. You've got to understand the bottom and know when you are close to a bank. Then you've got to know the direction of the current and whether it is setting up the right conditions. Marlin do pick positions and just wait there. It is easy to see that if they just milled around in bait schools they'd have the bait so hassled that it would be hard for them to catch these excited fish. You can prove it to yourself by going to the pier and watching the small bait schools. The predators are there, but they hang out on the outskirts of the school, down deep. They pick strategic positions and wait there for unwary stragglers to get too close."

To help you read the bottom you need a marine chart that shows bottom configurations as depth lines. Look for the 100-

The hook is set in a baited marlin, and he rears out of the water as though to gauge the mettle of his adversary before the battle begins. Photo by Peter Hoogs.

fathom line and watch for any bends in it that show "corners." These are the spots where currents can cause upwellings that bring feeding bait fish to the surface. The depth of 100 fathoms is prime territory since marlin don't seem to feel safe in shallower water—though they are certainly caught upon occasion right near shore. Freddy Rice thinks 120 fathoms may be better yet. From his years of fishing the Kona Coast, he can point to such corners occurring off Keāhole Light, Keauhou, Red Hill, Captain Cook, Hoʻokena, and Miloliʻi.

Once you've picked your spot and hooked your bait, how do you fish it? Your live-bait rod and its rig must be ready and in its rod holder even before you've hooked that bait. The special gear you need consists of a leader, hook, and bridle, all carefully chosen to give optimum results.

For Bart Miller there is no ideal leader. "Your best situation is a hookless, free-swimming bait. From there on, every step you take is backward."

Cable wire, the stuff usually chosen for plugs, is the worst kind for bait. Not only is it highly visible of itself, but it sets up turbulence in the water as it is pulled along. Its rough surface, which

you can feel by dragging a piece between your fingers, will chafe a
marlin's mouth while he is trying to swallow the bait and he'll
just spit it right back out.

Monofilament is less visible and very smooth, but it is easily
abraded by bills, cheeks, scales, and fins; so it breaks too easily.
Freddy Rice adds to its disadvantages the fact that it tends to float
a weakened live bait as the bait fish tires. Yet its weakness can be
its strength since it will cut immediately on a shark strike, thus
leaving you free to try for another bait and another marlin.

Bart chooses piano wire. It has a small diameter and swallows
easily, but that is about where its advantages end. It is the most
troublesome leader of all to work with, since it is stiff and brittle,
breaking like dry spaghetti when kinked. Bart knows its drawbacks, but feels that they can be managed.

"The secret is to keep a tight line so that the marlin cannot

Live bait fishing is just as effective for 'ahi as for marlin. Note that
Zander Budge is using a flying gaff. Once set, the gaff hook separates
from the handle and the fish is pulled in on the gaff rope seen running
alongside the handle.

swim across it and make a loop which will tighten into a kink, but you want to do that anyway. Yes, it is a tough leader to handle at gaff because you have to take double wraps over gloves to hold the fish—fishermen have lost a few fingers doing this. But total up some points on the plus side for the number of fish you can boat in a tangle. If a fish tangles with the leader in a bill wrap or body wrap, the wire holds its shape and bites into the flesh.''

To show that you can do it, note that Bart has landed several fish over 1,000 pounds on single strands of 315-pound-test wire. These big fish were black marlin that were taken during a journey to Cairns, Australia. "I'm not sure such light wire should be used on such giant fish," Bart adds, "but you get more strikes and more hookups.''

To say that your hook must be honed sharp is just the icing, it must be the right hook to start with, both in size and shape. Choose the typical big-game or "tuna" hook with a straight, knife-edge point. The bend should be pried open until the point is parallel to the shank to give the biggest bite possible.

Why a straight point, or rather, why not an offset point? When a marlin swallows the bait, the hook turns backward on its bridle and rests against the side of the bait. That means there is a 50-percent chance that the hook will stab back into the bait instead of into the billfish.

The hook should match the size of the bait, and the best way to determine this is to lay the hook against the side of the head with the point facing the tail—the gap should be as wide as the depth of the head. With an 8- or 10-pound bait, use a 16/0 hook. When Bart uses a 45-pound bait, he matches it with a 20/0 hook. The bigger the hook, the better the hookup.

There is an art to handling bait if you want it lively and fresh. Your bait will be a live 'ahi, *aku* (skipjack tuna), or *kawakawa* (bonito) caught on the grounds you will be fishing, from the school you hope your quarry is stalking. You want it undamaged and out of the water for no more than 10 seconds. When you pull him out of water, turn him on his back and tuck him under your arm, then hold your hand over his eyes for a second. This will quiet him down immediately. You can actually open your palm, and he will balance on his back without quivering. Then you can rig him without having to chase him all over the deck. Don't bother with a wounded or bleeding bait. An injured fish will just attract sharks.

The simplest live-bait rigging method is just to jam the hook up through the hard roof of the mouth being sure to get the point completely exposed. Then toss the bait back into the water so he can swim along behind. The chief disadvantage to this method is that it won't let the fish get its head down into a strong swimming position. Bart points out that it has another drawback—it interferes with the action of the hook when the marlin has swallowed it. Since it stays hooked to the bait, you are actually turning the bait in the marlin's stomach as you are trying to set the hook.

For a bait that will swim long and strong, use a bridle. This is just a loop of string tied to the hook at one end and to a bait needle at the other. The needle should have an open eye so that it can be disengaged in an instant once the bait is ready. The needle

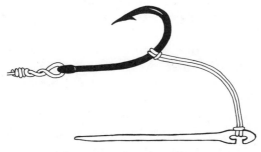

The bait bridle shown ready for use. Note the open eye of the needle so that the bridle can be slipped off quickly.

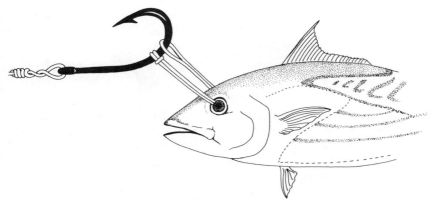

Live bait rigged with a bridle. The needle is slipped through the bait's eye socket without damaging eye. The loop is then disengaged from the needle and dropped over the point of the hook to secure the bait.

is run through the eye socket in front of the eye, and the loop is pulled back over the hook to complete the circle. Since the needle passes through a natural, sinuslike cavity in the bait, it does not damage the fish in any way. It allows the bait a natural, head-down swimming position, with the hook completely unencumbered.

"This is a very strong pulling point," according to Bart. "With a strong bridle, I once broke an 80-pound-test line when a porpoise grabbed the bait and hung on. The bridle just wouldn't tear away from the bait no matter how hard I pulled."

Strong bridles no longer interest Bart; he has switched to light cotton with a breaking point of approximately 15–20 pounds. "The hook turns backward on the bridle when the marlin swallows it, and it lays up against the thickest part of the bait. The weak bridle breaks when the angler sets the hook, and the point is completely free to do its job."

Be prepared for a strike anytime from the instant the bait is dropped back into the water. As a matter of fact, marlin will try to grab your bait when it is first hooked, and before it is even rigged. Imagine Darrel Skelton's surprise when a marlin raced in to attack a 200-pound yellowfin tuna being fought by the commanding officer of the Pearl Harbor naval base who was struggling to bring the big 'ahi to gaff on the *Mokunani*. The marlin, estimated to be near the half-ton mark, was obviously intent on a big dinner, and he probably got it since he succeeded in breaking the 'ahi off the line.

It is because marlin will attack so quickly that some anglers use what might be called the "instant rig." They tie an aku lure to a short leader and then to the hook of their live-bait rig. The instant the aku strikes the small feather lure he is ready to bait a marlin.

When towing a live bait, the angler should hold the line between his fingers and strip a large belly of slack line off the reel to be dragged in the water behind the boat. This belly is the "dropback" that allows the marlin to take the bait without feeling any resistance that might spook him and make him spit out the bait.

You will know when a strike is coming when you feel the nervous action of your bait instead of the steady swimming rhythm he uses until he spots the predator's charge. Don't drop the bait until you feel the definite strong pull of a big fish. Don't let your reflexes get the best of you and jerk back. Give the bait to the fish when he takes it and let him swallow it with the reel set at very

light drag or on free spool with ratchet. You want just enough
tension so the reel won't overrun and backlash, but not enough
for the fish to feel it and spook.

Most fish will snatch the bait and cruise to a stop to swallow it.
Hold your strike until he starts up again or you'll yank the bait
out of his mouth before he can get it turned and down. You can
strike by hand or by gunning the boat as you slide the drag lever
up to striking tension, while the rod remains in the holder. Freddy
Rice recounts a story that illustrates the advantage of the latter.

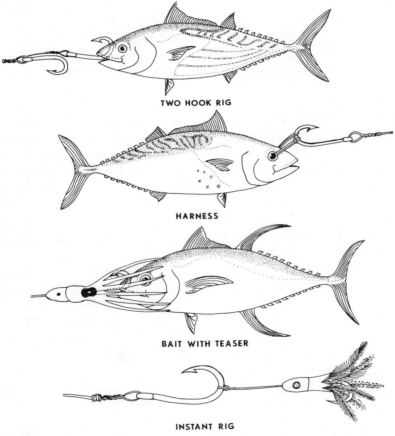

TWO HOOK RIG

HARNESS

BAIT WITH TEASER

INSTANT RIG

Four ways to rig a live bait for trolling. The first three are self-explanato-
ry. The "instant rig" *(bottom)* is trolled through the bait school until a
bait fish strikes the trailing feather. At that instant, the bait is rigged and
ready for marlin. Three different bait fish are shown: aku *(top)*,
kawakawa *(middle)*, and young 'ahi *(bottom)*.

When he picked up his rod to strike an unseen fish, he felt nothing but slack. Puzzled, he reeled in and found a broken line. A later conversation with charter captain Peter Nelson filled Freddy in on the fact that the fish had raced forward with the bait and leaped out of the water ahead of the boat. Peter estimated the weight of the marlin as 700 pounds. Gunning the motor would have kept the marlin behind the boat for the strike.

If the fish takes the bait and runs with it as he grabs it, it is often best to set the hook immediately and hope for the best, rather than continue the almost certain risk of having the fish spook. Each marlin species takes the bait differently. Striped marlin tend to bill the bait and play with it before committing themselves. Black marlin come in slow, like sharks, and take the bait slowly, with deliberation. The blues race in and snatch.

"Once in a while you'll notice that your bait has died for some unaccountable reason," according to Peter Hoogs, skipper of the *Pamela*. "There has been no solid evidence of a strike, but your bait just gives up and lies dead on the surface. Pull it in and you'll find that it has been rammed through with a marlin bill—a hole plugged right through the body from side to side. After the marlin killed the aku, for whatever reason in its violent, primitive mind, it just swam away and left it."

The possibility that the marlin was really interested in a meal when it speared the aku should not be ruled out. An aku taken from the belly of a marlin caught during the 1975 HIBT had a bill hole right behind its pectoral fins.

Though most live baits are members of the tuna family caught in the same waters the angler expects to fish, some boats use live 'ōpelu (mackerel scad) or akule (bigeye scad). These must be caught in advance and kept alive in a live-bait well with recirculating water. Once the boat reaches a spot where other fish have been seen, the crew can start bait fishing immediately, without depending on the fickle nature of the tunas already on the scene. Fran Weinberg kept a dozen 'ōpelu alive in the bait tanks of his 65-foot *Capricorn* for the entire week of the HIBT in 1972. The bait was just as rugged at the end of the week as in the beginning.

Before giving up on a live bait to try some other method, many knowledgeable fishermen try letting the bait sound. After being towed for a while, the bait will often dive for the bottom if the tension is released. As he plummets through the depths all alone, he is the perfect target for a deep-feeding billfish. If he won't swim down rigged with the bridle, try hooking him under the pectoral fin to change the angle of pull. When deep, the bait won't live long but will be almost as effective anyway.

Live baits swim deeper than lures, but they still operate within about 10 feet of the surface. The potential for catching big fish at greater depths has as yet only been hinted at because reliable and convenient methods have not been developed. Something to think about: during the slowest periods of the year for trollers, January through March, the commercial flag-line boats are bringing in fifty or more striped and black marlin a week per boat. Many of these fish are hooked on the ends of lines set at 30 to 40 fathoms. Former Kona charter captain Terry Truman took the lead in the Kona charter fishing derby one January with a hot streak of billfish caught while trolling live bait back and forth between Captain Cook and Kaiwi, weighted down with 30 pounds of weight to get it down deep and keep it there. The weight was tied to a handline and then to the swivel of the fighting line with a light breakaway string.

Most of what Bart Miller has been willing to share concerning live bait is part of the standard procedure employed by all topflight fishermen. Fishing dead bait is what sets Bart apart. His inspiration for perfecting his special techniques came from his experiences during a yearlong sojourn that took him from Fiji to Cairns to Bay of Islands, New Zealand, in successive fishing seasons as he followed the action to hit each place during peak fishing.

"I came back to Hawaii thinking I would set the world on fire with all of the wonderful things I'd learned in the South Pacific. It didn't happen that way. We don't have their great reefs, so we don't have the variety of baits, the ease of catching them, or the water conditions they have there.

"We skipped baits and caught a few fish, but I'd say the lure outfished the skipped baits. We tried all kinds, including mullet, all of the tunas, rainbow runners, flyingfish, etc. Then I began to realize how important the difference in water conditions was. Australian waters are rough and the baits are constantly tumbled automatically as they are trolled; this gives them an exciting appearance. Billfish are great hunters and aggressive creatures. They didn't evolve that way by attacking and eating the dead and dreary looking things we drag along on top of our placid waters."

In his extended experiments Bart discovered two things. First, the best dead bait is a yellowfin or bigeye tuna, and second, the bait must be rigged to swim actively *under* water, rather than dragged along the surface. He experimented with pulling points and ballast until he perfected a rigged bait that won't spin but rides on its side running to the right from 8 to 12 feet, turning its head, then running back to the left for the same distance before turning and repeating the process. Occasionally it breaks the surface and sometimes it dives a bit deeper, but mostly it stays under.

"I generally troll just one line at a time, but would almost certainly troll more if baits were easier to get and did not have such a high commercial value as food."

The monetary aspect assumes monumental proportions when you consider the size of the bait Bart is talking about. "I like to work with a ten-to-one ratio. I've reached a point where I'm only really interested in a fish that will take a 50-pound, or bigger, bait. This will be a marlin in excess of 500 pounds. A 50-pound tuna can be worth a hundred or more dollars on the market during some seasons of the year, so a trio of big baits would be a millionaire's dream.

"I regularly use a 20-pound bait, sometimes an ono or mahi-mahi, and that's a bait big enough to startle most people." With a 30-pound ono bait, Bart had a strike from a fish that pulled line from a brand new, 130-pound reel with nearly full drag so fast

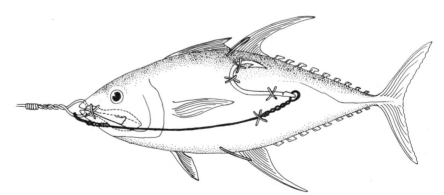

A rigged fresh tuna. After brining in salt water for toughness, the bait is ballasted with between 8 and 16 ounces of lead (inside mouth), and the fins are tied erect. The main leader takes the towing strain. The hook is sewed on in reverse because the bait is swallowed head first. Main leader pulls free of mouth when hook is set.

that it almost backlashed. "We had to chase it at 20 knots to keep any reserve on the reel at all. It finally threw the bait after we got fairly close to it. We aren't ready for the monsters yet—this fish would have been very close to 2,000 pounds."

The ten-to-one ratio may sound farfetched, but Bart has done it enough to know that it is a rule rather than an accident. "I once caught a 748-pound marlin that had a 65-pound tuna it its belly. The tail was still sticking out of its mouth when it struck the lure and it was in fresher condition when we boated the marlin than some of the baits I've taken out of a marlin's belly after a half-hour fight. I'd guess that it hadn't eaten that tuna more than a half-hour before it struck the lure."

With so many big fish to his credit, Bart does not agree that only the smaller marlin take baits while the bigger ones are more likely to be caught on plugs. His 111 marlin of 1972 averaged 300 pounds, so half were over this weight.

Freddy Rice explains the seeming lack of big fish boated on live bait as actually occurring because the big ones are more likely to break off when this method is used. They don't jump as much, but are more likely to take off like a rocket on a long run; thus they waste less energy. The deep hookup means that the wire will come out of the back corner of the marlin's mouth. This gives the angler much less leverage than he has on a plug-hooked fish where the hook is pulling from near the bill. When the fish is brought near the boat at the end of the fight, the mate has less control of the head on the deep hookup, so the fish can fight him all day until something breaks.

With all of the bait fish in the ocean when you toss yours back in, why does the marlin pick the one with the hook? Some anglers say it is a color difference, others that it is the uncommon action; still others say the bait stops reacting with the school and becomes the obvious straggler the marlin has been waiting for.

Whatever the reason, live baits take 'ahi with the same degree of effectiveness as marlin, and they account for big mahimahi, ono, and even *ulua* (jack), if you are willing to try a live bait in water under 100 feet deep.

But marlin and tuna are not the only big-game species in Hawai'i.

# 3
# Gods, Ghosts, and Fishermen
## CATCHING, AND AVOIDING, SHARKS

THERE ARE GODS in Hawaiian waters, and every fisherman is eventually forced to make his sacrifices to them. Whether he believes in them or not, they extract their pounds of flesh.

Tommy Rodenhurst knows, and from his stories, which carry just a mocking edge, it is hard to judge whether the swimming gods have been completely displaced by his adopted Christianity.

When Tommy entertains in his elegant South Kohala home, surrounded by the Chinese, Hawaiian, and New England antiques which reflect his ancestral background, he tests you with Oriental delicacies, measures you with Scotch, and then, if he finds you to be receptive, settles back to tell about the days of his boyhood in Kohala, a half-century ago.

Young Tommy and his cousin fished with an uncle who practiced the untraditional art of dynamiting. Uncle had learned a little from his mistakes, one of which had cost him a hand, until he knew just how long to hold the exploding stick before throwing it so that it blew a foot above the water's surface, thus ensuring a shock wave that would stun enough fish for a satisfying dinner.

On the occasion that would guarantee Tommy's eventual full head of gray hair, Uncle tossed his stick from a cliff rising 30 feet above the boys, and then sent them wading out to sort through the collection of concussed reef fish to pick the choicest for dinner. The fish would not stay comatose for long, so haste was of the essence, but one sight sent the boys paddling frantically to shore in fear. Three pairs of fins marked a trio of intruders silently working on Uncle's bonanza.

"Get back out there and get me my fish," Uncle shouted at the terrified boys.

"But Uncle, the *manō* will eat us," they wailed back.

"They won't hurt you. They are my *'aumākua*. Get me my fish."

Neither Uncle's wrath nor his faith in his 'aumākua, or family gods, would prod the boys back out into the water to face the feasting sharks.

Uncle scrambled down the cliff, balancing with his good arm and scolding the cowards for laziness that would masquerade as fear. Then he plunged into the water chanting to his 'aumākua.

With his one good hand, he gathered fish into his basket while smacking the greedy sharks with his stump if they got too close. Uncle would snatch a fish from the very jaws of the sharks, completely unafraid. When he had filled his basket, he waded back to the beach with the monster fish following in a line.

"And then," Tommy will tell you, "Uncle turned and tossed a fish to the first shark. The mano took it and swam out to sea. The other sharks waited their turn as each was tossed a fish and each disappeared."

In the Hawai'i of legends, sharks spawned humans, chosen maidens gave birth to sharks, priests who knew the proper prayers changed the ghosts of the dead into sharks, and sorcerers appeared as men to entice others into the ocean, where they were eaten by other sorcerers in their assumed form as sharks.

A man could watch the sharks near his village and know that they were his ancestors, his 'aumākua, who would protect him and guide his destiny. He could tell which shark was the reincarnation of each relative and always made sure they were well provided for with sacrifices, some human.

Modern fishermen don't make their sacrifices intentionally. It is when you have paid the price in time, money, effort, and vigilance to get a prized tuna, marlin, or wahoo on the end of your line that the 'aumākua of the ocean bring you to your knees— they've come to take your offering. They appear as formless blurs that destroy your catch just at the moment you've felt your marlin break from his exertion; just when you've begun to feel you really do have the strength to land your trophy.

Sometimes you can outwit these evil spirits, and it doesn't take chants or the intervention of a *kahuna* (priest). Jack Ross had just complimented his fishing guests on the progress they were making in their battles with a pair of big yellowfins, the 200-pound kind that run in the spring from Kaua'i to Kona, when his pleasure turned sour at the sight of a school of sharks. The big killers tore into one of the tuna while the other fled for its life, pulling hundreds of yards of line with it into the depths.

"Let him stay deep out of sight while we figure this out," Jack ordered. With the shreds of the first tuna bloodying the water at the stern, Jack took pot shots at the sharks with a rifle. But a rifle bullet makes very little impression on such mindless robots when they have the taste of blood on their tongues.

Half a fish may not be better than none, but in shark-infested waters, half a fish may be all you'll get. Photo courtesy of Steve Colewell.

"I guess it doesn't make any difference that we're out of ammo," Jack snarled. "There are just as many now as ever."

Jack hauled out a tangle of corroded wire and rusted hooks. Quickly, and with no explanation, he crimped the wire in 10-foot traces, with a hook at each end. He baited the hooks with chunks of tuna and dropped the lethal rigs overboard among the greedy sharks, who were eager to grab each end.

"That's known as a shark tug-of-war," he exclaimed with satisfaction. "And I don't care which one in each of those pairs wins." Four tandem rigs later the sharks had disappeared and Jack's happy group boated its unmarked tuna.

Other anglers have successfully driven off sharks using different methods. Sid Weinrich has perfected a technique that distracts the shark and keeps his mind occupied for hours. Sid keeps a short wire leader, with hook, attached to a bottle. When a shark makes his approach, Sid baits the bottle rig and drops it overboard. After swallowing the bait, the shark becomes annoyed by the antics of the bottle as it bobs along behind him. If he dives to get away from it, the bottle is pulled up against his flanks, bopping him in the ribs as it goes merrily along with him. Within a few minutes the puzzled shark will decide to take matters into its own mouth and try to crush the annoying stranger. Sid says that he has seen sharks chew on the bottle for hours, becoming more and more frustrated as the bottle pops back out of their mouths with the hard glass surfaces still intact.

Few fishermen intentionally set out to battle a shark. Shark fishing is an accident because the live baits that the toothed monsters prefer are the same ones chosen for their effectiveness in catching marlin and 'ahi. For many of us, though, the shark has a horrible attraction, perhaps spawned by the same kind of dread thrill that takes us one step closer to the edge of a cliff for a more frightening look into the terrors hidden in our souls.

A shark is an adversary as formidable as any we might conjure up in a nightmare. The fact that we can actually conquer these monsters makes it easier, perhaps, for us to drive other devils back into the shadows of our minds. That's why some of us don't curse the traditional gods when a shark engulfs the live bait we've lovingly set out to entice a magnificent marlin or titanic tuna.

Captain Zander Budge of Kawaihae and Kona, a skipper who'd like to see sharks get the acceptance as game fish that their

The shark family includes one of the world's greatest game fish, the mako. Few are caught in Hawai'i, but this 695 pounder proves that the occasional Kona visitor is usually spoiling for a fight. Photo by Jerry Seely.

strength deserves, tells a story that illustrates the obstacles to the development of "monster fishing" as a sport.

"A couple of fellows hired me last spring with the express wish to catch a shark. These fish like a live kawakawa or aku, but no schools had shown in several weeks, so I got ready a basket of chum and set it drifting with a large orange marker buoy to keep track of it.

"The idea was that we'd troll our favorite spots for other game fish and keep checking back with the buoy to see if any sharks had been attracted to the basket, which carried three or four cut-up fish.

"The first time we worked the area around the buoy, we baited up with a chunk of aku, and got an immediate strike. To our amazement, it turned out to be a 30-pound bull dolphin that put on a spectacular show and a tough battle before finally giving up in a final display of aerial fireworks, complete with all of the flashy color changes mahimahi are so famous for. Our guests were mighty impressed.

"The second approach was even more startling. A heavy strike, and we were battling a furious marlin.

"That's when the shark finally showed up. Just as a footnote to the point I'm going to make, this incident clearly shows that a shark is more readily attracted to a live fish in distress than by blood in the water.

"By now my party had lost all interest in shark fishing and didn't care about anything but the marlin. All of a sudden the greedy monster was an undesirable nuisance.

"Of course, we couldn't get the billfish near the boat as long as the shark was close, so we baited a heavy rig and hooked the shark. Then we horsed it in on the heavy gear and killed it with a powerhead. This dead shark still had its effect on the marlin, though, and when we worked him in, the billfish frantically powered around the boat and dived under us, tangling the line in the prop. Now, with another almost certain chance of losing the marlin generated by the presence of the shark, my party declared that they hoped every shark in the world would rot in hell. That is some change in opinion from a group eager to catch one just one hour before.

"Incredibly, I was able to pull up each part of the line with the gaff, cut it, splice it, and finally, boat the marlin.

"We ate the mahimahi, sold the marlin for fish cake, but could only dump the shark at sea. With no economic value, and overshadowed by the presence of other, more glamorous game fish, the shark is just an object of scorn."

One measure of the desirability of a fish, on the scales used by authors of angling literature, is its receptivity to an artificial lure. Undoubtedly, the fact that catfish and carp, say, like sharks, feed on refuse has made them less honorable than the noble trout, with its strange addiction to feathers, or the regal bass, the fish that thinks a chunk of wood with shiny whirling metal things at each end is an hors d'oeuvre.

Sharks do, on rare occasion, grab artificial trolling lures. Why such strikes are rare may be explained by the physiology of the fish and not his quirks of appetite. Hawaiian trollers move fast; an 8-knot speed is common. That means that any fish caught on a lure must be either very close to the path of the boat to see the lure before it flashes out of sight, or have extremely good eyesight to spot it at a distance and then track it in the race for the kill.

Some marine biologists say that the near-shore varieties of sharks are nearsighted. To satisfy myself on this point, I took a spinning rod down to the shallow waters near the submerged shark temple below Pu'ukoholā Heiau. Sharks have fed here since the days when human sacrifices were among the refuse they could savor.

Two black-tips cruised close enough for a series of casts with a swimming-minnow plug, a highly visible model 9 inches long. I had chosen the tackle primarily for its pinpoint casting ability, and not because there would be any real chance of landing a big fish with it.

The first cast dropped a dozen feet ahead of the lead shark and was ignored. Subsequent casts, placed closer and closer, drew no attention either. Finally, I dropped one 2 feet in front and repeated the twitching action of a crippled fish, which long practice had indicated as the best way to get such a plug mauled.

A swirl, a quick strike, a sudden break-off. The only thing different about that cast from each of the others was that it was within the shark's visual range.

The *mako* shark is the chief exception to the rule. It will take a trolled lure as eagerly as a marlin does. But the mako is so rare in Hawaiian waters that no handbook of Hawaiian fish even notes its presence.

The oceanic white tip is the most abundant big shark in tropical seas. Not even bullets will discourage it from pursuing its quarry. Surprisingly, it makes no effort to attack its constant companions, the banded pilot-fish. Photo courtesy of the National Marine Fisheries Service.

In May 1976 Rope Nelson boated a 695-pound mako after a three-hour battle that included several attacks on Nelson's boat, the *Blue Hawaii*.

"When he hit us the first time, it jarred the whole boat," Rope told me later, with the awe still in his voice put there by the impact of a fish strong enough to jolt a boat bigger than a railroad car.

Rope's mako was just under 11 feet long. Its jaws were sent to famed Florida taxidermist Jimmy Pfleuger to be mounted. Pfleuger told Nelson that it was the biggest mako he had ever worked on.

Rope is no stranger to sharks; among his catches is an 803-pound tiger shark reported to be the largest male tiger ever caught in the United States. That tiger had seven rows of teeth, each two and a quarter inches long—a grand total of 129 little white knives. The mako, by contrast, had only three rows of teeth, each an inch and a half long. It was the third mako Rope had captured in 29 years of fishing in Kona. Its steely blue hide was stripped to make drums in the old Hawaiian way; so the sound of its spirit lingers on. Its epitaph was simply stated by a bruised and tired Rope Nelson shortly after the fight, "I don't need any more of that."

How do they find their food if they don't see well? Sound and smell do the job, with a lot more emphasis on sound than most people realize. Rhett McNair is a diver who has devised a powerhead that fires underwater on contact. While developing it, he needed some free-swimming sharks to experiment with.

He fabricated a "shark caller," consisting of a gear which turned against what looks like the teeth of a comb. This little clicker could be adjusted to get the frequency of clicks Rhett needed to interest sharks. After a bit of experimentation on the bottom in 30 feet of water, the vibrations did their job and Rhett smacked the incoming sharks with his powerhead. Fortunately, the "bang stick" has always worked as well as the shark caller does.

The attractive powers of clicking noises are not a modern discovery. When Pacific islanders wanted to rid their waters of certain sharks which did not have desirable magical powers, they caught them and killed them by first tolling them in with special rattles. These were made from coconut half-shells, each having a hole bored through the center. The shells were then strung on a flexible stick bent into a hoop and tied together at the ends to look something like a tennis racket with bells on it.

Ancient sages explained away the attracting effect of the rattles as no more than the imitation of a school of bait fish, or, perhaps, as the raucous calls of seabirds feeding on such schools.

Terror tales associated with sharks describe them as bottomless pits, gorging themselves in insane fury on anything near at hand. Yes, it is true that sharks will often eat anything, including much that is inedible. It is probably not possible to name anything small enough to be swallowed that has not already been swallowed by a shark somewhere, including a keg of nails and a roll of tarred roofing paper. Imagine the consternation of the Hawaiian fishing crew that boated a shark and discovered a moccasin-type shoe in his belly!

But a puzzling fact is that sharks often spurn a free and easy meal. On several occasions, we have hooked aku and kawakawa from schools surrounded by sharks, and had the big killers sit right by our stern, tails crooked in the awkward fashion that keeps them

ready to pounce at a quick flick of a cocked tail, yet they have ignored the hooked fish and let us snake them in right past their
noses.

The history of the shark in Hawai'i is a tale of the long fall
from the heights of reverence to the depths of disdain. Yet the
shark may make a comeback in importance as a game fish. Even
Tommy Rodenhurst recently gave it a try. He is sure to release any
sharks that are hooked, of course, "just in case we might be
related."

# 4
# *The Offshore Middleweights*

HAWAI'I'S FAVORITES—MAHIMAHI, ONO, AND
ULUA—BY TROLLING

SOME FISHERMEN can't stand the nervous strain of being on a moving boat without dragging a lure in an attempt, however feeble, to catch a fish. It can be foolish, of course, to slow down to a normal trolling speed when you are on the way to some "hot spot." If you did, you'd be wasting time more wisely spent working more productive waters.

So there you go, speeding across the ocean hoping to find fish while ignoring the possibilities in the currents you cross. It's a classic dilemma and was the topic of conversation one perfect Hawaiian day as Zander Budge and I watched the wake race away from the stern of his boat, *Spooky Luki*. We were on our way from Kawaihae to fish the prime marlin grounds off Keāhole Light. We had no guarantee, either that we would find fish when we got there, or that we couldn't fill the fish box right where we were.

*Spooky Luki* sliced through the choppy waves at a hurrying 15 knots, the fastest she could make over this rough stretch, which always feels the force of the trade winds. Even for a pair of fishermen accustomed to the typical Hawaiian style of high-speed trolling, this was too fast for serious fishing.

But was it too fast to catch a fish? All fish react abnormally some of the time, and some fish are pretty peculiar all of the time. Maybe we *could* have it both ways and stir up some action with a crazy fish in the hour or so it would take to make Kona, while not bothering to slow down at all.

Zander hauled a giant bullet-shaped jig, with a leadhead, out of his tackle drawer and snapped it to the end of an 80-pound-class outfit. The jig was big enough to weigh a full pound and keep you from closing your thumb and forefinger around its shoulders. Zander had dressed it with scraps of vinyl skirts rescued from a half-dozen lures that had been chewed on by other fish.

A circus of colors, the monstrous thing was awesome. As heavy as it was, it stayed on top at the speed we pulled it. Sometimes it dove, but mostly it bounced. Its thrashing action reminded me of a puppy being hauled protestingly along on a leash to take its first bath.

Zander had chosen heavy tackle to withstand the battle of the lure, as much as to pull in any fish that the lure decided to attack on its way to Kona.

I thought you'd have to be crazy to believe that we had increased our odds of catching a fish even a fraction more than when we were towing no "lure" at all. To imagine any fish interested in challenging the "thing," as we had already begun calling it, was to conjure up a fish with the eyes of an eagle, the speed of a cheetah, and the mentality that caused extinction in dinosaurs.

A slashing high-speed strike is the trademark of the savage ono.

Before we got to Kona, we discovered two species of Hawaiian fish that had exactly those attributes. The first was a 40-pound ono, a long, metallic gray torpedo that zeroed in as swiftly and surely as any piece of naval armament could.

The strike of a strong fish on a big trolling reel is inimitable, and at this speed it was unimaginable. If you have ever heard the tires of an Indianapolis racer as they tried to keep the car out of a collision, then you have an accurate idea of the long scream that announced that first fish. There was no question of setting the hooks; we could probably have rammed them barb-deep into the hull of a destroyer at that speed.

The ono plays a one-run ball game, and it doesn't win for him any more often than it does for the Hawai'i Islanders. Overpowered, the fish gave up quickly. There is no ono in the world that could not be caught on 30-pound-test tackle, since the largest ever boated weighed 149 pounds, and we were using 80.

Our second surprise was a mahimahi. His strike still makes me wonder at the speed and visual acuity of this breed, both in the air and underwater. He first broke water at least 100 feet to the side of the wake and stayed on top until he caught the lure. He pounced on it like a diving hawk on a fleeing mouse.

I'm sure that these fish are as fast in the air as they are slicing their hatchet-flat bodies through the water, and their eyesight may be even sharper while flying. I once saw a mahimahi turn in the air to follow and snatch a banking flyingfish.

The mahimahi that grabbed the "thing" took it on the bounce from the air at the end of a jump. He was hooked *inside* the mouth, proof that he knew exactly where the lure was going and how to get there with it.

In true storybook fashion, we caught no fish when we reached the grounds. Our fishing day would have been entirely wasted without this experiment.

If high speed does not rule out catching mahimahi and ono, neither does slow motion. Once, when we were trying to sort out some problems with our CB radio, we stopped the boat and shut down the engines to get rid of all motor noise. We were as close to a dead stop as we could get without actually dropping anchor, and our lines were slanting steeply down into the water to prove it. A 36-pound mahimahi grabbed a drifting lure and started one of the toughest battles I've ever had with a fish of this size. Mahimahi have tremendous stamina under normal circumstances, but this one had not needed to expend energy to catch the lure in the first place, had not been dragged on the strike as usually happens, and was fought from a dead boat. He did not give up for 35 minutes, despite the constant pressure of a 50-pound-class outfit.

The exceptional endurance of a mahimahi against tackle designed for marlin and tuna surprises veteran anglers as well as newcomers, but when the tackle is scaled down to the fish's size, it can be nearly impossible to boat a big fish. A 40-pound mahimahi hooked on 20-pound-test spinning tackle aboard the *Catherine S* out of Honolulu wore out two anglers in a battle lasting an hour and three-quarters before finally succumbing to the efforts of skipper Lloyd Shelton.

The fellow who really wants to load up his coolers with mahimahi uses trolling only to locate the fish. The first mahimahi is the beginning and the end. With this fish subdued off the stern, the real action begins. The school remains with the hooked fish and can usually be seen hovering below their captive schoolmate, or keeping their distance off to the sides of the battle.

A cast lure will rarely work with these wary bystanders. Oh, they'll race in for a good look and get close enough to give you a heart attack, but then they just veer off. That's when you reach for a thawed-out squid, impale it on a 6/0 hook with a heavy monofilament leader and drift it back a dozen feet off the stern. Action can be instantaneous as three or four fish attack at once.

The school will stay only as long as the hooked member is not too close to the boat. If you try to hold him against the hull with a gaff, the others will disappear immediately.

Never go out without some kind of fresh bait if mahimahi are your quarry, but you can use belly strips cut from ono, aku, kawakawa, and even other mahimahi, if you don't have squid or 'ōpelu. This is the secret to catches that are counted in dozens.

Every ancient fishing mariner yearns for the sight of a drifting log. A barnacled trunk with a scattering of birds sets the mind reeling in drunken anticipation, and the body rocking as though to urge the boat to greater efforts. Can this be a mirage? Get there before the mirage disappears!

Why? Consider the morning we heard a call for assistance over the CB. Zander needed help, or so his mate on the *Spooky Luki*, Gary Moniz, told us. When we raced to the scene, we found all hands aboard the *Spooky Luki* tied into fish, with every line jerked tight as soon as it was put back out again. The mixed school of

A bull mahimahi can have a head as square as a barn door.

mahimahi and ono spread for a hundred yards around the drifting tree, and we hooked our first pair before we were even close enough to see its smooth, peeled trunk looping and bobbing with the waves.

For two hours we hooked and fought fish in an angling orgy approached in intensity only in our dreams. Then they just stopped biting. You could still see their multicolored, spangled skins as they played among the lures, but some primordial force had damped their urge to feed, and they would eat nothing, including our tasty squids.

The commercial sea lanes are host to many mahimahi because of the flotsam left by passing ships, which provides protection, shelter, and a parasite-cleaning station for mahimahi, ono, and small 'ahi. Drifting debris gathers colonies of life in the open ocean. Complex assemblages of species play hide and seek, with survival the stake for the winner.

Such colonies can be immense, like the one Manduke Baldwin and Sally and Freddy Rice discovered in March 1965. The focus was a log approximately 8 miles offshore from the "third flow," a black ribbon of lava snaking toward the sea in South Kona.

"We could see dozens of mahimahi, but they refused to bite," Freddy recounted. "After a few frustrating passes with our lures near the log, a marlin appeared in our wake, directly behind the boat. He was stalking a pair of big mahimahi swimming frantically along under our boat, seeking the protection of its hull. One mahimahi tried to make a break for it back to the log, but he was playing the marlin's game—he was cut down before he got a dozen feet. In four hours we hooked and lost three marlin that broke our lines."

Such colonies are semipermanent "condominiums," staying together as long as the drifting object remains afloat. During the 1967 HIBT, some of the best marlin fishing occurred in the vicinity of a large, half-submerged tree trunk that stayed between the second and third flows for several days, then drifted south toward Miloli'i. As the log moved, so did the concentration of marlin strikes.

A "log" can be anything from a single coconut to the floating body of a dead shark. Jack Ross once caught a mahimahi from the shadow of a drifting shark carcass, but even that is not the strangest piece of flotsam that ever harbored a colony of game fish. Let Tommy Rodenhurst tell the tale:

"It was out in the Moloka'i Channel, just off 'Īlio Point, a great black shape in the distance, bobbing up and down like a giant balloon only half full of air. As we approached, a rancid smell nearly overcame us, and we knew for sure it was a dead whale. The whale's oil had spilled out of him making a slick for a hundred yards around, flattening the water like a lake. It was like looking through a window pane into the depths. Packed against each other like the feathers on a peacock were the brilliant blue backs of hundreds of mahimahi. We'd get upwind of the overpowering odor to store up some clean air in our lungs, then we'd make a pass with the reel drags as tight as we dared. As fast as we'd hook up a few mahimahi, we'd drag them back into clean air again to fight them. I swear we'd still be out there fighting fish to this day, if the smell hadn't finally driven us away."

Schooling mahimahi draw enough comfort from running with the pack that they lose much of their natural fear of other creatures. The Aukaka with Dave Nottage as skipper encountered a giant school, numbering in the hundreds, while crossing the Moloka'i Channel. The fish would not strike at either lures or bait. Dennis Kirwin, an accomplished diver, was on board and led an underwater foray with spear guns. They got four mahimahi that were comfortable enough among the divers to get too close.

All fish seem to turn their interest in feeding on and off. It may make no sense whatsoever that a mahimahi will totally disregard a succulent meal capable of driving it mad with hunger when the tide changes, but it is true.

The golden dolphin is most likely to be a surface feeder during the high-tide change. The low change is next best, and a steep-rising tide rates third. One morning when we had had no action of any kind for several hours, we were startled into battle for a solid half hour of repeated strikes from mahimahi, before the school disappeared. Naturally, we thought we had just found, and then lost, a wandering bunch of rampaging fish, but we discovered a new dimension when we started to contact other boats by radio and learned of similar experiences during the same period.

For approximately one-half hour at the top of the tide every boat strung out along 10 miles of coastline had struggled with a half-dozen or more strikes—and then nothing. Our fish were filled with bottom creatures like shrimp and spiny puffers; obviously they had been foraging deep and came up for a change of diet under the mysterious power of moon, tide, and current.

Ono will strike at anything that moves, including swivels, leaders, knots, the V which the line makes as it cuts the surface, and, of course, artificial lures of any and every kind, from the simplest to the most farfetched. Despite their great speed and maneuverability, they do prefer an easy target, however, and will make their first choice a deep-running, straight-tracking lure. Kid McCoy and Charlie Campbell proved this on a trip to South Point that produced twenty-nine ono, most of which were caught on a heavy lure of Kid's own design. The lure was a piece of chrome tubing filled with lead around a small diameter pipe, and with the flat face cut exactly perpendicular to the leader. Since the line always angles down into the water from the tip of a trolling rod, the flat face is always digging in, regardless of how the lure turns; so the heavy weight pulls the lure along 5 or 6 feet below the surface. An attached plastic skirt just serves to hide the hooks and complete the shape. You can't argue action, color, shape, or any other nuance of the lure maker's trade with a pair of fellows busily cleaning a half ton of ono.

When the ono's mind is made up, his strike is as quick as a lightning bolt, and charged with the same power. I like to watch the lures as they track through the wake, searching for a game fish to fool; hence I've seen many ono streak in to destroy a lure with their powerful jaws and knife-edge teeth.

I can recall being startled out of a sea-induced trance by a long, mysterious shape powering through the sky 15 feet above the water and steadily pumping its tail, as though mastering the air the way it masters the sea. The only sound had been the jerk of the outrigger tip, but the airborne ono didn't even break the rubber band as he realized the outrigger lure in his mouth was a phony—then dropped back to the water's surface, with the discarded lure falling next to it. Neither made a bigger splash than the other as they hit together. To prove I wasn't dreaming, I hauled in and inspected the half of the lure which the ono left me.

Often, an acrobatic ono misses when he tries for a super strike. We spotted a small ono in the air an instant before one of our flatline reels screamed out, so we were amazed to find ourselves fighting a fish with three times the power of the one we saw attack. We could only surmise that a much bigger fish had shouldered the other out of the way and gobbled the lure. It proved to be the same 20 pounder, but fighting backward. He had missed the lure with his bite, but smacked it with his tail on the

way past. The lure had flipped around his caudal joint and snagged the leader on the other side, lassoing him like a steer. It was a
chance in a million, but if you fish long enough, you can see
nearly everything.

For every fish that strikes a lure, how many are not fooled? How
many are attracted enough to follow behind the strange contrap-
tion, only to turn away as though definitely able to ascertain that
the thing is as inedible as you and I know it to be? When you
reach the end of one of those fishing days, hopefully rare, which
are barren of any action, you are tempted to say that the fish just
weren't there. Pride refuses to allow us to believe that we just did
not have the skill to outsmart them.

Yet there is very strong evidence that this may be the case. In
other words, lure action, color, and size just are not enough sometimes to persuade a Hawaiian fish that a bellyful of calories is
there for the eating. You don't need to spend the day watching
the wake with polarized binoculars to satisfy yourself that mahimahi, ono, ulua, and others swim through the baits chuckling to
themselves about the obvious artificiality of your "old reliables."
Instead, follow the lead of several successful fishermen and add
some flavor to your lure.

One way is to take a 10-ounce leadhead with no skirt and tie on
fresh strips cut from the belly of an ono. Make these by first trim-
ming the silvery under section of the ono until it is an even
quarter-inch thick. Then cut the strips three-quarters of an inch
wide and about a foot long. Tie these to the stem around the
head, and you have a lure that will troll at 8 knots without breaking up and will leave a trail of flavor behind it to satisfy the most
skeptical fish.

On days when the fish are actively feeding, it will do you no

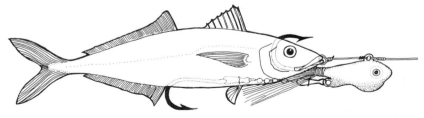

A small 'ōpelu rigged with a 2-ounce jig swims with a lively wriggling action at low trolling speeds. The bait should be flexed to loosen backbone.

more good than any other lure. When they are just window-shop-
ping the other lures, however, this tasty combination is the
answer—especially for ono and ulua.

The idea of marrying an artificial lure to a natural bait is not
new, but getting an attractor that is streamlined and more subtle
than a meatball can be a problem, especially when the only strip
bait you can get is squid. Squid strips tend to rip off at trolling
speeds if they are just hooked once on the ends. If you try to hook
them more than once, they bunch up into twisting chunks.

Hawaiian fishermen beat both problems by wrapping a tiny,
stainless steel treble hook onto the leader with Monel wire just

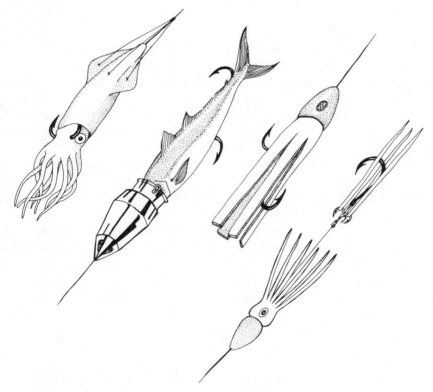

A rigged squid trolls best when the body is tied to the leader with
strands of thread. A small 'ōpelu trolls well with its head inserted inside
the hollow center of a jet lure. Hooks trail next to the bait. Strips of ono
belly make a succulent skirt for a large leadhead. Strips of squid can be
attached under a lure skirt by wiring a small treble hook to the leader.

ahead of the hook of the trolling feather lure. With the points bent in to keep them from snagging on the skirt, they provide three places to attach as many as three strips of squid. The treble hook pulls up underneath the skirt so that the squid strips can be hooked once at their very ends. They will be protected by the skirt from the streaming force of the current, which would otherwise yank them off. The master hook follows along in the midst of the fluttering streamers where it does not interfere with their action but is ready to stab even the short strikers.

Another natural-artificial combination, which dates back to the earliest days of fishing, is lures adorned with strips of *lai* (leatherback) skin. The lai is a sharp-toothed fish with the appearance of an elongated *pāpio* (young jack). It has a tough, leathery, metallic-colored hide that will last for years when dried. Every time it is used it soaks up water to regain flexibility, and it retains its silvery luster until ripped apart by many fish.

Unfortunately, the acrobatic and fast-striking lai has become a rarity along the shoreline and skins are at a premium. Anglers like Eddie Laau of Kawaihae swear by mahimahi skin as a substitute. It won't last as long as the lai skin, and it has a different, though appealing, color. It is easily stripped from the fish, preserves well when dried, and does not shed its tiny, pointed scales. Eddie can cite many examples of days when not only mahimahi and ono, but 'ahi and marlin have chosen the sweet smell of fish-flesh-festooned lures over the tasteless plastic kind.

Night-feeding fish, like the ulua which are also caught occasionally by trollers, cannot depend on sight to find food in the black depths. They must rely heavily on smell, or on the feel of the vibrations of passing creatures. The bigger ulua are primarily bottom feeders, though Zander Budge once encountered a big school that was chasing bait on the surface in 200 feet of water. This unusual school-feeding activity is very typical of the jack crevalle, a very close cousin of the many Hawaiian jacks lumped under the title ulua, but the crevalle is not found in local waters.

The ulua's normal tendency to seek security among the coral heads means that trollers must work waters less than 100 feet deep if they want to outsmart and outmuscle these brutes. The shallower you go, the tighter your drag setting must be. When a good ulua hits, he'll try to bury himself in the rocks for protection, and you've got to keep him from making it, or lose him to a broken

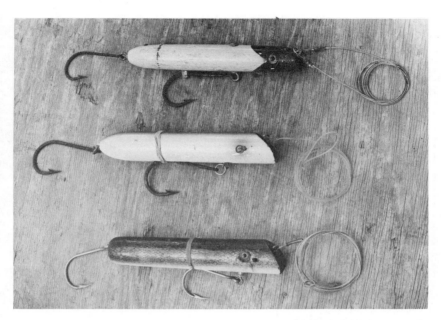

The commercially made "Tarp-Oreno" *(top)* evolved into the homemade "taperina" *(bottom)* in the hands of Hawai'i's lure makers. In the process it developed a new tapered shape that trolls well at twice the speed of the original. The plug in the middle is a commercially made lure adapted from the teasers made famous by Zane Grey.

line. With a normal drag setting you'll be wound up in coral before you can even grab the rod. You need to use the tight setting to pull the fish into deeper water immediately.

When I saw Kwanji Fukuyama haul a 100-pound ulua out of his fish box—a giant fish caught in waters many anglers troll almost daily—I thought the answer must be magic. My boat had never caught an ulua of any size by trolling, let alone one with shoulders as broad as my own.

"That's because you don't use taperinas," Kwanji said. The mysterious taperina is a broomstick with a pair of hooks on it. It is descended from an oversize, freshwater bass lure, marketed commercially under the name "Tarp-Oreno" and the big brother of the still popular "Bass-Oreno." At one time all Hawaiian trolling plugs were adaptations of these wooden monsters before plastics technology changed the rules of the game. The local corruption of the name matches the home-grown industry that features craftsmen who whittle and tune their wooden puppets to quiver and dance at the end of a line.

I became a fervent believer in this lure after watching Mateo Alcoran battle a 71-pound mahimahi hooked solidly by the prongs of a "tap." The fish took an hour and a half to subdue, cleaving its big bull head through the currents, its square brow seemingly as wide as a door. Twice it took the gaff from Mateo's hands before he could heave its bulk aboard. When asked to describe the lure's action, Mateo told me that it "swims way down and only comes back up when it grabs a fish."

The channeled front end works against the opposing force of the lure's buoyancy to produce a wriggling swimming vibration. It's this vibration that seems to be the secret of its mastery of big fish, and of ulua especially. Though the lure is no longer available commercially, its action is duplicated by other giant swimming lures including the balsa-wood minnows perfected in Finland. Of these, the Rapala lure tracks best at the necessary 6- or 7-knot trolling speed.

Like most game fish, ulua can be caught on nearly anything when their mood is right. And the mood takes them nearly all of the time along remote shorelines where few boats ever pass—places like South Point and the Hāmākua Coast of the Big Island, or the windward reefs of the neighbor islands.

We were working one such region, near the Coast Guard station

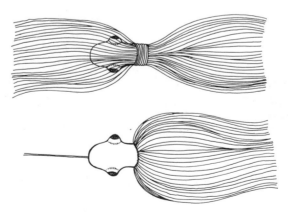

The "Hawaiian ghost" is an excellent lure for small game fish. Strands of nylon filament are tied on in a bunch at their middle, but flow backward over the lure in use.

A 100-pound ulua can bring a satisfied smile to any angler's face, even an old hand like Kwanji Fukuyama.

off 'Upolu Point, trying hard to take an ulua big enough to win the prize in the Kawaihae Trolling Club's spring tournament. We were doing everything "right": swimming wooden plugs right up in the shallows, something the bigger boats didn't dare try. Beyond us was *Spooky Luki* fishing the deeper water with conventional lures—all wrong for ulua, of course. We could not muster a strike of any kind, but turned our heads in time to see Zander hook up a strong fish. His 25 pounder won the ulua prize. With some embarrassment, Zander confessed that he hooked the fish on a standard blue Hawaiian trolling plug; nothing special about it except the fact that I had made it. A dozen others, all from the same mold, had spent the day unused in my box.

No matter how many rules of fishing you think you've learned, there is always a fish, somewhere, ready to break them.

# 5
# The Offshore Lightweights

## TROLLING FOR SMALL GAME

AS THE BOAT edged into the pier, the happy group aboard greeted their waiting families with superlatives about the great day of fishing they'd just enjoyed. Yet no flags flew from the mast and no big fish were on display. Instead, the skipper opened his ice chest and began unloading fish after fish—all assorted aku and kawakawa, and all under 15 pounds.

When he had added the fortieth or fiftieth plump bonito to the pile, he shrugged and explained, "We tried to talk them into fishing for marlin and tuna—all they wanted to do was catch bait." But the twinkle in his eye countered his nonchalant manner and gave away the fact that he, too, was well pleased with a trip that had been full of action and of satisfied customers.

One of the latter confided that he had never caught a fish as big as 10 pounds before and did not even know another fisherman that had. "These fish never quit hitting; we were pulling in an aku or kawakawa nearly all of the time. Sometimes we had four on at once with everyone howling and fighting fish. There wasn't a guy on board that didn't catch his share. If we'd gone for bigger game most of us would have been disappointed spectators while maybe one lucky fellow worked on a marlin or tuna for a couple of hours."

Hawaiian anglers are spoiled. The presence of giant fish that may run as heavy as half a ton tends to overshadow the tremendous offshore sport with small game on light tackle. Aku and kawakawa are among the smallest of the tuna family found in local waters, but they suffer from no inferiority complex when hooked on tackle scaled to their size. There is probably no fish of either species which could not be successfully landed on 20-pound-test trolling tackle, yet most fishermen tend to overpower them with gear ranging from 50-pound-test on up, since catching the bonito is just the first step in live-bait fishing for the real giants.

The aku is the skipjack tuna, sometimes called oceanic bonito, and the kawakawa masquerades under such names as black skipjack, little tuna, false albacore (actually a misnomer since this is a similar species found elsewhere), or just plain "bonito." Though similar enough in appearance to fool the *malihini* (newcomer), the two actually have different shapes, markings, and habits. The aku has black stripes on its belly, and the kawakawa has wavy lines only on its back and several spots on each side of its belly just behind the pectoral fins.

Aku travel in immense schools, feeding frantically at every opportunity. They provide Hawai'i's fishermen with dependable sport during their summer migration. Photo courtesy of the National Marine Fisheries Service.

Aku are the more abundant of the two species since they are pelagic fish which migrate in large schools delivering a constantly changing population. Kawakawa are occasionally mixed in with the aku schools but are more often found in groups of two or three. During some seasons, big schools of tiny kawakawa (called *oi oi*) appear. Generally, kawakawa are more land-oriented and stay in the shallower ocean waters outside the deep drop-offs along the reefs. Their stomachs are kept filled by foraging on crustacea near the bottom, but they regularly come to the surface whenever food is abundant there.

Sometimes large, scattered schools of big kawakawa gather for several days along the lee shores of all islands and startle fishermen with their willingness to strike anything. On one such day we found a few birds scattered over many acres. None were actively feeding—just hovering a dozen feet above the surface as though watching and waiting. Experience told us that such bird activity meant a school of fish too deep to promise action. That's why we nearly jumped out of our skins with the screech of the first reel.

Within seconds we were hooked up on three lines. The mystery of the triple strike lay in the lures. Each was a plug of marlin size, roughly 10 inches from plastic scoop to the tips of the rubber tails. Yet all three fish were kawakawa. True, they averaged 15 pounds, not too small a size to hit such a plug if they were mahimahi or ono. But kawakawa are not so well equipped to be aggressive feeders. They can scarcely scratch you with their tiny teeth and must swallow whole anything they catch, rather than chopping it to pieces. Generally, they avoid any lure bigger than a 1-ounce trolling feather.

We puzzled over what had caused such a marked personality change, especially as the fish box continued to fill with others from the widespread school. Each was lifted aboard carefully without gaffing, since all tunas are very bloody fish, and each was packed on ice, of course. Bloody fish spoil rapidly.

Since all were hooked on our biggest lures and our heaviest tackle, we had to give up fishing for other species. Despite overpowering tackle, these kawakawa gave a very good account of themselves; so we did not begrudge them their takeover of all the water for miles in every direction.

Soon we came upon a strange sight that explained much of the unusual behavior. A pair of excited birds danced above a dark spot in the water with their claws never more than inches from the surface. As we drew closer the shadow of what we had thought to be one large slow-moving creature became distinguishable as a massed ball of 'ōpelu, each one doing its best to get into the center of the pile.

Teamwork by an assortment of predators kept the 'ōpelu packed without hope of escape. Below them were the big kawakawa ready to pick off any that tried to plunge into the depths. Around them circled a big 'ahi, working them together like a sheep dog herding its flock. Above them were the birds, each trying to sink its claws into the flashing, rolling mackerel as they tumbled together in panic below trying to get into the center to use their friends as a living shield.

Once in a while a terrified 'ōpelu would try to escape and the 'ahi would suck him in at the end of a short brutal run, like a linebacker smothering the quarterback. Or a kawakawa would grab as much as he could hang on to and do his best to swallow as his brothers yanked on any part sticking out of his mouth.

By pulling in the flatlines and maneuvering the outrigger lines

An overeager kawakawa breaks up a ball of bait fish. Photo by National Marine Fisheries Service.

through the ball again and again, we could count on catching kawakawa until we tired of a sport that eventually became as controlled as a shooting gallery. Many of these fish had one or more 'ōpelu between 8 and 12 inches long swallowed live in their bellies.

Much of the trolling for aku and kawakawa is incidental to fishing for their bigger cousins. The top spots in the trolling wake for lures, therefore, are usually reserved for more desirable fish. The small feathers the welterweights usually prefer are kept in close where they won't tangle with the higher-priority lures. Since aku or kawakawa will strike these shortlines regardless of their proximity to the motor, the myth has grown that this is the location desired by the fish.

Fishermen who would like to prove this false can do so by trolling a pair of identical quarter-ounce feathers, one on the short flatline and one on the long outrigger 60 or 70 yards back. Three or four times as many of the small tunas will be caught on the outrigger on most boats. Some fishermen will feel that this is a waste of a key wake position. Others, the live-baiters, will argue that a method that produces three times as much marlin and 'ahi bait as any other is hardly a waste of anything at all.

When doing this it pays to switch to light piano-wire leaders, even though wire is slightly less desirable in aku fishing than monofilament nylon (called *suji* by the old-timers). That miniature lure, straggling along far back in the wake, is an inviting target for every kind of sharp-toothed fish including the biggest. Our little outrigger feather has taken mahimahi up to 45 pounds, ono as big as 60 pounds, and an occasional 40-pound yellowfin. It even took a rap from a marlin that lost sight of the tiny thing as he raced toward it and missed.

Color may also be an important determinant with these tiny powerhouses. One trip on the *Spooky Luki*, intended primarily to catch sashimi fish for a party, opened our eyes to the possibility that kawakawa can be crazy over chartreuse. We trolled a pair of identical small jigs with hooks, leaders, and tackle of the same size off the corner rods—lines stretched to the same spot so the lures ran side by side a few feet apart. One lure had a bright, yellow-green plastic skirt, the other was white. Against the overcast late afternoon sky, the chartreuse lure was always hit first and enticed fourteen kawakawa while the white drew only six.

Proper tackle for small tunas can be as light as you like. The biggest aku rarely exceed 40 pounds, and the record on flimsy 6-pound-test is a 21 pounder. Twelve-pound class makes aku fishing great sport. Of course, if your interest in tiny tuna is as a bait fish, then you'll want to use heavy gear to subdue the bait fish and get it in quickly before it has a chance to fight itself to death or attract a shark to finish the fight for you.

Now that the kawakawa has finally been recognized as a game fish by the IGFA there is added incentive to fishing for them on very light tackle. At this writing, the world records in most line-test classes are vacant, a fact I learned to my great chagrin. It was just after I had cleaned a 15-pound kawakawa taken on a regulation 20-pound-class outfit that I remembered the vacancy in that class. The minimum qualifying weight was a mere 9 pounds. I had just destroyed a certain record! Even had the line overtested, forcing the submission into the 30-pound class, it still would have been a record since that class was vacant, too.

In waters where big fish abound and aku and kawakawa, even of the size and fighting prowess of those found in Hawai'i, are considered no more than bait, these sport fish are regularly downgraded. The fact that probably 90 percent or more of the estimated 40 million American fishermen have never caught a fish as big and tough as a typical aku should bring things into perspective. That mob of 36 million anglers would be very content to change places with any fellow who was dissatisfied fighting an aku.

According to Freddy Rice, there are three distinct subpopulations of aku that make up the total population available to fishermen. The biggest, called *otadi* weigh 20 pounds or more and show up in Kona in August, staying until as late as October. These are the backbone of the Hawaiian tuna fishery. In fact, Hawai'i may be the only place where aku of this size are abundant enough to support commercial fishing. These are two or more years old, a fact which suggests a rapid rate of growth.

Hawaiian waters also appear to host a subpopulation of non-migratory fish which remain year round within a relatively small geographic area near their original spawning grounds, unlike the traveling otadi. In June and August of 1962, two otadi were caught locally that had been tagged two years before along the Baja California coast. Since then a total of eight aku from Baja have been captured in Hawai'i. One such fish, taken in 1975, had grown from 4½ pounds to 21 pounds in the 14 months since it was tagged. Its length had increased from 18 to 30 inches during its 2,750-mile journey. Interestingly, all of these Baja fish have been recovered in years when the commercial catch rate has been below average. Freddy Rice notes that the only tagged marlin he has ever heard of being recovered in Hawaiian waters had also gotten its marker in Baja waters 2 years before its capture.

The third subpopulation are the migratory aku from the large stock that supplies the eastern Pacific fishery. These are spawned in the equatorial central Pacific. They are the small young aku which move to the coast of California and South America and then return to the central Pacific where they turn up in Hawaiian waters as part of the good summer catch.

Even nonmigratory fish do a lot of traveling, though most of it is in circles. Biologist Heeney Yuen of the National Marine Fisheries Service has reported that the tagging of a big aku with an acoustical sonar device showed that the fish kept its position on the bank during the day while running far offshore during the night—then returning to almost its exact daytime location. Yuen's team of researchers, aboard the research vessel *Townsend Cromwell*, tracked an aku school with sonar gear for five days and nights near Ka'ula Island off Kaua'i. They found that the school traveled as far as 60 miles from its daytime station every night.

Kawakawa are known to chase bait into shallow water upon occasion, at which time they may be caught by shore fishermen. Such occurrences are rare in Hawai'i, though common off Florida where fishing piers extend far offshore.

Many aku are caught by blind trolling. There may be no evidence of any kind that a school is in the area—no birds, no surface splashes, no feeding bait fish—and the aku lines will zing out. Spectacular fishing occurs only when the schools are churning the surface to foam in a frenzy of feeding. Such schools can stretch for miles. Francis Ruddles reported an aku school that stretched from Māhukona to 'Anaeho'omalu Bay 20 miles to the south and consisted of fish breaking water in an unbroken line the entire length. This school was still there two days later for me to see for myself.

Marine biologist John Naughton of the NMFS described a scene that occurred on an exploratory trip into Pacific waters rarely traveled. He saw what he was sure was an uncharted reef or atoll complete with the white water of waves breaking across the coral. As he approached he discovered that the commotion was caused by a furious school of aku beating the surface to a milky foam for miles.

Such gigantic accumulations of excited fish do not always spell fishing action. After working one big school for a full day without success of any kind, we directed our queries to marine biologists about the phenomenon. The fish were so thick and so active that we could feel them bumping the bottom of the hull in their blind fever. The biologists speculated that the schools were spawning and had interests other than eating at the time. We missed our chance of verifying this by not being aware of the possibility. Ruddles had succeeded in boating several fish by simply stopping his boat in the school and letting the lines sink down through the tumbling mass of underwater acrobats until the fish wrapped themselves in the line and could be pulled in. The next time it happens we'll check for gravid females.

Even when schools are feeding they can be frustrating to work. They tend to get one track minds and program themselves to attack one kind of food, rejecting all others if there is plenty. Peter Budge reported a frustrating morning trying to hook aku from a school that was driving flyingfish into the air for acres around the boat. They struck none of the usual lures. Yet if Peter had had a mālolo to drift into the school he probably would have caught fish.

During certain seasons all aku are crammed with squid. At such times pink and red lures, leadheads with plastic skirts, of a size comparable to the squid, are the top producers. Aku are so heavily preyed upon by all bigger fish that they have learned to run at the sight of trouble. The racing shadow and sound of a boat will often drive them away or chase them down into the depths except on the occasions when spawning or intense feeding causes them to ignore danger. When they are spooky it is best to circle the school with lines set as far back as possible, even on the outriggers, and thereby pull the lines through the school without having the boat go near the fish. Sometimes the sight of the boat only causes the school to go down slightly and then return to the surface once the wake has begun to settle. That is when the longlines really do the trick.

For the feeding sprees when aku hit anything that moves anywhere they can find it, shortlines become practical. Some trollers attach a pair of cleats about a foot apart inside each gunnel. These provide storage for a pair of stout handlines which can be readily wrapped around them and kept tangle-free until feeding aku schools are sighted. Handlines are tied to shock absorbers made from surgical tubing to keep them from breaking on a strike. There is little sport involved because the aku is yanked to the surface as soon as he is hooked, then skitters across the surface helplessly.

To increase the catch on days when aku are finicky, trollers use 30-pound-test monofilament leaders. Decreased visibility means more fish. Small lures are better than big ones. Quarter-ounce feathers work best for fish around 5 pounds; eighth- and sixteenth-ounce pearlheads will often work when larger ones are rejected. Big aku occasionally take feathers up to 4 or 5 ounces, but such times are rare.

George Parker believes in finesse when he wants an aku. He uses no leader or swivel to distract fish but runs the monofilament line right through the lure to the hook. That means he needs a lure that will track dead straight, since no swivel is there to take up the twist. His choice is a small vinyl squid with a tiny lead inside. This lead can be an egg-shaped sinker with a center hole or a bullet-nosed "worm" weight, so called because it was developed to use with plastic worms in catching freshwater bass.

On a rare day when even this degree of subterfuge is not enough, the addition of a thin strip of frozen squid will turn the lookers into biters. The strip bait is attached by running the point of the hook through the wider end of the tough white lace of skin. The point of the strip dangles just outside the end of the skirt, a tantalizing bit of taste, smell, and action.

When aku are feeding on small shiny fish, such as *nehu* (anchovy), the addition of strips of bright plastic mylar can turn a dead lure into a killer. Hooks must match the size of the lure and should be no bigger than necessary to run with the point outside the skirt, or they will draw fewer strikes. Such hooks should be of moderately heavy wire or they will open on the strike before they can penetrate if they hit a hard part.

Most hookups will occur in the corner of the mouth as the fish turns to run with his fresh caught kill. Many fish are lost when the point fails to penetrate the palate, since the point will sometimes head in that direction. Others are lost when the hook is swallowed and catches on the gills, thus tearing loose and leaving a crippled fish to wander, bleeding, until a shark snaps him up.

One of the greatest spinning-tackle sports possible is casting to feeding aku with a small silver spoon from the bow of an open boat. Often a school that is too skittish to let a fast moving boat maneuver its trailing lines over it will hold position as a slow or drifting boat approaches. Sometimes a boat stopping to pull in a hooked aku will find that the drifting hull has lost its terror and the aku continue to break water all around. Then a spin caster can marvel at the speed and power of a strong fish on a limber rod.

Jigging a lure through a school so that it darts and stops will also enhance its effect to draw more strikes. On one occasion when our lures remained untouched as we passed near a school, I started to strip some loose coils of poorly wound line from a reel as the lure trailed in the water. The pulsating action thus imparted made the lure so much more attractive than three others that it was the only one to draw a strike. Fearful of backlashing the loosely wound line I screwed the drag tight and hauled in the fish. Then I set out again to get rid of those loose coils in the same way with the same consequences: two or three pulls and another aku.

Commercial aku boats use a refined hook-and-line technique. Such boats are built with live bait wells filled at the start of each operation by a netting trip for nehu. When the aku school is spotted the boats head into it. If the school swims deeper, the boats make a slow circle around the spot, tossing live bait into their wake. The combination of the live bait and the spray of sea water thrown out by special sprayers mounted along the sides of the boat overcomes the tunas' fear of the sampan, and they race right up to the stern for a handout. Thick bamboo poles with strong lines are brought into play, and the aku quickly snatch the shiny lures offered at the ends of the lines. With no hesitation the fisherman pulls the fish clear of the water before it knows anything is amiss and can start to pull back. The aku flash their silver sides against the sky for a second, beating their tails furiously in the air, before they disappear over the fisherman's shoulder and down into the hold. Their action then frees them from the barbless hook and the lure is returned to the water in another second to fool another fish.

Hungry aku will perform surprising feats to get food. At times the lure doesn't even have to be in the water. Once a pair of aku lines tangled on the *Spooky Luki* so that one lure dangled a few inches above the surface as it was being reeled in to get the mess sorted out. An aku burst out of the water and clamped down on the swinging bait.

Since new discoveries about aku are being made all of the time, perhaps it is fitting that we leave the subject right there, hanging in midair.

# 6
# *The Fight From Strike to Gaff*
## HOW TO BOAT ANY FISH

IF YOU CAN BOAT a Pacific blue marlin, you can land any fish in the ocean. When tackle is scaled down to match the fish, the principles involved in fighting and gaffing a 500-pound marlin on 130-pound-test tackle are similar to those needed to subdue a 50-pound mahimahi on 12. The major difference is the size of the fish relative to the strength of the man who must beat him. More muscle is needed, more strength, endurance, and time; and there is more danger to the gaffer in the final moments.

Small fish of any species are more manageable by men who can overpower them by their superior size and weight at gaff, but the fish can still inflict casualties in their panic when near the boat. No matter what fish you try for, if you can learn to beat a marlin you will have no trouble landing any other.

A marlin bill is a killing weapon well designed for its purpose, and the fish will use it on the man if he gets the chance. For four hours Toots Tsutahara of the *Coreene C* helped angler Ross Wall in his fight with a big marlin. Six times Toots had his hands on the leader, and each time the marlin pulled free. The already enraged fish became maddened completely out of control when he tangled his bill in the prop. When Tsutahara again tried to gaff him, he leaped right into the boat after the two men, barely missing both and driving his bill into the top of the starboard icebox. Unable to strike a killing blow with its bill, the marlin thrashed with his huge tail forcing Wall over the stern and nearly into the water with the rod and reel still harnessed to him. One smack of the tail tore a fighting chair loose from bolts strong enough to hold the weight of a man fighting a big fish. Fortunately, no one was hurt, and Tsutahara finally got control again, but only after belting the fish with a weighted club.

The marlin Robert Kiehn brought to gaff had better aim. He leaped at skipper Darrel Skelton on the *Mokunani* as he leaned over the stern to gaff him. Though he missed Skelton, he smacked Kiehn in the chest with his bill and flailed the tip across Kiehn's cheek, drawing blood on both scores.

When Larry Clapp tried to hold a marlin at gaff, the fish yanked him overboard. Clapp was agile enough to get back aboard, very quickly, of course, and still gaff the marlin.

George Parker had a violent billfish ram its spike right through the planking of his *Mona H.*

A hooked marlin attacked the *Malia,* splitting her planking and breaking off its own bill. With the boat leaking at an alarming rate, angler Aka Hodgins' only comment was, "Main thing, we caught the marlin." Fortunately, owner Freddy Rice was able to call ahead to commercial fisherman Bob Leslie to get the drydock cradle ready, and the *Malia* went up on dry land as soon as it made port.

Is any further discussion necessary? Billfish are dangerous and must be handled with care and good sense.

That's rule number one, but from there on, there is very little agreement among anglers on how to strike, fight, gaff, and boat a fish. When a fish hits a trolled lure, should you strike it or will the speed of the boat do it for you? Should you gun the engine in hopes of increasing the pressure on the hook point, or should you back down immediately to save line? Should you chase the fish or fight him from a dead boat?

Surprisingly, the answers to such seemingly elementary questions are still cause for debate among many anglers of different persuasions but with enough experience to mount telling arguments on all sides of each question. Add to the confusion the individual character of each marlin encountered and you've got controversy that will forever defy resolution.

Strike the fish? Rope Nelson says, "The marlin doesn't have

hands to put the hook in his mouth, you've got to do it for him.''
Another fisherman will say that the point of a hook traveling at 8
knots on a line set with 20 pounds of pressure will sink as deep as
you'll need it, and setting the hook will just pull it loose. Then
the argument will rage back to the other side when a fellow like
Freddy Rice reminds you that you drive a nail into a board by tap-
ping it, not pushing it; the former is the equivalent of the quick
pull on a tight line, which is what striking means.

If you are really lucky, the fish will do it for you by slapping the
leader hard with his tail when he jumps, thus setting it hard
enough to drive the point right through his bony bill. Striking
can't hurt and may help. Any hook pulled out by the power of a
quick upward sweep of the rod against a drag tightened just long
enough to get the job done wouldn't have stayed in until the end
of the fight anyway unless luck, God, and the fish are all on the
angler's side during the whole battle.

The boat should not be slowed until the fish is struck and the
angler is in the fighting chair. The strike can be no more than a
quick increase and decrease of the drag lever with the rod in the

Keep a marlin jumping and he'll usually beat himself trying to shake the
hook. This black marlin leaped 43 times during the fight and was gentle
as a lamb at gaff. Photo by Tony Rutgers.

holder. But an experienced fisherman can draw the rod from its holder, increase the drag for a second while sweeping the rod up once or twice, then drop into the fighting chair as he releases tension back to normal.

Only billfish have bills, and the long noses make a difference in the way you strike. Most fish will have the hook in their mouth or will have the point snagged somewhere on the head. A hard upward sweep helps the point penetrate. The difference with marlin is the possibility that the leader is wrapped around the bill, and the hook may have no contact with the fish at all. Some experts can tell by the feel of the rod in their hands whether the hook is solidly against bone or the leader is sliding on the bill. There is no advantage to striking a bill-wrapped fish.

A well-hooked billfish feels the steel and jumps immediately. A marlin that runs may well be bill-wrapped. An 'ahi runs like an express train straight away from the boat on a strike. So does an ono, but the toothy torpedo uses up everything on this run and generally quits. The mahimahi gets right into the air when it hits, then continues to leap spectacularly throughout most of the fight unless hooked in a vital spot. An ulua goes right for the bottom.

Those are the standard patterns, and the only rule of nature is that all rules have exceptions. Occasionally an 'ahi will bound across the surface like a blunt billfish and a mahimahi won't show a fin until gaffed.

Once the fish is struck, the boat handler must take his cues from what the fish is doing and the speed and power with which he is doing it. Obviously, a fish hell-bent on stripping all of the line from a reel with a full-power run straight away from the boat requires different tactics than the fish that turns and runs parallel to the boat's heading. A fish hooked in the lower jaw may drown himself with his every effort, since his mouth is continually forced open when he tries to pull; a tail-wrapped fish may stay fresh forever like the 183-pound 'ahi that outwitted George Parker and Dan Wallace on the *Kona Queen* for four and a half hours.

What the fisherman does first in the early going depends on the way the fish acts. It is nearly always smart to keep the boat sliding forward until all lines are picked up. This keeps the fighting line from slacking, strips additional line to ensure that the fish will not be near the boat while green, and gets the fish clear of all other lines. But a screamer on light tackle may require that the boat be backed down on the fish immediately. Zander Budge had an 'ahi strip all of the 30-pound-test line from a 6/0 reel despite backing down as fast as *Spooky Luki* would go, almost from the instant of the strike with all other lines reversing around the bow in a great tangle.

One school of thought says that the boat should be moving toward the fish as long as line is leaving the reel once the other lines are out of the way. Another says that the easiest work for the angler comes when the skipper turns to run parallel with the fish so that a belly of line forms between the running fish and boat on the same heading. The belly gives enough drag to beat the fish while holding back from a direction that keeps him from sounding. A line being pulled sideways through the water can cause enough drag to break itself. This type of battle requires an alert skipper with nothing to do but watch the fish and quickly change direction accordingly. One nonattentive instant may allow the fish to cut across the bow or under the boat, with a broken line the almost certain result.

An angler who really works hard on his fish, giving it no quarter and himself no respite, follows the rule that the line must always be moving. It either goes out or comes in. If the fish isn't taking line the angler must; otherwise, the fish is using his weight to keep the strain while his muscles recover.

It is here that inexperienced fishermen confuse the advantages of rod and reel by trying to winch the line in under reel power only, a nearly impossible job. The rod is a lever which pries the fish toward the boat with upward sweeps, "pumps," from a nearly horizontal position to a nearly vertical one. The angle between rod and line at the top of the lift must not close beyond a right angle or the power of the fish becomes vectored down into the butt, with the possibility of a broken rod as the result. The downward pump is the time when line is picked up by the reel, all the while being guided back and forth across the spool. Cross winding is important so that line lies across itself on the spool rather than in perfectly parallel turns that cut down between each other to bury themselves and sabotage the battle on the next strong run.

When the first run is over, many skippers prefer to keep the fish behind the boat and fighting straight back off the stern. Freddy Rice keeps the line running out over the port corner of the transom. At least one other skipper works the fish by turning the chair sideways so that the line runs over the port gunnel and the fish is kept in the middle of a circling boat. Fran Weinberg on his huge

A portable deck chair, moved to the bow, can be a help when chasing a fast-running fish. Note the use of a shoulder harness clipped to the rings on the reel.

fishing cruiser *Capricorn* likes to walk around the boat with the rod butt in a belly socket and the rod itself supported by a shoulder harness attached to the reel rings. With a big fish that promises a long bout, Fran chooses to fight from the bow while seated in a movable fighting chair. That way his skipper, John Kilgore, can remain on the flying bridge for maximum visibility and work the boat forward toward the fish.

One of the toughest problems for the angler is the fish that dives for the bottom in desperation and kills himself with the effort. A big dead fish deep at the end of a long line can be all but unmovable. Rope Nelson has perfected a way of planing the fish to the surface. It takes determination and a bit of line on the reel to begin with. After setting the drag as tight as the angler can handle, Rope pushes the boat forward letting line slowly slide off the reel. Either the fish comes up, or the line comes to an end. If the latter happens, Rope backs down on the fish while the angler recovers line until the boat is straight up over the dead fish, which should not now be as deep as before. The process begins again and continues until the fish hits the surface. A dead fish can rarely be hauled straight up; it must be vectored up with the force applied by line at an angle.

A big marlin can ram itself right into the ocean bottom in its fury. It happened to Murray Heminger, Jr., off the old Kona Airport. The water wasn't too deep, so Murray went down with an Aqua-lung, broke the marlin free and brought it home to weigh in at 400 pounds.

A spare flying gaff will quickly rig a marlin for towing home. The gaff is set in the belly between the pelvic fins. A ring is slid down the gaff rope and over the bill and lower jaw to keep the mouth closed. Then a half-hitch is thrown around the bill.

When the fish "breaks" and is too exhausted to generate another run away from the boat, it can be pumped within gaffing range. The rest of the job belongs to the crew. In most cases the angler will now have nothing left to do but stay ready in case of unexpected difficulties. Any fish small enough to fit into the boat's fish box can be brought aboard while live, whether it is an aku, ono, mahimahi, ulua, or 'ahi. No such fish should ever be lifted aboard by the line or leader, but should be picked up with gaff or net. The latter is the preferred instrument with any small bloody fish like aku, kawakawa, or small 'ahi. The only exception is when the tuna will be used for bait; tangling it in the mesh of the net may create enough handling problems to weaken the bait before it can be rigged. The angler who makes it a habit to forgo net or gaff can expect to lose a lot of fish.

It is the volatile jumper, the mahimahi or marlin, that causes *pilikia* at gaff. The runners are generally so exhausted when pulled to the boat that they seem resigned to their fate. While gaffing a 35-pound ono for Dick Ednie, I drew the fish alongside and then watched the plug come free from the strain. The ono just lay on the surface until I made a desperate lunge with the hand gaff, which the ono obligingly swam right onto.

More mahimahi are lost at gaff than at any other stage of the fight. This is partly due to the perversity of the fish, but mostly because the gaffer becomes overeager and stops using his head. If you make a pass at a frantic dolphin and you miss because the crazy creature decided at that precise instant to jump into the boat and try to push you overboard—well, that's just the well-known lunacy of the species. But if you miss because you haven't figured out which way the gaff hook is pointing, that is poor preparation on your part, and you probably don't deserve to be that close to the fish anyway. To guarantee that they'll know which way the prong is pointing, many gaffers twist a stainless steel screw into the hand hold of the gaff opposite the side the hook sprouts from and just at the forward end of the handle wrap. Without taking his eyes off the fish, the gaffer can feel for the screw head with his thumb to make sure he has the gaff turned the way he wants it.

Stainless steel gaffs tend to be blunt and to get dull fast. Regular attention with a file is a must, since your safest bet in working with an active fish is to drive the gaff hook in until it comes out the other side. A 6-foot gaff with a 4-inch hook is standard for mahimahi and ono.

If a mahimahi does get free of the gaff when you've got him aboard (and this happens even to the best blue-water men) he'll cause a lot of trouble as he thrashes wildly about, throwing blood all over the cabin while doing his best to beat your brains out with any part of his body he can throw at you. You can try grabbing him again with the gaff, but you will probably end up just marking your boat trim or your crew. Harry Foster always brought a towel aboard and kept it handy for just such an emergency. He'd make like a bullfighter and try to get the towel over the mahimahi's eyes to blind it. This tended to calm the fish down. Zander Budge goes for the caudal peduncle (that's the wrist-like part of the body just in front of the tail) and squeezes down on it as hard as he can. He says the mahimahi usually goes limp.

The tail of a mahimahi is such a sensitive zone that he may gyrate like a Tahitian dancer when you touch him. Don't try to grab him by the gills unless you've got gloves on; the gill rakers will slice your fingers into neat strips. When you've got the gaff in, try to get the fish into the fish box without touching anything. Stunned mahimahi come back to life as go-go dancers the minute they feel contact.

Keep the gaff and leader well separated when you reach out to place the hook. One quick twist can wrap the wire around the gaff, thus immobilizing the gaff and pulling the hooks free. One major contributing factor to poor gaffing is the panic the gaffer feels when he sees how the fish is hooked. Mahimahi jaws are long and narrow, so these fish don't always get hooked firmly inside the mouth. The barbs frequently take hold somewhere outside the gill covers or even up on the hump. When the gaffer discovers that the only thing holding him to the fish is a half-inch strip of skin, he tends to hurry the job and lose the fish.

Where should you gaff? Behind the pectoral fins is a secure place but sometimes injures the meat or the body cavity enough to make it undesirable when the fish is served. The lower jaw is less secure but protects the fillets, but like the skipper told me when I was about to gaff my first mahimahi, gaff him wherever he'll let you.

Marlin can present the same kinds of problems and their size rapidly magnifies the difficulties to gargantuan proportions. Freddy Rice tells a tale that illustrates one approach veteran big-game fishermen employ. ''An embarrassing experience taught me a

Mahimahi can be very docile near the boat—until they feel the gaff. A second after this picture was snapped, this fish was 3 feet in the air!

lesson I never forgot," Freddy said, "and it may be the reason my wife Sally later got her world-record fish."

Freddy's lesson came when he was pulling in the leader preparatory to gaffing a wild, 250-pound marlin. The thrashing fish turned and tried to run full speed straight away from the boat. Faced with the pounding tail, Freddy let go of the wire and the fight started over again.

"We finally got the fish, but as we started cleaning up, Butch Chee, skipper of our boat *Malia,* said in a very quiet voice, 'You know, my father never let go of a leader.'

"I felt small enough to fit in the bucket, but I never forgot it. On a later trip when Sally and I were fishing alone, except for our six-month-old daughter, we hooked a good fish on Sally's line. After 30 minutes the fish was in back of the boat, but it was still green.

"We decided to go for it anyway since the water was choppy and the northbound current was heading us steadily toward rough seas that we were sure to reach in a long fight. The marlin played see-saw back and forth off the stern, and several attempts to hold him failed. So we decided to back down on the leader the next time he crossed.

"We backed down, and as the leader came up I put the boat back into forward and grabbed the wire. It was a full five minutes of bedlam, ending with the marlin completely clearing the water in a last-ditch effort before finally coming alongside the boat where I was able to set the big gaff, a second gaff, the yacht hook, and several ropes."

This 623-pound fish held the women's all-tackle record until it was beaten nineteen months later—by a lady fishing on the *Malia*.

With all of the big fish experience on the *Malia,* dating from the days of the late and revered Henry Chee, it may be instructive to study their system, and Freddy was good enough to share it.

A big flying gaff is set up with the hook over the starboard side and the handle back into the cabin along the starboard gunnel. A smaller flying gaff is laid across the transom. The big gaff's rope is

Ono are easy at gaff, but only if the gaffer makes sure the razor jaws are kept out of reach of the crew.

kept coiled and tied on the starboard side, with the small gaff's line kept separated from it on the port. A hand gaff is in its carrying hook under the transom, and a yacht buoy hook with heavy nylon rope is laid on the deck out of the way.

Both flying gaffs have barbs, and the hooks are firmly tied in to the detachable handles with hitches of wrapping string to make sure the hook does not pull away from the handle without a tug strong enough to bury the point solidly. Other skippers accomplish the same thing by cinching the gaff rope around the handle with half-hitches of the gaff rope itself. This means that the handle will go overboard after gaffing, but it is still firmly tied to the gaff rope.

When the leader comes up, the crew on the *Malia* takes it and brings the marlin up with determined hand-over-hand pulls. When the leader is in hand, the angler sits ready—some skippers prefer that the reel's clicker is put back on at this point so that everyone aboard will be instantly alerted if the leader gets away from the crew.

Since the stern of the *Malia* is broad and uncluttered, the crew member is able to drop the recovered line on the deck to one side of where he is standing. This routine is different from that followed on many boats where recovered leader is always kept in the water. Freddy says that dropping the wire overboard is dangerous because a wild fish can weave wire and gaffs into a liberating tangle. Detractors suggest that the coiled wire inside the boat is a potential hazard if, for any reason at all, the crew does lose its grip on the leader.

With the crew holding the wire, the gaffer picks up the long-handled gaff and positions himself straight behind the leader puller so that he can go to either side of the wire man to set the first gaff. A choice spot to gaff is the hump between head and dorsal fin. Good gaffers avoid the sensitive last third of the body and the easily torn belly region.

With the leader and first gaff line helping to hold the fish, a second gaff is put into place near the head so that the head can be pulled up and controlled. Then the yacht hook is set in the lower jaw. Its spring-loaded closing prong cannot be shaken free by the fish. The yacht-hook line is hitched around the bill so that the crew has complete control of the fish and can pull it into position for stunning with a forceful blow of the killing hammer or club right on top of the head.

Being prepared for the worst is the best mental attitude. Fortunately, most marlin are easy at gaff, since they tend to fight themselves into total exhaustion. Exceptions include the fish that is stunned at the hookup and comes in completely green after no fight at all, and the fish that is hurt by the hook and swims toward the boat to take the pressure off the painful tearing in his throat. He, too, can be mean at gaff, since he has his full strength.

With expert boat handling there may be no upper limit to the size of a fish that can be taken on light tackle. Such fragile equipment as 20- and 30-pound-test line can beat fish weighing 15 to 20 times the breaking strength of the line. For example, a 430-pound blue has been taken on 20-pound-test and an 816-pound black on 30.

Can you really put enough strain on a healthy, full-strength, 800-pound fish with 30-pound-test line to wear him down and beat him, when in actual fact your drag setting probably won't exceed 20 pounds of pull? Even if it can be done, wouldn't it take hours, stretching into days? Or is there some "trick" to it?

Actually, it can be done in minutes. Steve Zuckerman's former world-record blue, a 430-pound fish caught with skipper Bart Miller on 30-pound line, took only 20 minutes from strike to gaff.

Therein lies a controversy concerning sporting ethics, because the secret is to get to the fish *before* he does his heavy fighting, not after. The fish must be hooked on bait so that it has no clue that anything is amiss. A plug-hooked fish knows immediately that something is wrong and goes within an instant into a series of frantic escape tactics. Such a fish must be beaten with the drag of the reel constantly eroding his strength. On the other hand, a fish that eats a bait and notices nothing out of the ordinary can sometimes be approached by the boat as the angler works full speed to recover line left slack by the rapidly diminishing distance. Actually, the battle begins when the gaff is set.

Bart Miller talked about the procedure and its ramifications. "I've taken several monsters in Australia that were thousand pounders, one in five, one in about nine minutes. In the 1973 HIBT we took a 629 pounder in eight minutes. To understand and appreciate this, a person must look at it in all of its light. For every one that I've taken that way I've lost sixty or more.

"My wire man must take his life in his hands, literally. Once the fish is within the legal length of the gaff handle, the entire weight of the responsibility is on the gaff man. With a fish that green, the gaffer must set the big hook absolutely perfectly, or you'll have the fish on only for a few seconds before he tears free from the gaff.

"The angler is working flat-out the whole time, even though it may only be for five or ten minutes. There are few people who can run full speed for five minutes, or even talk as fast as they can for that length of time. The skipper is trying to stay close to a fish and still keep the line tight, with all of the many problems this involves. And then all of this has to converge at one time and click. It's like a racing car coming into a pit stop during an important race and it's got a carburetor problem, needs fuel, needs to have all tires changed, get all this done, and still get back on the track because there are only a few seconds separating the leaders.

"It's all teamwork and I carry extra men just for that. When we miss a fish or lose one, we discuss why we did and what we'll do in the future to make sure it doesn't happen again.

"The 629-pound marlin in the 1973 tournament made us win the Henry Chee award. When I saw the size of him and the match-up with the angler's experience and condition, I didn't think we'd be able to boat that fish on 80-pound line after a long fight without having to substitute a new angler and disqualify the fish. In all fairness to the man on the rod, I could very well have been wrong. But here was the opportunity, I had to make a decision, and I grabbed the leader.

"Within the blink of an eye, it pulled me the length of the deck, broke my finger, and chipped my shoulder bone. We gambled and we made it, but I had to fish the remaining two days with the injuries and ended up in the emergency room at the hospital.

"I think that when it is told that way, it is a lot different than someone saying, 'Ah, you just back up on him and kill him before he even knows what happened.'"

# 7
# *Small Boats and Big Fish*
## EQUIPPING A BOAT FOR HAWAI'I'S FISHING

WHAT "SMALL BOAT" MEANS to you may depend on whether you are the captain of an aircraft carrier or a kayak. By any man's definition, most of the boats that chase big fish in Hawaiian waters are small; 19 feet would be nearly average and some run as small as 12. Size seems to be no handicap as far as the fish are concerned. Consider the following story.

On a day early in May, Zander Budge launched his skiff and headed out along the Kona coast of the Big Island. The skiff was made of wood and was a mere 14 feet long. Fourteen feet! Barely more than three times the size of a typical bathtub. Fourteen feet of boat and what Zander intended was to challenge the biggest billfish in the world.

One by one he dropped three lines back into the wake. Each was baited with a home-made plug cast from plastic resin in Zander's garage. The baits plunged along behind the little boat, splashing, then diving, occasionally hunting from side to side. Each did its best to goad a billfish into striking. One did its job very well. One bait executed a pretty little jump, then dove right between the jaws of a huge Pacific blue marlin that had raced in to intercept it. The lure had no chance of escaping, for the mouth that opened under it was as big around as a basketball hoop.

The splash was big enough to be heard over the drone of the 28-horse outboard motor. The sound of the 12/0 reel as the 80-pound line was dragged from it hit at the guts with the same emotional impact as an ambulance siren heard on a still night. A moment exciting enough to be almost terrifying—but Zander was well prepared for battle. Many other marlin had provided the drill to get him ready for a big one. His harness was already on and he clipped the reel to it as soon as he had set the hook. With the rod thus in fighting position he was able to crank in the other lines without neglecting the giant fish that raced steadily away from the boat.

The little boat had been designed for just this kind of action, and controls could be reached easily from the fighting chair. "Chair" may not be the proper term. Zander fought his fish from a seated position on the fish box with the rod's butt firmly held in a gimbal he had fashioned from sections of brass tubing.

The man and the little boat relentlessly pressed the big fish. In just one hour it was pulled near enough to gaff. Even with the gaff set in his lower jaw the fish still had the power to be dangerous. A fish this big could easily break such a small boat to pieces. With gloved hands Zander drew the gaff line in until the marlin could be stunned with a blow on its head. Two half-hitches of the gaff line around the bill secured it for towing back to port.

Five hundred and seventy-five pounds. At the time, it became a new IGFA record for 80-pound-class tackle. In the many years since this episode the record has been broken and Budge has deserted small boats to become a professional skipper chasing fish with the kind of elegant sportfisherman usually associated with big game and blue water. And in those years the "mosquito fleet" of boats 19 feet long and under has grown steadily. Every weekend hundreds of miniature craft set out from ports all across the island chain to search for fish that are frequently too big to be brought on board. Mainland anglers who are accustomed to chasing billfish, tuna, dolphin, and wahoo in 30- or 40-foot cruisers are generally very much surprised to find that such luxury is not necessary here. Prime fishing grounds start at the harbor mouth, which obviates the long run to fishing territory so typical along the shallow water of the continental shelf.

Skiff fishing is nowhere near as comfortable, of course, but a skiff does not require a big crew or a big bank balance to maintain it. A fisherman can put his 16 footer in and pull it out by himself

The outboard-powered trailerable fiberglass boat can be turned into a miniature sportfisherman with every fishing feature of a larger craft— except, perhaps, comfort.

and can also handle every phase of the fish catching operation without help.

It is, of course, never wise to fish alone. Even with a maximum of safety precautions, accidents can happen, and an extra pair of hands can make a life or death difference.

Are small boats as effective as the big ones? Some boats definitely seem to be better fish getters than others. There may be something about the wake or the throb of the motor that will attract or repel fish. Size is not the deciding factor. Records of local club tournaments from Kaua'i to Kawaihae prove, however, that the small-boat fishermen can outfish their colleagues in the giant cruisers often enough to show that the amount of deck an angler stands on is less important than everything else he has working in his favor.

Paradoxically, most big boats catch more fish than most small ones. There is no contradiction here. The greater comfort aboard the big boats enables the fisherman to stay at his task longer and explore water no skiff man would dare try because of roughness or distance from home.

Strangely enough, lures that are killers on one boat don't necessarily attract fish on another, and this is especially true for exchanges between craft of different sizes. Butch Chee amends this rule even further by stating that the same lure will have different results fished at different spots in the wake of the same boat. Whether a lure is run on the front or back of a wave, or in a turbulent or calm spot of the wake, affects its action and its appeal.

Zander Budge once loaned me a plug that was his top producer. A flat-nosed straight runner with a blue and yellow insert, it was number one for months on end—on his boat. I made a rubber mold of it and turned out exact copies. After five trips and no luck, despite hopscotching the lures all over the wake among others that were catching fish, I disgustedly gave the pair I'd made back to Zander. On the very next trip he had one cut in half by a 30-pound ono and lost the other to a marlin that was too big to handle on the 20-pound rod it hit.

Outfitting a boat is a labor of love, despite the cynic's definition that "a boat is a hole in the water into which a man pours money." Perhaps it is true for some that "the two happiest days of a man's life are the day he buys it and the day he sells it." Each item of equipment is lovingly debated and pondered over— outriggers, for example.

No boat is too small for outriggers, though many fishermen regard them as "too much humbug" since they are more difficult to tend than flatlines. Why outriggers? They prevent tangles between different longlines, some as much as a hundred yards back, by holding the lines up off the water so that the flatlines can pass back and forth under them. This also puts less line in the water which may spook a fish. Fish can swim across a dragging line while trying to intercept a lure on another line and cut off the long one. The long wands impart more action to lures since they are always lifting the front end, and because they transmit the dipping action of the boat, which sweeps the outrigger tip forward and back, causing the lure to dart and settle.

Outriggers also allow you to maneuver around a school of fish or a floating object with the boat while dragging the lure close to the target. With live or fresh baits, the outrigger provides an automatic dropback of slack line, giving the attacking fish a chance to swallow the bait. Such a dropback is completely undesirable in lure fishing, of course, because the slack allows the fish to spit out the phony. To prevent dropback, Hawaiian fishermen employ a "stinger" line which runs down from the tip of the outrigger to a height at which the angler can grab it for attachment to the trolling line. One strong attachment is made by tightly wrapping a rubber band around the trolling line and then snapping both ends into a safety-pin-type snap at the end of the stinger. On the strike the band breaks after it has started driving the hook point into the fish's jaws. Once the rubber band is tied, line is pulled off the reel while it is vectored upward by the pull of the outrigger until it reaches the height desired. Generally, on the strike the trolling line is pulled straight and starts the reel turning before the rubber band breaks so that there is no dropback of any kind.

Stingers should be made from stiff heavy cord to decrease their tendency to whip forward when released and wrap around the

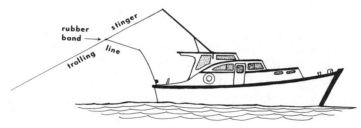

A stinger line allows the angler to use outriggers with artificial lures by eliminating dropback. The hook is set on a strike when the fish breaks the rubber band.

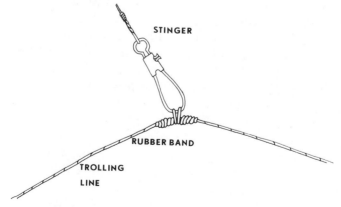

To attach the stinger, one end of the rubber band is looped over the open snap. The other end is wrapped tightly around the trolling line a dozen times, then it too is looped over the snap.

outrigger pole, causing a tangle which can frequently be undone only by demounting the outrigger from its holder.

The disadvantages of outriggers are, of course, numerous. Stinger lines can be hard to retrieve in a wind; they may blow back across the line while a fish is being fought and tangle with the fighting line. Once the band is tied, the length of trolling line cannot be adjusted. If a fish hits a different line, the rubber band must be undone before the outrigger line can be retrieved.

Clothespin outrigger snaps run up and down the pole on pulley lines solve some of the problems, but they give a dropback and don't generally hold the bigger plugs without marring the line. A popular solution in Kona is to tie the rubber band to a large glass or metal ring and thence to a very short stinger line run up to the top of the outrigger pole after the trolling line is passed through the ring. Line length can be adjusted through the ring, and the lure can be reeled all the way in without being dismounted. On a strike, the ring breaks free and slides down the line as the fish is fought.

A few small-boat fishermen avoid the problems while securing many of the advantages by mounting extra-long trolling rods from holders that rise a foot or two above the gunnels. Thus the outrigger and rod are the same piece of equipment.

To make the job of working with outriggers easier, the holder for the rod being served by the 'rigger should be a minimum of 4 feet forward of the stern transom. This gives the fisherman enough room to make the attachments without taking the rod from the holder.

Standard boat equipment should also include a fish box capable of handling fish up to 5 feet long. This should be as close to the side over which fish will be gaffed and pulled aboard as possible, to reduce the distance needed to carry an active fish on the gaff. Lids should be nonhinged so that they can be removed entirely to keep the box open with no chance of closing before the fish is dropped in. Fish boxes can double as fighting seats, but this is not really an efficient arrangement since the box cannot be opened while the angler sits on it. He must get up from his seat and open the box before the gaffed fish can be put away.

One way to compromise is to position the fish box across the boat with two lids that separate in the center and a gimbal on each side of the center line. While an angler sits on one side to fight the fish, the other lid is open. Double strikes become

Rod holders should be sturdy, heavily chromed, and mounted at an angle to slant rods back. Safety lines insure against loss of equipment on a heavy strike.

pandemonium no matter what happens, but one fish is handled at a time.

Insides of fish boxes should be glassed and resined smooth for sanitary cleaning. The latter should be done after each day's use with a strong chlorine solution.

Each trolling rod should be protected with a heavy safety line mounted to the structure of the boat and tipped with a sturdy noncorrosive snap that can be attached to the reel rings. Rod butts break occasionally on heavy strikes, and the safety lines salvage thousands of dollars worth of equipment in Hawai'i annually. On a small boat the safety line can be long enough to allow the rod to be carried to the fighting seat without being detached. Many new fishermen are startled by the amount of pull from a heavy fish— enough to tear the rod from their grasp if they aren't prepared for it.

Two types of rod holders are available: the "flushmount" and "sidemount" fittings. The former fits through a hole in the deck leaving no protruding parts except for the flange. It holds the rod at a predetermined angle to the deck, though the amount of slant varies with the manufacturer. Unfortunately, of those on the market you can choose only between installations that point the plane of the rod in one of two perpendicular directions, either straight back or straight out to the side. Bolting it in straight back is poor because it does not allow enough spread to keep the lures from tangling unless the stern is very wide. The straight-out choice gives a few more feet of needed spread but leaves you victim to the flying loop of line that forms as the rod jerks back and forth from the action of the lure. This loop catches the rod tip and means an instantaneous break-off when a fish strikes. When this happens you are lucky if it is only the line that breaks and not the rod.

The perfect flushmount would let you bisect the angle between straight out and straight back for spread without danger. Nobody makes one that does this, however, so you have to modify existing equipment. One way is to remove the pin at the base of the holder before mounting it. No matter what mounting angle you choose, you can swivel the rod accordingly. Its drawback is that it lets the rod butt slide down into the holder until it jams tight, making it difficult to withdraw under the pressure of a heavy fish. The best bet is to remove the pin and reposition it by drilling new holes after the mounting angle is determined. Someday someone will market port and starboard flushmounts and the problem will disappear.

To install a flushmount, reinforce the deck from underneath with a wood panel to which the holder is bolted. This means cutting an elliptical hole with a coping saw and half-round file. Use bolts, not screws, for maximum support. Make sure these are of a metal compatible with that of the holder to avoid corrosion caused by the "two-metal" effect, electrolysis.

Sidemounts are strong inexpensive holders used where spread is no problem, such as for rods that are serviced by outriggers or for short wakelines. No holder should ever be set so that it carries the rod in an exactly vertical position. This position causes maximum friction of the line on the guides while a fish is making the reel whistle.

Safety equipment is essential. Two motors are a must anytime you leave the harbor, even if you have all of the tools and parts for minor repairs. There is little you can do with a wrench and screw driver if you break a connecting rod and shoot it out through your engine housing. The second motor may be a match of your first to provide a dual unit that powers you all of the time, or you can rely on an auxiliary kicker.

The matched pair is the better choice for those who can afford it. Many inboard-powered craft operate with twin screws as standard equipment. The I/O or inboard-outboard intermediate craft generally have just one power plant; so the spare kicker is a must. The outboard-powered hull is about the only place you have a choice between dual drive and auxiliary assistance. Preference for twin outboard pushers is based purely on the need for a second engine big enough to get you home on time regardless of the weather and water conditions. A small auxiliary engine may not be strong enough to shove the boat against wind and current before nightfall turns a minor mishap into a frightening experience.

The matched pair is not without its disadvantages, of course, including price as a starter. Twin forties, for example, weigh more than a single eighty, so the additional weight of the pair cuts down on the equal power. Optimum emergency use comes when each engine is hooked to the steering separately. A single cable with a solid connection to both engines may not allow you to tilt the damaged motor to keep it out of the way. The drag of the dead lower unit can slow you down appreciably, as well as making steering a muscle-building operation. The key is to unhook the dead engine from the steering so that it can be tilted separately. All connections should be kept well oiled and the bolts turned occasionally so that disconnection can be done with ease.

With small hulls, the auxiliary that is used only in emergencies is not only cheaper, but will do the job. A 10-horse spare may run a light 16-foot glass hull as fast as 3 or 4 knots when the standard prop is replaced by a three-blade pusher. Run any emergency-only spare motor as often as possible. A good habit is to run the spare on the hose at the end of each trip. Better yet, keep a barrel of fresh water to run it in and you'll make the seals and pump last longer. Using only fresh water as a coolant avoids the problem of unnecessarily corroding the system.

Carry a pair of paddles anyway. One paddle won't do much good unless you need to travel in a circle. The pair will take you as far as your energy will allow, very slowly of course, as well as getting you out of tight spots in harbors where a couple of quick strokes may be all you need to avoid unscheduled encounters.

Fortunately, typical Hawaiian weather conditions along lee coasts are an advantage to the fellow who finds himself listening to the horrifying silence of a dead engine. As the land mass heats up from the sun, a convection current forms in the atmosphere above the land-water junction, causing the cooler air above the ocean to be pulled toward shore. Thus a pair of perspiring paddlers can plan on having the wind at their backs to help push them home. This same shorebound wind has gotten stranded fishermen out of paddling altogether if they've had the foresight to coddle themselves with the comfort of a canvas cover. This top can usually be tilted into a position to catch the breeze well enough to slide the boat steadily onward.

Sometimes the best bet is to stay in one place if current and wind are too strong to allow you to make headway in the direction you want to go. Hawaiian waters are deep, so that anchoring may be difficult without a few tricks. If you fish beyond the 100-fathom ledge and need to anchor in an emergency, you may not want to haul that thousand feet of anchor line back up, even if you had it in the first place. *Akamai* (clever) Hawaiian anglers beat the problem by carrying a spool of heavy monofilament fishing line in the 100- to 150-pound-test range, as well as an inexpensive hook-type anchor. In an emergency, the mono lets the anchor drop to the bottom with very little drag, yet it is strong enough to hold a fairly large boat. There is enough stretch in 1,000 feet of nylon line to make breaking it nearly impossible.

Radio equipment is now within the financial reach of so many boat owners that small transmitters and receivers are common on board. The radio is a sensible necessity for the man who needs the security of an immediate search when he is in trouble.

There is one time when none of this equipment is of any use. That time is when a wave hits and the boat is flooded before any message can be sent. Two men and two boys fishing off Mākaha, Oʻahu, in the middle of the night were capsized while trying to pull up the anchor after fishing for ʻōpelu. The next morning other fishermen found the debris, floating ice chests and gas cans.

Since the point can be made without telling a tragic story, this one has a happy ending. Small boat fishermen feel a close bond because of the fragile nature of their détente with the sea. This lucky crew was found by a boat from the swarm of "mosquito fleeters" who were unwilling to assume the worst from the evi-

A well-equipped medium-sized fishing boat has *(1)* a swim step for carrying big fish, *(2)* two engines, *(3)* rod holders spaced for convenient use, *(4)* steep, strong outriggers, *(5)* racks to store rods out of the way when fighting a fish, *(6)* a fighting chair with removable back, *(7)* a flying bridge with a second set of controls, *(8)* an automatic pilot, *(9)* a depth recorder capable of reading to a depth of at least 100 fathoms, *(10)* a canvas top for sun protection, *(11)* ship-to-ship and ship-to-shore radio equipment—and a safe port to return to.

dence and went out to find them. All four fishermen were discovered in good health clinging to the bow of their drifting boat, the only part still above water.

Many boats are made with flotation below the flooring. They will automatically "turn turtle" when flooded. New designs have flotation up the sides. Under rough conditions, these will also flip. A team of boat builders in Kamuela has designed a 19-footer especially for Hawaiian waters, and the boat features flotation up the sides, as well as a floodable compartment in the centerline below the deck to act as ballast. Ken Smith, who designed the boat for the firm called Glass Pros, says they've had as many as fourteen people in a flooded boat without capsizing.

It is wise to get into the habit of leaving word with someone at home about when you will be back and where you will be fishing. An immediate search when you are overdue could mean life instead of death.

Don't rely on flares. Yes, they can be lifesavers, but there have been examples along the Kona Coast of boats drifting within sight of shore for days and not being found despite peppering the sky with fireworks.

If you won't wear a life jacket, at least keep flotation cushions aboard. They'll float to the surface out of most kinds of wreckage to provide any survivors with something to cling to.

Minor safety precautions include such items as shoes, sunglasses, and water. Monte Richards, Jr., insists on the shoes. Hooks are meant for piercing flesh, and so are fins and teeth. In a lifetime of fishing there will be many times when such sharp implements end up at your feet. Monte was once impaled through the heel by a hook sticking out of the mouth of a whirling bull mahimahi—an excruciating experience as the fish flipped and yanked. Jack Ross insists on the glasses. When you have a fish near the boat and you are pulling on the leader, your eyes are very vulnerable to the thrown lure and hooks that often come flying out of the middle of the spray. You can last a lot longer on an unscheduled drift toward Australia with a good supply of water. One excellent way to carry it is by freezing it in plastic jugs placed in the fish box for double duty.

Like the fisherman who calls himself Captain Tuna, the Chicken of the Sea, the most important thing you want to get when you leave the harbor is back.

# 8
# *Where Are the Fish?*

USING BIRDS, CURRENTS, TIDES, TEMPERATURES
TO FIND FISH

ALL ANIMALS, land and sea, respond to unseen forces according to rules which span the range from the mystic to the scientific. Ancient Hawaiian fisherman, modern rancher, futuristic scientist, each has observed the phenomena. The Hawaiians generated a fishing and farming calendar designed to predict the best times for planting crops, poking for squid, netting akule, or handlining 'ahi. South Kona ranchers report that cattle feed, change locations, and settle down to rest according to definite cycles which depend as much on barometric pressure changes and moon phases as on time of day and temperature. Leading outdoor magazines publish charts purporting to project the times of day corresponding to active periods which apply as much to birds and beasts as to marlin and *manini*. At least one computer firm compiles data to feed its mechanical marvel and translates the resulting bleeps into black bars spanning optimum time periods for hunting and fishing.

One purpose of studying the past is to predict the future, to formulate a structure in which success can be repeated and failure explained. But wordless creatures cannot describe their instinctive motivations any more than voluble humans can; theories about finny behavior are crude and not perfectly reliable. The best that any angler can do is to select the conditions of time, season, current, tide, moon, temperature, and locale that seem most promising and hope that his luck complements his intelligence to provide the remaining ingredient.

For most fishermen this means merely fishing where they can, when they can. For the angler who has the leisure to pick and choose his hours and the mobility to go wherever his whim commands, studying the gleanings of other prophets provides satisfaction even when it doesn't produce fish.

Occasionally the offshore angler can rely on birds to find fish for him. Flocks of small dark terns, *noio,* looking black against the sea or sky, mark tuna schools. Usually noio follow aku and kawakawa; sometimes they work schools of 'ahi; once in a while they mark a concentration of fish of all species including aku, kawakawa, 'ahi, ono, mahimahi, sharks, and marlin.

When mahimahi are actively hunting mālolo, they are frequently accompanied by hungry *'iwa.* These big hovering birds soar above the green backs in anticipation of the moment when the mahimahi drive the flyingfish into the air and into the 'iwas' claws. The 'iwa, or man-of-war bird, rides the air currents barely flicking a wing tip as it glides along marking the school for any fisherman within a few miles. Once in a while, an angler chasing an 'iwa is startled to discover that this bird will follow marlin as well.

Boobies, relatives of the Atlantic gannets, also mark big fish, but need not wait until their finny friends chase bait fish into the air. A booby will plunge deep into the water to chase food, catching its prey before it returns to the surface.

Strangely, seabirds are not often fooled for more than a moment by the lures as they race along behind the boat. A quick look is all most birds need to discover that something is wrong. One exception is the albatross, a big bird perfectly capable of catching a lure, hooking itself, and pulling line off the reel in a wild screaming melee that ends only when the fisherman reels him in and works him free. The unappreciative hooked albatross is big enough and scared enough to slash the fisherman with beak and talons as the poor fellow tries to release the feathered fury and get his lure back.

Bird action can tell a lot about fish action. The more birds, the bigger the school. Erratic diving birds, circling fast, mean small aku. Often, high-flying birds that dive and rise steeply are follow-

The noio, small black terns, travel with aku schools. They can indicate
the presence not only of aku, but of 'ahi, mahimahi, and even marlin.
Photo courtesy of the National Marine Fisheries Service.

ing 'ahi or mahimahi. Freddy Rice suggests that the erratic
touching of the water surface by the birds helps bring the bait fish
up to the top where the feeding aku can herd them from the bottom. Scattered birds mean the bait fish have sounded. So do sitting birds clustered on the surface bobbing up and down like a

duck hunter's decoys. When the birds are sitting, according to pioneering angler Olney Roy, it can mean that the school went down because a marlin came in to feed. Thus the sounding school has left a hungry marlin on the surface in just the right mood to take a well-trolled lure.

A similar occurrence may be announced by the presence of swooping birds that work back and forth. It can mean that bait fish are deep and staying down to keep out of the reach of a marauding marlin. Big fish find it easier to catch aku when the tuna are flattened against the surface or the bottom. Any chase becomes two-dimensional instead of three.

Traveling birds mean traveling bait fish. Big fish don't usually try to keep up with fast moving aku but are content to stay behind to pick off the stragglers.

Working against the birds with live bait can produce strikes. Searching birds tell the direction of the current, according to Bob Leslie; they don't have to work as hard if they fly against the current and let it bring food to them. In Leslie's words, "Birds are no damn fools; they know that fish feed against the current."

When birds feed they send out a screeching signal that other birds can hear for miles. The sight of groups of birds steadily flying together alerts the smart fisherman to the possibility that they are responding to feeding birds somewhere out of sight. That is when their direction of flight does not indicate the current direction.

The current is the main determining factor in where fish feed and why Hawai'i is a mecca for gamefishing. An underwater ledge is only as good as the current which strikes it. Change the direction of the water flow, change its strength, and you change the population of fish that feed in its eddies.

The Hawaiian Islands sit like a fence across the prevailing California current, which flows from east to west. A backwash, or wake, is formed which may extend as far west as Johnston Island when the current is strong enough. In the winter months the flow is from east southeast but switches to east northeast during typical trade wind conditions from June to September. A pair of eddies swirl in the wake to the southwest of the islands causing countercurrents that pull the larger fish and bait fish back into the lee coast ledges. Like the converging whirls made by eggbeaters, the eddies stir the ocean; a clockwise spiral on the southern edge, a counterclockwise whirl from the north.

These eddies are carried westward at a speed of approximately 5 nautical miles a day. The result is a continual change in the swirl pattern, with one eddy predominating as the other breaks away and slides out of the system. Thus the countercurrents formed at the convergence can oscillate back and forth along the coastlines bringing marine life to shore at different points each day.

Of course, the whole pattern is played out on such a gigantic scale that it produces little visible effect on the surface of the ocean. This evidence is collected by painstaking measurements made from research vessels, the study of miniature models which attempt to duplicate the pattern of flow and restraint, and the direct evidence of screaming reels.

Good fishing can occur only where fish are concentrated, not scattered one per square mile. A pair of billiard balls rolling at random across a giant pool table will meet less often than a hundred banging from cushion to cushion on the same field. Fish concentrate in nutrient-rich anomalies along the surface.

The flow of the ocean currents against a rising bottom ledge brings the nutrient-rich cold waters up from the depths with their load of food. Water at depths is rich in nutrients for the same

Summer current flow strikes the islands from the east northeast. The islands interrupt the flow and cause a turbulent wake in their lee. Eddies are created in the wake in a pattern somewhat similar at times to the simplified drawing above. The whole pattern slides westward at about 5 nautical miles per day, causing the structure of the eddies to change constantly, with one or another predominating. The vortices where the currents join cause upwellings. The eddies pull these nutrient-rich waters to the surface regions near the lee coasts. Back currents frequently flow in reverse through the interisland channels.

reason it is cold. Its temperature is low because it lies outside the
region illuminated and warmed by the sun, and that is also why
the nutrient salts are there. Open-ocean plants, chiefly phyto-
plankton (microscopic diatoms and simple algae), must rely on the
sun for photosynthesis, the process through which they convert in-
organic salts into the living matter of their cell structure; hence,
the plants cannot use any nutrients that drop below the zone
penetrated by the sun's rays.

Yet every creature must die, and if it is not devoured before it
drops below the illuminated zone, its substance is lost to the food
chain at the surface. Bacteria capable of living in the depths will,
of course, break down the tissues of the dead organisms as they
sink to the bottom regardless of how deep they go. The nutrient
salts resulting from bacterial decomposition are dissolved in the
cold waters and remain trapped there because the greater density
of the colder water forces it to remain below the warmer surface
layers. Only when a current strikes a near-vertical surface with
enough force to overcome the density difference will these nutrients return to the feeding zone of game fish.

Rising and falling masses of water change the surface temperature. Whereas most fish will tolerate fairly wide ranges of temperature variation, they will not usually swim across a thermal barrier,
a sharp line of demarcation between waters differing by several degrees. Any skin diver can feel this barrier by diving below the surface warm layer, usually several feet thick in near-shore waters,
down into the shockingly cold layer underneath, a change of only
a few degrees. Indeed, purse seining depends on dropping a net
around a school of fish that will refuse to dive out the bottom to
safety if the lower edge of the net hangs below a sharp temperature drop. Such methods are unreliable in local waters because the
temperature may remain constant from the surface down to depths
as great as 600 feet during strong, prolonged trade wind conditions because of their stirring effect.

Possible associations between temperature and the migration
depths of big-game fish have made the study of underwater thermal gradients (thermoclines) of great interest to marlin hunters.
The NMFS has provided George Parker with a special electronic
gadget for determining temperatures down to extreme depths. A
lead weight is dropped overboard and pays out a thin copper
signal line from the end of a spool attached to the probe and
another spool attached to a recorder in the boat. He has gathered

Concentrations of mahimahi are often found around drifting debris.
Photo courtesy of the National Marine Fisheries Service.

enough data to hazard some guesses about fish and temperature
correlations. Though he speaks as a layman and not a scientist, his
words are those of a fisherman with several decades of experience
in mid-Pacific waters.

"There does seem to be a thermocline here that rises or falls—or
at least there is a place in the depths where the temperature
changes abruptly," Parker maintains. "During the winter, the surface warm water layer is thicker and goes deeper. In the summer it
is thinner; its bottom is not so far down. Scientists tell me that the
blue marlin migrates along the bottom of this warm water
layer—in the warm water but just above the cold. Since this layer
is thinner in the summer, the fish are closer to the surface and
easier for us to catch by normal trolling methods.

"Sometimes the temperature break is at 100 feet; at others it is
as deep as 200 or more. In the winter it fluctuates between 150
and 200. In the summer it is as shallow as 100, and this makes a
difference in the surface fishing. The winter surface temperature
may range from 73 to 76 degrees [Fahrenheit] down to the 200-

foot mark, then it plunges rapidly to 55 degrees by the time the probe hits 800 feet.''

This means a change of nearly 20 degrees in an underlying layer 600-feet thick when there has been no change in the top 200.

In lee areas where the water is calm, scientists have noted a heating effect from the sun that can change the surface temperature as much as 2 degrees to depths as great as 10 feet. It may be that under such conditions a trolled bait traveling at the surface may draw no strikes merely because of this thermal ''barrier.'' Zander Budge, in his experiments with a downrigger that pulls lures along 20 feet under the surface, has discovered that there are days when fish will hit the deep lure and ignore the shallower ones.

Some data seem to suggest that yellowfin tuna occur in waters from 64 to 88 degrees Fahrenheit with continually fishable concentrations between 68 and 84. Their close relatives, the bigeye tuna, are found in colder waters in a band centered on 60 degrees. Striped marlin are most prevalent in waters from 68 to 77 degrees, while the Pacific blue prefers temperatures of 77 to 82 degrees. Comparing the different marlin preferences, it is easy to see why the stripes outnumber the blues in the colder months while the reverse is true from June to September.

Blacks frequent the warmest range, running from 77 to 87 degrees. Aku like their bath no lower than 68. Generally, in Hawai'i this means that the warmer the water the better the fishing, at least on the surface. Since the eddying currents can rapidly change the temperature of the water, fishing can literally go from cold to hot from day-to-day. Freddy Rice's records suggest that the best fishing in Kona comes when water temperatures range from 78 to 82 degrees.

Temperature, current, salinity, barometric pressure—each of these factors is useful to the angler only if it can be forecast, or at least determined, and then understood. It is the difficulty of discovering and using these data that causes fishermen to ignore them. The one ocean feature that is predictable is the tide; so it is the tide chart to which the angler turns as a guide, and it does not fail him.

Feeding phenomena are related enough to tides and tide changes to make study of the relationship valuable. Planners of the HIBT, for example, have kept exhaustive records of their success that point to the period beginning at the low tide change and extending for two hours afterward as the time when the most

Ono are lone wolves, but occasionally school up for fast action when conditions are to their liking. This free-swimming trio was attracted by a school of bait fish seeking the shelter of a log. Photo by Peter Hoogs.

strikes are recorded. Freddy Rice quotes Olney Roy as saying that the most important tide change is the last one before sunset because it is the last time that day-feeders will have to catch food until the next day.

The Hawaiians believed that the worst tide was the ʻaʻole tide. It occurs when moon and tide conspire to produce an unfavorable combination. The high tide change comes around the middle of the day and slides downhill the rest of the day while the new moon is giving way to the full.

Yet the same moon period can be an excellent producer on a sharp rising tide; HIBT officials plan the tournament to begin with the new moon if the low tide occurs during the morning. The full-moon days can also be a period when many small ʻahi are feeding at the surface.

The difference between high tide and low tide in the central Pacific is a matter of a scant foot or two, and a fish is in no position to see any rise or fall in the water level anyway. Is it possible for fish to tell what the tide is doing? The mechanism used may be in doubt, but the fact that some sensor does the job is indisputable. If a cow can tell the change of tide, a fish can. A strange comment, perhaps, but Freddy Rice claims that wild cattle in Hawai'i had to rely for water on the brackish ponds left along the shoreline when the tide dropped. From personal observation, Freddy asserts that no matter how far from the ocean they were, the cattle knew when the time was right for them to return to the tide pools for a drink. If a cow can, a fish can.

One possible advantage of the low tide for the big fish, Freddy speculates, is the fact that a low tide pulls smaller fish away from the shoreline. Hence, schools of 'ōpelu, for example, tend to spill over into the deeper drops where the bigger fish feel safe enough to hunt them during the day. "Trolling close to shore along the lava flows in south Kona is usually best at low tide as a result," he adds. "When the marlin come into the Kona waters to feed they aren't concerned that they are close to an island. A 100-foot drop-off at 100 fathoms is the same to them be it 50 yards offshore, as is the case at the third flow, or out in the middle of the ocean at Penguin Banks."

Ono and mahimahi are found everywhere from mid-ocean waters to hidden bays where they occasionally astonish shore casters by grabbing slide baits. Berns Bree makes a habit of outfishing everyone from his home port by working this green water early in the morning while big fish are still in the shallows looking for an easy meal. Many of the most successful mahimahi trollers zigzag the 25-fathom line as they work along the coast looking for underwater ledges and canyons capable of swirling ocean currents toward the surface.

Mālolo are a sure indicator of water that will interest mahimahi and ono. When a school of flyingfish flashes skyward far enough away from the boat to satisfy the angler that it wasn't the boat that scared them, it means fish are feeding. Unfortunately, mahimahi can be finicky and refuse anything but mālolo when they are in this mood. The result for the fisherman is a frustrating chase from school to leaping school. Several expert anglers prefer to stay with a shoal of mālolo, regardless of whether there are any immediate signs of big fish. They feel that all of the conditions are right to attract game fish, and the chances are as good there as they would be anyplace else. The mālolo provide a natural living chum.

The wise fisherman keeps a careful account of the conditions existing after each day's fishing, whether good or bad. Time, temperature, location, tide, current, barometric pressure, wind, season, all should be recorded, if not on paper, at least in the mind of the man who hopes to be a better fisherman tomorrow than he is today.

# 9
# *The Silent Shadow*

## DRIFT FISHING FOR EVERYTHING

THE PINK GLOW crept along the edges of Mauna Kea. Then, as
though emboldened by the ease of its victory over the soft black-
ness now ready to release its 10-hour hold on the ocean world, it
flooded across the sky in ever brighter colors to reveal a windless
sea spreading ahead of us in smooth sleep. The lights flecking the
solid black landmass to the east winked out as we passed. Our
wake disturbed the surface for only a few seconds—the ocean can
be a reluctant riser trying to retain its comfortable repose.

We scanned the liquid mirror searching for a skiff. Its owner
had told us he'd be spending the night bottom fishing and would
welcome a "good morning" visit from us as we tried for an early
start at trolling. When the boat showed ahead of us there was no
sign of life, but Kimo responded to the sound of our approaching
motor and relaxed our fears with a wave. Then he signaled for us
to come close for a look at his catch. The broad arrow of a head
that emerged from the fish box was big enough to swallow Kimo's
own. The long muscular body kept rising out of the box until
Kimo had pulled it up as high as his hat, yet the tail still stayed
hidden below the gunnel. This giant barracuda was the biggest
fish we'd seen all week caught by any method. And it was caught

Barracuda get big in deep offshore waters. This fish was caught at night on a live ʻōpelu bait fished at the bottom, 200 feet down.

on a live bait fished on the bottom of 200 feet of ocean in the middle of the night.

To the troller the sea is a vast, blue, inanimate desert broken only by the occasional flurry of a school of fish splashing the surface in a brief frenzy of hunger. Once he turns off the throbbing intrusion of his engine and his boat glides to a stop, its drifting silent shadow is soon joined by others that seek its quiet protection. Small fish, maybe just an inch or two long, appear from no reasonable place to hide in the furry growth along the hull line. Flashes of ʻōpelu roll upward from the depths. Eventually, they will be joined by predators, the mahimahi, ono, 'ahi, even aku, that constantly hunt for bellyfuls of the tasty mackerel.

Drift fishing produces the greatest poundage of fish at the lowest fishing cost of any method possible. It is perhaps the hardest kind of work, but, on a calm sea, day or night, it can be a satisfying experience with nearly constant action of some kind.

Fishing a drifting boat is more common than anchoring. Most waters are so deep that anchoring is either impossible or so difficult as to be a complete waste of the time necessary to haul and coil hundreds of fathoms of anchor line. There are methods possible for getting a heavy anchor hook down and getting it back. But if the bottom fisherman can be successful without doing it he will probably choose just to drift, a practice which has been described as the slowest form of trolling since it does present a moving bait to a constantly changing group of fish as the boat slides along with wind and current.

What can you expect to catch? It depends on the depth fished and whether the bait is lowered all the way to the bottom, floated along the surface, or fished somewhere in between. Drifting fishermen have caught every kind of fish found in Hawaiian waters, including the marlins and tunas, mahimahi and ono, and all other fish usually thought of as for trolling only.

Snappers are the top prize because of their exceptional eating qualities. They are also caught at the greatest depths. 'Paka are the more common and shallower water species. They can be caught at depths of 70 fathoms (6 feet to a fathom, remember). In some waters, depending on the bottom temperature, they may be in such relatively shallow depths as 50 fathoms. They attain a maximum length of about 3 feet.

The Japanese fishermen looked at the onaga, the brilliant, fiery red snapper, and saw its long graceful tail. Thus they gave it the Japanese name "long tail." The Hawaiians were more impressed with the unmatchably vivid, glowing scarlet back and rosy pink sides. They named it 'ula'ula. Almost as impressive are the giant eyes adapted for vision in the darkness at the bottom of deep waters 100 to 200 fathoms down.

For fishermen who don't want to try to find the bottom in waters that deep, there are other fish much closer to shore. Kāhala (amberjack), uku (gray snapper), kākū (barracuda), 'a'awa (wrasse), nabeta, ulua, and Hawaiian salmon can be caught in depths less than 300 feet, and the succulent hīnālea (wrasse)

Drift fishermen can catch a mixed bag of surface and bottom fish when conditions are right.

known as the *pō'ou* (commonly slurred to sound like pow-wow) is found along the sandy, rubbly bottom in 100 feet of water.

Winter is bottom fishing time in Hawai'i. This is partly because the medium-sized game fish that keep the trollers happy in other seasons are not quite as common, and partly because the market value for snappers jumps markedly upward. The holidays give commercial anglers added incentive because many local residents don't feel the new year has been properly celebrated without a bright red steamed snapper on display, served whole to their guests.

According to records kept by the Hawai'i Division of Fish and Game of the sale of commercial species, December is the peak snapper fishing month, with January through March not far behind. The kāhala is another important bottom feeder which is on the increase in January, though peak fishing doesn't occur until as late as March. These tough fighters get big. A Kona fish of 120 pounds once held the world record.

Occasionally, kāhala are caught by trolling during these winter months, but the greatest percentage are hauled from the depths by hand. Kāhala meat tends to be wormy, which turns some people away, but the parasites can be consumed along with the cooked meat without ill effect.

The uku is the only member of the family with any reputation as a fighter. It does not become abundant until later in the year, with the peak season occurring in June.

'Ō'io (bonefish) of a size that would make shore fishermen around the world sob in despair are occasionally hauled up from sandy bottoms a hundred or more feet deep. Rainbow runners, the Hawaiian salmon, are more frequently caught by bottom bouncers than any other way. Among species that can only be caught at

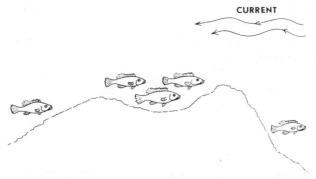

Bottom and current conditions conducive to successful fishing in deep water. The greatest number of fish are found in a depression right behind the upward slope of a bottom ledge when the current is striking that slope.

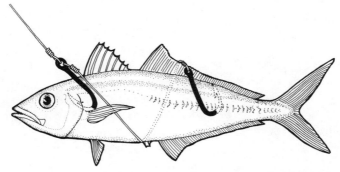

Big bottom fish like a whole 'ōpelu. Rig a dead bait by hooking it behind the head below the backbone. A trailing hook through the tail increases the chances of a hookup.

depth is the *hāpu'u*, black sea bass, a deep-sea grouper. Most of the shallow-water groupers found throughout the tropical waters of the world are absent in Hawai'i, yet, at least two deep-water species are found. The spotted grouper, a black fish with round white markings, reaches at least 5 feet in length, while occasional reports come in from scuba divers of a giant weighing nearly half a ton, with a mouth as big as a cave.

Drifters who work the intermediate depths, or swim a bait at the surface, work their handlines from short rods and big reels. When a heavy strike from an oversize 'ahi, or even a marlin, comes on the handline, the fisherman lets go quickly and takes the power of the run on the reel's drag with the rod held firmly in the holder, but usually not before the quick pull on the handline has sliced deep into the tough skin of the uncovered palm. Marlin of 700 and more pounds have been boated by handline fishermen drifting for smaller fish.

Many fish choose the deep layers because of the colder temperatures existing away from the surface. Such species as albacore, bigeye tuna, broadbill swordfish, and sailfish are often caught on commercial longline gear at depths of 20 or more fathoms, but are rarely found in the warmer Hawaiian surface waters. These same species are reported from surface waters in other climates.

The right conditions of wind and current are essential for a successful drift. Few experiences are more uncomfortable than bottom fishing from a boat bouncing like a basketball. Calm days are not

The deep-water red snappers include the onaga *(top)* and the 'ula'ula *(bottom),* distinguishable only by the differing lengths of their tails.

'Ōpakapaka can grow to be a yard long, a tight fit even for the largest of ice chests.

really required by the fish—they probably don't even feel the difference at 100 fathoms—but they certainly add to the enjoyment for the angler. On the other hand, a good current is absolutely necessary. Not only does it provide the steady movement that is the angler's traveling ticket, but it sets up the kinds of conditions that make fish feed.

Little can be told about deeper currents from what is happening on the surface. Bottom currents can run strongly in directions at right angles to and even directly opposite the run of the surface.

Currents bring food to fish which do not have to leave the security of the reef to hunt for it. The more cautious fish will not come out of hiding at all if the current does not increase their chances of getting a meal. Although maps are available to indicate the prevailing surface currents, they can't tell the whole story with its daily variations; you'll learn more about the currents in the waters available to you from a half-dozen fishing trips than from the same time spent perusing atlases.

The current can be too strong. Its strength determines the amount of weight you'll need to touch bottom. Some days 10 or 12 ounces is plenty. On others, 2 or 3 pounds is a minimum. Occasionally, no amount of weight is practical because the drag of the water against the line will float everything but the anchor.

Most experienced bottom fishermen have their productive spots marked by triangulation of shore reference points. Unless you can

Deep-water groupers grow to enormous sizes, like this 490-pound black sea bass, probably the largest Hawaiian grouper ever photographed.

talk a fellow into letting you know his glory holes, you've got to find your own. Few anglers will be willing to give you a map to their buried treasure trove of 'paka and onaga unless you are willing to marry the ugly daughter or go in half on a new boat. A commercial fisherman can look forward to a lifetime of financial security as long as no one else cleans out his gold mine.

How do you find your own? A depth recorder is a great help. It tells you when you are over water deep enough, and it shows the sharp rises and dips in the bottom. At times the action will be on the upcurrent side of the rise, at other times feeding fish will be found in pockets and dips where the current makes eddies that drop food into slower waters. No matter how expensive the initial investment is, the depth recorder eventually pays for itself.

Some of these electronic gadgets just blip out a light on a rotating dial. You must watch the dial to keep track of depth changes. The best recorders keep the record for you by means of a stylus that marks the bottom changes on a paper drum. The result is a cross-sectional picture of the ocean floor contour. Electronic wizardry has produced recorders that will even give some idea of the bottom consistency from the type of mark made on the drum, either sharp for a hard rock bottom, or fuzzy for a muck floor. These supersensitive sensors can sometimes even spot schools of fish lying above the bottom.

If you must explore without electronic eyes, you need an efficient procedure for marking your spot once you've found it. You must learn the type of bottom and the depth of the species you want to find. It is a great waste of time hunting 'paka, for example, in waters less than 50 fathoms and onaga at less than 70, though both may run in much deeper water depending on the prevailing bottom temperature. My first onaga was hauled up from 144 fathoms, according to the orange blip on the rotating dial. Line markings are rough indicators of depth; their accuracy depends on the amount of belly bent into the flexible strand by the current. About all you can tell for sure is that the bottom is no deeper than the length of line you've dropped.

Start by drifting with a baited line and a marker line. The latter is a heavily weighted line lowered to the same depth as the baited line, but with no hooks on the bottom and a float tied in on the surface end. The bottom weight is kept a few feet above the bottom by one man while the other is fishing. As soon as the fisherman feels a bite, his partner lets the weight plummet the extra feet to the bottom and tosses the float over the side. Thus, the float marks the exact spot in the drift where the strike occurred and will stay there for the remainder of the expedition as long as the weight is heavy enough. An excellent supply of such heavy weights can be made at very little cost from discarded food cans filled with concrete loaded with pebbles. A wire loop stuck in before the mortar hardens provides an attaching ring.

If the strike turns out to be a valued fish, the crew should return to the marker and find shore reference points for permanent triangulation which makes the marker no longer necessary.

Why the emphasis on pinpoint accuracy? Hard broken bottoms supply the necessary environment for bottom feeders, rather than the soft muddy or sandy ocean floor frequently found in the lees of large islands. Corals diminish in extent and type as depths increase and light decreases. Off most Hawaiian shorelines living coral reefs disappear at more than 200 feet because there is not enough light to support them. Bottom fish are oriented to physical features such as rocks, caves, banks, shelves, and steep inclines of all sorts; hence they tend to remain in fixed locales as feeding stations. They change their habitat only when fluctuations in water temperature and salinity, with their resultant effect on food supply, fall outside the range they can tolerate.

The latter happens most often along the innermost portion of the range of the species. We've caught 'paka along a 70-fathom shelf on one day, and have been completely unable to find them two days later despite intensive effort along the same shore markings.

The mixing effect of trade winds determines how thick the surface-water layers of homogeneous temperature are. The longer and stronger the winds, the deeper the stirred warm surface waters penetrate. Temperatures at the 400-foot level may vary from 78 to 80 degrees Fahrenheit after extended periods of strong winds, then may turn as cold as 68 degrees when the surface waters remain calm for many weeks. Deep water fish are able to tolerate some change, but wide differences drive them to new locations.

Bottom-fishing equipment is not a sporting proposition. There is no such thing as "light tackle" when the job to be done is dragging heavily weighted lines up from the great depths loaded with fish that are quickly rendered nearly lifeless by the pressure change. This is not "sport" in the classic sense of magnificent battles with equipment balanced to prolong the great struggles of sprinting, leaping fish.

Tradition decrees heavy handlines of hard, braided nylon so stiff that it refuses to tangle when coiled in a big plastic tub at the fisherman's feet. The dark purple line is gained slowly in hand-over-hand pulls, as the line comes up during as much as five minutes of muscle-cramping work. Whatever thrill exists is in the capture. Whatever battle exists is in the overcoming of environmental obstacles. Each man to his own definition of "sport."

Large-diameter lines are easy to handle with fingers and palms, but they require much more weight than thin lines. Breaking with tradition, many bottom fishermen are now discovering the advantages of using short stiff rods with giant trolling reels that have spool diameters large enough to speed the line with ever-multiplying cranks of the handle. The efficient storage on a 16/0 reel eliminates the tangles and makes the thin lines a good choice.

Monofilament testing 50 or more pounds is the least expensive and hence most popular. Its relatively large diameter and tendency to float make it less desirable than braided Dacron.

Monel wire or braided stainless steel lines are small in diameter, flexible, and sink rapidly with half as much weight as monofilament. They slice down so straight that there is almost no shock absorbing belly, so every bite is felt quickly and easily. Less line is out, so it is rapidly pulled in, and every wiggle of the fish is transmitted on the way up.

Does that make wire the perfect deepline? Some say yes, but its disadvantages far outweigh its advantages. Wire can be mean stuff to handle, since a kink will break it, and it will spring into a tangle on the reel spool if not enough tension is applied to keep the spool from turning a fraction of an rpm too fast. It must be worked from a short stiff rod with carbide ring guides capable of withstanding the cutting effect of the abrasive metal surface. Worst of all, the weight of the line continues pulling downward after the sinker touches bottom. That may mean that you'll never even know you are down because the line just keeps rolling off the reel.

Regardless of what the Atlantic Ocean experts say, wire is best avoided. But, if you think you can figure ways of mastering the metal monster, make sure you spool on more wire than you need to touch bottom, at least 10 percent more. The joint between wire line and woven backing is necessarily a very weak link. If you snag the bottom while the connection is out, you will break it off right there and lose the whole line section.

The popular wire size is 45-pound-test, and the dropper loop to the sinker at the bottom of the rig must be 20-pound-test or less to reduce the risk of having to break off all of the wire if the sinker snags.

Most anglers rig their hooks on long leaders that can be detached from the mainline with a snap connector. The hooks are strung out along the leader with short leaders of their own tied in to three-way crossline swivels. A minimum of six hooks is the normal choice, since so much time is lost in the ascent and descent of the line between boat and bottom that the fisherman wants to make each drop worth the considerable effort.

Tangled leaders can be a problem because the descending baits pull the leaders back against the mainline where their spinning action wraps the hooks around the line. Early Hawaiian fishermen learned to defeat this problem with bamboo spreaders that held the hooks away from the line. Modern fishermen accomplish the same result with heavy wire spreaders that attach to the mainline at their centers, then hold a hook at each end on a short leader. As the sinker pulls the spreader into the depths, the rig looks like an airplane wing with twirling decorations at the tips. The dropper loop to the sinker from the center of the bottom spreader should be longer than the leaders on the bottom hooks so that they cannot catch in the rocks and endanger the whole rig.

The secret to the entire operation is the modern version of the Hawaiian hook invented primarily to do this job. When the line is on the bottom it must be left there until all of the baits are found by fish, in order to have maximum efficiency. That means that the hooks must have such holding power that the fish cannot get away from them. To accomplish this, the Polynesian deep-sea fisherman invented a hook with a point that rolls in toward the shank, mak-

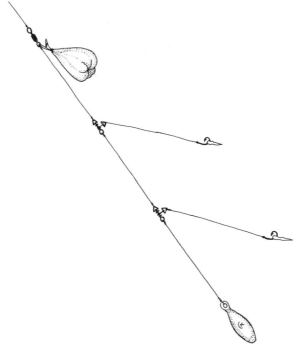

One typical bottom-fishing rig has the palu bag at the top and crossline swivels as the attachment points for hooks. Six or more hooks would be used to take maximum advantage of the long drop to the bottom.

ing a nearly full circle. With the very special way it is tied onto
the leader, it makes an escape-proof trap. As the fish takes the
bait he slides his jaw into the gap between point and shank. The
special leader tie-in helps direct the jaw into the trap. When the
fish discovers the resistance and starts to pull, the leader draws the
point through the jaw and around in a circle. The rotating hook
point will not let go, no matter how the fish shakes his head. The
fisherman should not try to set the hook at the strike by jerking it.
Not only will this not help, it might actually interfere with action.

For maximum efficiency, the bait must be the toughest fish
meat possible, kawakawa belly, or aku belly. Soft flesh is easily
stripped from the hook without requiring the fish to clamp down
hard and turn to pull. On a recent trip using just 'ōpelu chunks as
bait, we lost five baits for every fish hooked. Yet 'ōpelu definitely
*is* the food most likely to attract an onaga to the hook. The secret
to successfully using it is salt. Kept in an icy brine, the 'ōpelu
strips toughen into durable baits.

'Paka seem to prefer squid strips to anything else. We've alter-
nated the tough white slices with fillets of many kinds of fish, but
the biggest catches go to squid hooks.

In shallower waters, live baits are always worth a try since the
biggest fish tend to be predators rather than scavengers. Uku,
kākū, ulua, rainbow runner—all like a whole, small, live 'ōpelu.

To bring the fish to the baits, Hawaiian anglers have developed
techniques of chumming found nowhere else in the world. *Palu* is
the word for it, and local fishermen know how to palu by remote
control. Right above the hooks on a bottom-fishing rig is a long
cone-shaped denim bag. In its open end the fisherman stuffs a
mixture of canned sardines, tinned mackerel, or ground fresh
'ōpelu combined with crushed crackers and salt water in a watery
gruel that rapidly disperses when set free in the water. The open
end of the cone is tucked in to shut it, and it stays closed until the
sinker hits bottom. A hard yank forces the chum out of the bag,
and the tasty bits drift toward the bottom to draw snappers to all
of the hooks. Some fishermen put a pebble or two in the palu bag
to help force it open. Others choose to tie the palu up in a plain
brown paper bag that will soak through from the water and break
with a hard yank at the right time.

Two effects attest to the value of this palu addition. Snappers
are just as often caught on the top hook as the bottom, and a

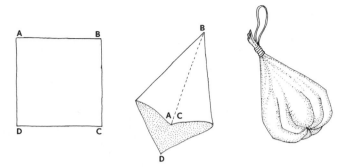

An 8-inch square of denim makes a satisfactory palu bag when a pair of adjacent sides are stitched together. Complete it by tying on a loop of cord at the point of the cone for attachment to the snap swivel on the fishing line. Fill it with chum, and tuck the opening in to shut it.

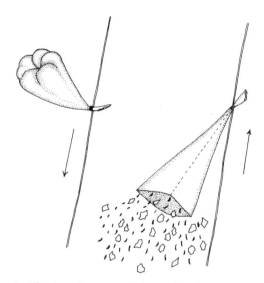

The closed bag holds the chum until it reaches bottom. A sharp upward jerk releases the chum to attract fish.

steady transition in the nature of the fish caught can definitely be noticed when anchoring is possible. First, the small ones get the hooks. Eventually, the palu draws in the big ones. If the anchor holds bottom, the big onaga are the prize.

This same palu mixture can be used to attract fish of all sizes. A skiff fisherman can anchor his boat along an ʻōpelu *koʻa* (fishing grounds) in 20 or 30 fathoms and palu to start a cycle that begins with small fish and ends with big game. With a large palu bag at the end of a handline, he lowers the mixture 20 or 30 feet below his hull, then jerks it to cause an underwater explosion that generates a cloud of food particles. Peering through his glass-bottomed box, he watches the palu disperse, repeating the process as often as needed until finally the milky cloud is replaced by a dark ball of swirling 'ōpelu.

These fish can be hooked on tiny white flies (wisps of filaments tied to small hooks with red thread wraps) or led over the mouth of a bag net where they can be scooped up in a quick swoop. 'Ōpelu help the netting process by their instinctual tendency to dive for the bottom when frightened—right into the mouth of the waiting net.

The palu bag helped this fat pair of gindai find the hooks of a spreader rig.

Attracted by the action of the 'ōpelu ball, mahimahi and ono circle the mass of living food, eager to pick off the stragglers. A hooked 'ōpelu drifting off on a big hook becomes a target the game fish cannot resist, and any fisherman willing to turn his attention away from catching 'ōpelu is rewarded with as much fight as he can handle.

Drift fishing is the only method that allows the angler to work many different levels at the same time and still cover a broad range of fishing territory. The drifter can simultaneously bounce the bottom or float a bait at any level in between, where temperature layers cause fish to congregate. Indeed, if he has the stamina and is willing to yo-yo a heavy metal lure back and forth between bottom and surface, he can test all levels for productivity.

Even when 'ōpelu are not available, the bottom fisherman can get a live bait for surface action. Any small bottom fish will do; a 1-pound pāpio, for example, is a perfect surface bait because of its hardiness. Such baits cannot be fish pulled from extreme depths, of course. When a deep-water fish starts coming up, his air sac expands from the reduced pressure; he gets the "bends." One result is that he will continue to come to the surface even if he does shake free from the hook. Boaters often find disabled fish with

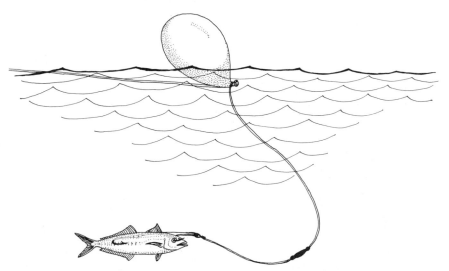

A live or fresh bait can be drifted at the surface and held away from the boat by a balloon. When a fish strikes, the balloon is pulled under and breaks.

bloated bladders swimming feebly upside down along the surface down current of bottom fishermen.

To be used as a surface bait the bladder should be perforated with a small thin needle inserted into the side of the belly. It will then live for a short time on the surface. If returned to the bottom immediately, a bloated fish can be used as a live bait at the depth from which it was pulled. Water pressure normalizes the swim bladder.

Whole dead baits, such as ʻōpelu and akule, can be drifted on the surface and will take mahimahi and ono. To keep it near the surface the bait is rigged with a large float, such as a small plastic bottle, large hunk of cork, or a piece of Styrofoam. A balloon is a good choice because it breaks during the fight with whatever fish is hooked and leaves the line unencumbered. Such baits attract

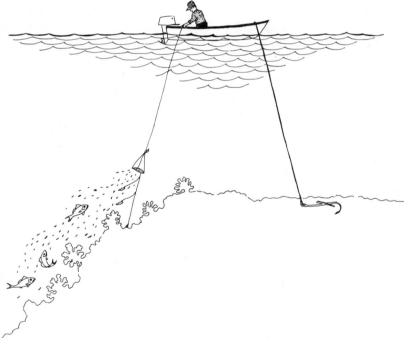

A successful bottom-fishing technique used at Penguin Banks is to anchor in the shallow (20- to 25-fathom) water near the steep dropoff at the edge and then use chum to bring the ʻpaka up out of the deep water. The current often flows from the shallows into the depths. At first, fishing is slow until the chum spreads and reaches the ʻpaka.

sharks as well as the more desirable game fish. The angler who
wants to avoid a prolonged fight with an unwanted shark will rig
his hook with a short wire leader just long enough to ward off the
teeth of an ono or mahimahi. If a shark swallows the bait, he will
turn and hit the line with his rough tail and break off.

Such drifted dead baits should be hooked through the head to
give the most natural kind of appearance when pushed around by
surface currents. A one-hook rig should pass down through the top
of the head of the 'ōpelu or akule and out the lower jaw. A pair
of hooks rigged in tandem is more effective to insure that the fish
doesn't take half the bait without getting the hook. The first hook
runs through the eyes, while the second passes through the back
just behind the fattest part of the bait.

Many 'ahi are caught by fishermen drifting lines at mid-depths
ranging from 15 to 50 fathoms. No special tactic for finding fish is
needed other than knowing the existence of some well-publicized
'ahi ko'a. An 'ahi ko'a is a place where temperature, current, and
natural food combine to provide a feeding ground for yellowfin
tuna. On most weekends you can spot such places from the con-
gregation of small boats drifting together within talking distance
of each other. Some of the 'ahi ko'a along the Kona Coast collect
as many as two dozen boats at a time.

So little light penetrates into the great depths that there is probably very little difference to the fish between day and night.
Though such fish as 'paka and onaga have huge eyes, they must
also be able to find food with other senses. During daylight hours
they use their eyes primarily to distinguish food as shadows and
shapes against the lighter background above. Such contrast may
indicate why night fishing is most successful on bright moonlit
nights.

The boat fisherman used to trolling for eight hours a day accompanied by the constant throb of an engine discovers an entirely
different world when he shuts it off. A world very much worth exploring.

# 10
# *Slide Baits and Lantern Lights*

## ULUA FROM SHORE

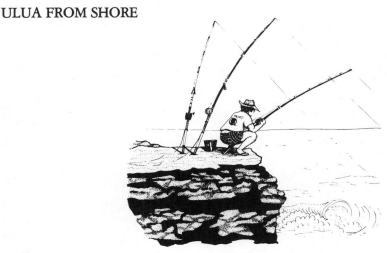

HAWAI'I may be the only place in the world where a man can stand on shore and cast a line to a fish weighing as much as 150 pounds. Add to this potential the mystique of starry nights and rugged cliffed shorelines and you have a sport at once thrilling and dangerous.

The quarry and the obstacles are uniquely Hawaiian, so the methods developed to overcome both are different from anything seen elsewhere in the fishing world. Slide-bait fishing with super-sized surf tackle is the method, ulua are the prize. Sometimes other fish are caught as well; a run of kāhala may rip through the deep lines, a rare school of 'ahi or mahimahi finds the baits, but most fish caught by this method are ulua. On one very strange night at O'ahu's top night spot, "Bamboo Ridge," all lines were sent screaming out at once as bells attached to the rod tips jangled in metallic chorus, but the blundering creature that had started it all just waved goodbye with a hugh tail as it inadvertently stripped the lines. A whale tale, that is. Other unwanted creatures include the ubiquitous morays willing to twist up the leaders any time an ulua doesn't find the bait first.

Slide-bait fishing was developed by local shore casters to catch ulua in the face of a combination of physical difficulties encountered in few other places. To find ulua near shore you must often fish from cliffs 20 or more feet above the water. With the spread of residential development to all but the remotest places, anglers on the more populous islands are forced to retreat to perches that would seem inaccessible to a Big Island bighorn sheep. In addition, the ulua fisherman must contend with a coral bottom and very deep, 100 feet or more, fishing water. South Point on the Big Island is a good example since it offers some of the best ulua fishing in Hawai'i; its inshore waters drop to 150 feet right at the shore fisherman's feet.

Deep waters add to the length of line needed to reach the spot and then fight a fish capable of taking 200 yards more. When the cast is made, the angler must keep his thumbs off the spool as the sinker drops so that line continuously rolls off. If he doesn't keep feeding line, the sinker will swing through the depths on its tether until it ends up right back at the fisherman's feet.

The coral bottom just about guarantees that the sinker will hang up on the bottom on every cast. Few sinkers are retrieved, except by scuba divers interested in supplementing their income with the sale of lead. The metal deposits at popular ulua holes are mineable with economic benefits.

Big fish require big baits—so big that a fellow interested in casting both lead and bait might consider practicing for the hammer throw in the next Olympics as a warm-up. Contemplate a bait that might be a whole octopus, or at least a good chunk with several legs. Fish with enormous appetites must find the bait in the first place, and great size of serving is a help. A 10-inch fillet of moray eel would be a small bait. A whole, live bottom fish like an 'āweoweo (bigeye) might be a typical entrée. One adventurous fellow uses a whole aku.

Zander Budge once demonstrated to a throng of several hundred people that an ulua will gladly swallow a couple of 5-pound aku whole. While weighing in a marlin at the Kona pier, Zander noticed a dark shadow under his boat. He tossed it a 5-pound aku which it enjoyed with one gulp. Then he fed it another, with hook and line, and the crowded gallery watched while Billy Budge fought a 63-pound ulua to gaff before their startled eyes.

The point is, no one can cast a bait this size. Indeed, trying to toss off a lot of 75- to 100-yard casts with a 12-foot rod before or after a working day when you'd rather be sleeping—that makes very hard work of a good sport.

The early morning light finds a slide-bait fisherman hooked up and fighting.

For the slide baiter none of these are problems; his method avoids them all. He selects and sets up his camp while it is still light. He picks the section of bottom he wants to fish while there is still sun enough to find it. He makes one perfect cast with a hookless, baitless line. If it doesn't reach the right spot, he hauls it in immediately before it can settle and snag, then tries again until he is satisfied. He knows that he can put all of his effort into it because he is probably not going to have to do it more than a few times the whole night. Indeed, it may be the only cast he'll have to make unless a fish is hooked.

When a cast is right, the fisherman lets it settle until it catches. Positive anchoring is necessary, and slide baiters have developed special casting weights with soft wires molded in to make the

sinker hold without moving. The added advantage of the wires is
that they will bend when the time comes to release the sinker if a
fish strikes or the fisherman quits fishing.

With the sinker holding well, the line is pulled tight and the
rod is put in a holder. Rod holders at popular spots are chipped
into the rocks with heavy hammer and masonry drill. A rod butt is
wedged into such a hole with a wooden triangle so that the rod
cannot be pulled free by a solid ulua strike. Occasionally, safety
lines are tied to the rods and anchored around boulders.

Nothing can happen, of course, until there is a bait on the line.
A special leader is used with a hook at one end and a connector at
the other. The connector can be a split ring or a pigtail loop.
Either can be attached to the line without breaking it and will

The "bamboo forest" sprouts overnight at Hawai'i's best surf-casting
ledges. Note the trolling reels adapted for casting, the two-piece rods
with fiberglass tips joined to bamboo shafts, and the bells to alert sleeping anglers when a fish strikes.

slide down the line into the depths as long as the angle is steep enough. Pigtail loops have the advantage over the traditional split rings because they are less apt to damage the line when being attached. Of the several styles available, the best is a loop of brass wire with a single twist around the main stem.

The line should run freely through the loop of the connector and let the bait slide down until it reaches a predetermined "stop" near the sinker end of the line. This stop can be a swivel much bigger than the opening in the slide connection so that the fish cannot pull the leader right off the line.

Sometimes, when the cliff is not very high above the water, the bait may just hang without sliding unless it is tossed to get it started. Once it hits the water the lubrication should keep it gradually moving downward. If not, a small bit of lead pinched onto the leader may help.

At regular intervals throughout the night other baits can be slid down without pulling in the line if the fisherman feels the bait has been chewed off by small fish or is hidden by the coral.

Small live fish are sometimes good baits because they can be hooked from around the rocks early in the evening and will attract ulua with their vibrations while not drawing strikes from other small fish. These live baits can be kept handy in enclosed tide pools until ready for use. One trick with small live baits is to make a second stop in the line from 10 to 30 feet from the end so that the bait stays well above the bottom. This stop can be a wrapping of dental floss with just enough thickness to retard the sliding ring, or perhaps a blood knot in the line with the ends left a quarter inch long rather than being snipped in close. The important thing is that the stop must slide through the guides on the cast and retrieve.

A durable but very small bait for this use is the ugly but lively "jumping jack" found in all saltwater tide pools. Though it breaks the "big bait" rule, it has been proved surprisingly effective since it stays alive for a long time if the hook is in a nonvital spot. These fish are easily caught since they are transfixed for a few seconds by the glare of a bright light.

Care in handling lights is important. They should never be shown on the water because they will scare ulua away. Anglers who dispute this maintain that a stationary light is no problem as long as no one walks by it in such a way as to throw moving shadows on the water. A moving light definitely chases fish away.

Fishermen have used this fact to herd hooked ulua away from potential snags by shining a light in the water between fish and hazard.

Heavy tackle is a necessity, though an occasional freak occurrence happens, like the feat of the North Kohala fisherman who landed a 100-pound ulua on a 15-pound-test spinning rig.

Veteran fishermen like Mickey Waddoups choose rods, reels, and lines more massive than surf fishermen elsewhere would dream possible. But Mickey's credentials as an ulua fisherman are so impressive that his methods are worth detailed study.

Mickey is a fisherman-rancher with the hallowed South Point fishing areas at his doorstep. For him, Hawai'i's best ulua holes are almost walking distance from home. His top catch is a 120

The preferred casting weight for slide-baiting has soft wires molded in to grab the coral. On a strike, or when the fisherman wants to reel in the line, the wire hooks straighten and the weight is pulled free.

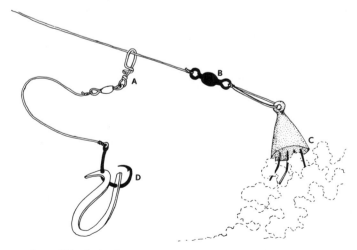

The complete slide-bait rig has a slide (A), a stop (B), casting weight (C), and baited hook (D).

pounder. While fighting this fish, a second ulua struck another rig and stripped it while Mickey could do nothing but ignore the tortured scream of the reel. After landing the big one, Mickey's next cast found a little 55-pound ulua within fifteen minutes. This two-hour total of 175 pounds of ulua is more than many ulua fishermen catch in a year, or even a lifetime. Within a week, Mickey had added a 100 pounder to the total.

Surprisingly, all three fish were caught between twelve and four o'clock—in the afternoon! That's a time when most ulua fishermen are resting up from a hard night on the cliffs.

"Good gear is the secret," says Mickey. "You won't get very many ulua strikes, so you must make every one count by having tackle strong enough to overcome all of the possible problems a big fish can cause. I use a 6/0 reel loaded with 80-pound-test monofilament. That's a trolling reel used for casting. The only modification is the removal of the harness rings because the line can snag one on the cast. The rod is half glass and half bamboo. A trolling rod blank is joined to a bamboo shaft to provide the needed length and stiffness. This requires a 10-ounce sinker with soft wires. Such a rig can toss off a 100-yard cast. Each hook is a number 52, Hawaiian rolled-in-point model rigged with 6 feet of number 15 piano wire. My best bait is a fillet cut from a spotted moray. The cut bait is about 8 inches long and rigged folded over."

Mickey likes the eel bait because it is less often bothered by other eels. During the day he may choose a live bait, either a *menpachi* (red squirrelfish) or *mamo* (damselfish) if he can get one. He avoids octopus baits because they attract eels.

As far as conditions go, Mickey likes a rising tide, but he does not feel that this is as important as getting the right moon phase. Day or night he chooses a big moon, with top preference going to the fourth night after the full moon.

As evidence that the full moon works, fisherman-agronomist Eddie Hosaka (author of the classic 1944 work *Sportfishing in Hawaii*) used a full moon one July night in 1959 to catch 21 ulua, the largest being a 111 pounder.

Mickey believes that the ulua run starts in May and lasts until August, even though some fish can be caught all year around.

Gaffing an ulua from a ledge far above the water is very tricky. It must be done with a bridge gaff, a large weighted multipronged grapnell that is lowered to a spot at the base of the cliff and kept

there until the hooked ulua is led over it. Then a quick snatch
hooks the ulua in the body muscle whereby it can be pulled up
the face of the cliff. As a safety precaution, experts do not reel up
the slack as the fish is brought up. The line is kept loose in case
the ulua gets away from the gaff and drops back down to the water. If the line were reeled tight, the weight of the fish would pull
it free from the hook.

A highly successful variation on the bridge gaff is a sliding gaff
which is attached to the line itself by means of a split ring. It will
slide down to the ulua and stay right on target no matter where
the fish goes.

Ulua like a free handout and will stake a claim to a spot where
fishermen are known to clean their catch. Sonny Martinson was
cleaning fish on the pier in Kawaihae Harbor when he spotted a
large ulua working its way through the scraps in the water below.
Borrowing a hand gaff from his brother-in-law, Lala Laau, on the
boat *Waiulaula* which was docked nearby, Sonny ambushed the
unwary ulua. Before it could dig its tail in, Sonny had the 50
pounder on the dock.

Jim Wallace of Kaua'i reported a tale of an all-night expedition
on Kaua'i near 'Ele'ele that produced no fish all night but still
ended happily. In the morning the disgruntled group broke camp
and tossed away the left-over bait. These bits of eel attracted a big
black ulua. Itsu Sakata glimpsed the fish and immediately threw
him a line. The ulua grabbed the bait and fought furiously. When
it could finally be weighed, it stretched the scale to 80 pounds.

Chumming is, of course, a standard technique in most waters,
but it has an unfortunate effect when tried along Hawai'i's coastline. It draws moray eels, sharks, and puffer fish with jaws like
wire cutters. All of these will swallow ulua baits, with the eels being the most common offenders.

Morays as big as the 85-inch, 64-pound, spotted *puhi* caught by
Hilo fisherman Masayuki Mitsuda while on a South Point adven-
ture can keep you too busy for serious fishing. Eels are pests which
give a very unexciting fight, swallow the bait so far down into
their needle-lined jaws that getting the hook back is nearly impossible, and twirl the line into a horrendous tangle. When an eel
tries to escape from some natural enemy like an ulua or octopus
that has grabbed it, the flexible creature will tie itself into an
overhand knot and push the loop along its body to force the at-
tacker to let go. When they do this repeatedly to the "predator"

that has them hooked on the end of a line, it ties that line into a slimy series of knotted loops.

Since eels are such ulua delicacies, it is very natural that they should be afraid of the powerful brutes. One South Point fisherman told me he always knew when a school of ulua was working the water because the eels stopped biting. They could feel the vibrations of the big fish and immediately went into hiding.

No fisherman should contemplate night fishing on steep remote crags without taking stock of the danger involved. Many fishermen have been killed when unexpected and unseen waves swept them from their perches into pounding surf from which no escape is possible. Many others have fallen to the rocks below, suffering permanently crippling injuries. The well-known fishing ledges are marked by images of Ō-Jizō-san, the Japanese deity who protects travelers, children, and fishermen. It was the immigrant from Japan who developed many of the techniques of ulua fishing, and his sons continue the sport under the watchful eyes of the old-country deities.

One modern invention that has added immeasurably to the safety of the sport is the battery-powered headlamp which always points in the direction the fisherman is looking, while his hands are thus free to carry equipment or grab a handhold. At well-traveled outcrops, fishermen have painted white footprints, lines, and other markers along the way so that the path can be readily picked out by the thin pencils of light in the black of night.

It is not all arduous work. Catnaps are possible for the angler with foresight to attach a bell to the rod near its tip. With each rod wrapped in a different pattern of colorful reflective tape, instant identification becomes possible for the befuddled anglers who wake to the sound of the jangling bells and flash their headlamps along the line of rods to find the one bent deep in a fighting arc.

One problem that still remains with slide-bait fishing, according to Mickey Waddoups, is its effectiveness. Whereas many methods of fishing tend to skim off the most gullible, least wary, or some other small percentage of fish, slide baiting is irresistible and is capable of fishing out a spot if not judiciously controlled by the anglers themselves.

# 11
# *Whipping Inshore*
## SMALL GAME ON SPINNING TACKLE

IT WAS the most promising spot I had seen all morning, but I knew how difficult it would be. To reach the point that brought the whole cove into casting range would mean a rough hike across black ‘a‘ā lava. Even then I would have to teeter on a chunk of rock that would be awash on every wave. It would be tricky, but it also looked as though it would be worth the effort. I had already struggled out to many places that had looked equally promising, however, and my fish bag was still empty.

With the sweat drawn by the morning sun running down out of my hair to tickle its way through my eyebrows, I squatted on my heels to cut a fresh strip of squid and survey the easiest path across the coarse, tar-black rock pile that separated me from the ocean.

If you were to construct a model of the lava tongue I was viewing, to get the feel of what it was like underfoot, you would shatter glass bottles until the pieces were gravel size and then mix the sharp-cornered chunks in the driest cement that would solidify. There is a saying that the Hawaiians discovered hamburger by chasing a cow through a lava field.

The fact that I had only about a hundred feet left to go decided me. I wiped the back of my hand across my eyes for the hundredth time that hour, instantly regretting it because of the raw, stinging flap of skin that had started the day as an eyelid, and began picking my way out to the perch I had decided on. The canvas Japanese *tabi* on my feet protected me with their auto-tire soles, and I reached the spot with only one strawberry on the side of my calf where I had stumbled into a rough boulder welded to the surrounding lava. The ocean was now literally at my feet.

When I first started pursuing this kind of sport, I learned that rule number one was to keep one eye on the waves. Today, most were providing me with a cooling, knee-deep foot-soak, but there are always the mavericks that rush at you unexpectedly to drag you off the rocks if you are not quick enough to get back to safety. And safety means that dry spot you have already mentally checked out, representing a place where no wave has touched in the past half hour or so.

With both feet planted in relatively firm positions, I sent the half-ounce lead out on a 40-yard arc while it hauled its hook load of squid on a 2-foot leash behind it. As I started cranking the reel, the slim gray lead scooted back toward me under the surface, and the white strip wriggled in line behind it, following along in the approved fashion.

Beautifully done, but entirely unnoticed by any fish. Ten or fifteen casts went out, each one perfect, with a retrieve to match— and no action at all. On each retrieve I had whipped the rod tip back and forth in unison with the crank of the reel, and the bait had been positively succulent. I had covered the surface in 10-degree increments everywhere I could reach. In short, I had gone through exactly the same routine that had produced hundreds of pāpio, kākū, lai and *moi* (threadfin) in the past.

I gauged the depth of the water, perhaps 10 feet, and waited for the next wave to pass me on its rush up the cove. I timed the cast so that it would hit just behind the crest of the wave as it came abreast of me and then let the sinker settle in the smooth water for a few seconds. When it had sunk as much as I dared let it without touching the bottom (and a guaranteed snag), I swung the rod tip up 4 feet and let it settle back again for another second or two. The next lift brought my heart up with it.

There is no possibility of mistaking the feeling that is transmitted through your rod when a pāpio tries to take a bait away from you, for he hits it on a dead run and accelerates away. The first run is often a determined rush for the nearest exit that will get the fish away from the shallows. As this one ploughed steadily along

The ultimate light-tackle challenge. With surf, lava, coral and a stubborn fish all conspiring against him, the whipper can expect to land only one husky pāpio in ten strikes.

on a course toward Australia, I worried again about my selection of a 15-pound-test line. The fish could not break the line by pulling, of course, the drag would see to that. But one touch of the line on a coral head or lava projection and there would only be that exasperated sensation of giddiness that comes when you first realize that the line has no weight. This is a very familiar feeling in the repertoire of agonies that haunt pāpio fishermen when their midnight dreams turn to angling.

The first run took far more line than I should have let it. The tighter the line, the more easily it snaps when nicked by a sharp outcrop, so I tend to fish with a lighter drag setting than I should. I almost dreaded stopping the fish, since I knew he would switch to a more dangerous tactic. His second maneuver was sure to be to hunt for a hole in the bottom. As I felt the run peter out, I gambled. I twisted the drag nut just enough to give me as much pull as the line could take, and then hauled back with all of my strength. The pāpio had two options: he could dive, which my haul was designed to stop, or he could start running again, which would probably have pulled something apart. This time I won. The strong pull dragged the pāpio's head up to the surface about 75 yards out.

Hope changed to satisfaction because I knew that the combination of the height of my perch and the 9-foot length of the rod held above my head would be enough to keep the pāpio on the surface. The war wasn't over, but the deciding battle had just been won.

The only tough part left was the last-ditch dive the pāpio would make when he got close to the rock I was working from. The first pāpio I had ever hooked had won on that trick, but few have since. There was no doubt that he would try for a hole at my feet if I let him; so I didn't bring him up to the rock until I had chosen the wave I needed to boost him into the tide pool next to me. The wave came in as a heavy swell that matched the lift of the rod just enough to get the fish above the rim and into the pool.

If this were a superdramatic fish story, the hook would drop out at this instant, but I had spent too much time putting a point on that carefully chosen hook to have any pilikia. It took a knife to get the hook out of that sturdy 8 pounder.

Only an 8-pound fish? In a book filled with the accounts of the capture of giant marlin, huge tuna, tackle-breaking ulua, and many other streamlined titans, why tell the tale of a fish so small? Because the man who whips the shorelines and reefs has the purest, simplest, least-cluttered, and, in many ways, most satisfying sport of all anglers.

His gear is simple, but enough of a mechanical joy to delight him in its rhythmic flex and turn. His communion with the never-silent sea is not interrupted by the whumping of a grumbling motor, the smell of unnatural gasoline or diesel fumes, the dependence on any other person, or the nagging thought of how much everything is costing him.

It is not just that the cost of one day's offshore charter will keep five whippers fishing for a year—it is the peace and pleasure of being lost with one's own thoughts; unraveling the tangles of daily living with the shooting loops of line, away from the sights, sounds, and smells of civilization.

The man who catches a fish whipping owes no one for his success. But right there is the rub. Success along the shoreline is a steadily diminishing commodity. Civilization hounds the fish as much as it does the fisherman. Good fishing spots disappear with each new development and its burden of people and their effluent.

Perhaps the descriptions of the methods and techniques of whipping may serve future generations not as a guideline, but only as a history.

All young ulua of any of the dozen Hawaiian species are called pāpio. They don't lose this designation until they can overbalance a 10-pound weight. "Whipping" for pāpio is just about the only type of fishing in which local anglers use tackle their mainland counterparts would call light. The whipper usually tosses a small lure, like a quarter-ounce jig, and must have a line thin enough to give distance to his casts. But even here the whipper does not go to line as fine as the spin caster of other ports who might choose 6-pound-test line or even lighter. So few fish could be hauled out from among the jagged features of the Hawaiian bottom on 6-pound-test line that it would be no sport at all to use it. Ten-pound-test lines give an extra margin of support, and 15-test is the choice when lures are replaced by bait that can be cast with the addition of an ounce or so of lead.

Since a jig has no action of its own, being just a bit of lead molded around a small hook and finished off with a wisp of deer hair for a tail, all of the enticing movement must be provided by the caster. The rhythmic flicking of the rod tip does it. To get it you must have a tip limber enough to pick up the action imparted by a combination of rolling movements of the wrists while both work to crank in the lure. The hand that holds the rod moves back and forth like that of the angry lady scolding the neighbor's child with waggling finger. The reel hand is thus nearly stationary as it pushes down on the handle when the rod comes up, then pulls back as the rod flicks forward.

The little jig pulses under the surface, flexing and kicking its tail, darting right and left, up and down, splashing the surface at times, and always acting very much alive.

The angler follows the lure through Polaroid glasses which cut the surface glare. He stays alert for the flash of a fish rushing at the lure. He has to be as quick as the fish. He must react in the instant of the strike to jerk the rod tip and thus bury the hook in the tough pāpio jaws or between the kākū teeth before the fish ejects the fake food, because the fish will spit the tasteless chunk out as fast as he grabbed it if the angler lets him.

Often a pāpio hunts the lure in a parallel path that keeps him hidden from the fisherman. He tracks it nearly to the unexpecting angler's tabi tops before he flashes into sight and explodes the water with the fury of his charge—and the jerk which sets the hook is nothing more than a startled reflex.

No angler gets closer to his sport than the whipper who wades the shallow fringing reefs of Moloka'i or O'ahu. He can surround himself with productive water a hundred yards or more in any direction as he literally gets in among the fish up to his knees, and even up to his armpits if he is especially eager.

The practiced whipper is always ready to lift his rod tip when fighting a pāpio, to haul the silver fighter's nose up just before he starts for the bottom. And finally, perhaps as he tries to avoid being tied up in his own line by the fish swimming back and forth through his legs, he slides the fish into his net (a must for the reefer) and quits holding his breath.

To get the most action from a jig the experienced fisherman chooses the smallest one he can cast since the eighth-ounce lure responds more eagerly to twitches than one only double its size. This lure is tied on with an open loop rather than a cinched knot. The freedom of the loop means the lure does not have to flex the line to dart downwards. This fastening is made by first passing the end of the leader through the eye of the lure, doubling it back on itself for 6 inches or so, and then tying a standard end loop of the type you would use if the lure weren't there.

Barracuda like jigs as much as anything else you can feed them on most days, but they will cut right through a monofilament leader on the strike. To defeat their sharp fangs you'll need a thin wisp of wire for a leader. The visibility of the wire will decrease the amount of action you have from pāpio, and you should switch back to monofilament if you notice any packs of pāpio racing along with the lure but not willing to strike at it. Thin wire rusts through in very short order. Fortunately, it is so inexpensive that it can easily be replaced before every trip.

A jig-caught fish even fights differently than one caught on a bait rig where he is hampered by the constant downward pull of the casting weight. One morning as the dawn first pinked the sky, I set the hook in the jaws of a fish that jumped repeatedly until netted. To my great surprise it was a moi—the first leaping moi I had ever encountered.

The ulua family are noted night feeders and that makes them

Concentration and determination show on the face of an angler who has been tricked too often by the unexpected last ditch dive and roll of a Moloka'i 'ō'io. When this one rolled, the angler was ready.

smell feeders. But when they are in the mood for a fast lure it doesn't matter that the lead and feathers have no appealing aroma. Occasionally, though, the cold metal must be enhanced with natural flavor. Diggie Yamamoto took Ken Ozaki, Mas Kurashima, and me trolling inside the reef on Moloka'i with our spinning gear to locate some spots for whipping. We trailed three identical white jigs, except that mine had a thin shoelace strip of squid dangling from the hook. My lure took the first three fish until Ken and Mas started cutting bait for their lures.

Though the jig is the traditional lure for whipping, the small "swimming-minnow" plugs will actually outfish them. These are the baitfish replicas copied from the balsa wood minnow with plastic lip first handcrafted in Finland. Now many are made in the

United States, including the Cotton Cordell "Redfin," the "Rapala," the "Rebel," and the Gladding "Sea Bee."

The formula for success with these is simple. Throw it as far as you can, then race it back as fast as it will go without spinning out. It should track straight while swimming with a steady vibrating kick of the tail hook. Fast retrieves are for pāpio; for kākū, alternate quick returns with "crippled-minnow" retrieves. Do this by letting the lure settle for an instant, then work it back in short pulls. After each pull, stop for a second to let the lure wobble back toward the surface. The kākū just slide out of nowhere and suck it in. Then everything stops for a second until you set the hook and the long, slim barracuda rears up into the air to try to fling the thing back at you. If no strikes come in a dozen casts, move down the shoreline another 30 feet and repeat the series.

Where exceptionally long casts and strong lines are required to reach and beach the fish, bait is the answer. That's because it can be trailed slowly behind a casting lead heavy enough to pull a 15- or 20-pound-test line off a big spinning reel.

Though pāpio can be caught on nearly any kind of bait, the first choice of the whipper is a live "jumping jack," probably the ugliest fish God ever made. This blenny can jump from tide pool to tide pool to avoid the fastest man with a scoop net, or he can dart into a tiny crevice where no one can reach him. A few minutes after you've left a tide pool in disgust, the little blankety-blanks swim nonchalantly out of hiding and dare you into some more panting, redfaced exercise.

As a young lad, Peter Budge earned the respect of his fellow fishermen by being able to catch them in broad daylight. His method required teamwork and timing. He stationed himself at an opening between rocks where the waves wash back and forth from the open sea. His partner rushed at the tide pool just as the waves started sucking out past Peter's ambush. Then Peter quickly scooped the mocking blennies as they thought they were escaping.

You can avoid all the exercise by hunting blennies at night, when a sudden bright light stops them cold for a few seconds allowing time for an easy scoop. Needless to say, they must be stored in a large container, carefully covered.

Squid is the easiest and least expensive bait to get, since it can be purchased in frozen packages in most food stores. This is not to be confused with the creature known colloquially in Hawai'i as squid. The local nomenclature is shifted one cycle out of phase—

the octopus is called squid, the true squid is known as cuttlefish, and fortunately, the true cuttlefish is absent or the chain would continue to regress. That's why many fishermen have simply started over again in a new language, Japanese, and call the octopus *tako* while the true squid is *ika*.

Frozen shrimp imported from the mainland (hence called "California shrimp" even though it is probably netted off Costa Rica) is readily available but very expensive. Local shrimp, the tiny translucent *'ōpae* and the larger reddish *'ōpae-lōlō*, can be netted in calm shallow waters at night. They are tough to keep alive, though that's the way they make the best baits.

The problem of keeping live bait is not nearly so difficult for the whipper who hunts his quarry at the edges of the inshore reefs, rather than the rocky coasts. The reef fisherman constantly wades through shallow water in continuous search of the channels that provide highways for fish coming up onto the flats to feed. These fellows find it no problem to tow a floating bait container behind them. The live bait stays quite happy in the constantly changing water.

With all of his gear stowed in convenient places, the reef fisherman is a strange sight. All of the equipment must be kept above the high-water mark on his body, deeper than which he will not venture. Hanging around his neck and resting on his chest is a knapsack for hooks, lures, swivels, spare leader, and casting weights—maybe even a spare reel with heavier line for the time when he switches from lures to bait. Also around his neck but hanging under his right shoulder is his combination bait and fish bag. It's probably been lovingly sewn out of an old rice bag by his

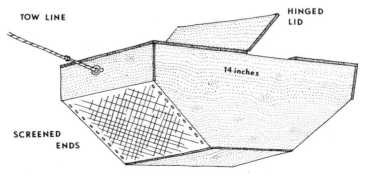

A floating box for live bait can easily be made from scrap lumber. The whipper can tow it behind him as he wades the reef.

sister-in-law. Around that same neck but under his left shoulder is the landing net suspended from an elastic band. Towing along behind him like a puppy is the floating live-bait well. Clamped between his teeth is a plug of tobacco to ward off the pangs of thirst from a half dozen hours away from fresh water. And, in certain special seasons, stuck in his right ear is a plug leading from a radio tuned to the broadcast of the Hawai'i Islanders baseball game.

A new and highly effective lure for small pāpio is something that doesn't look like anything at all. It is a slice of transparent soft plastic called a minnow strip. Even though it is colorless, it refracts light rays enough to be visible in the water and brings all kinds of fish up for a taste.

Why this attraction? Many kinds of sea life are transparent when small—fish, squids, and shrimp among them. This lure, which may not look like any one of them in particular, must remind young predators of such delicious little creatures. Henry Doi first showed me how successful it was—he even caught an akule with it—and told me how to rig it by hooking it through one prong of a small treble hook leaving the other two exposed to catch on a striking fish.

If such a shapeless piece of plastic works, why not one made from the same stuff but in the shape of a shrimp? Thomas Takamoto used just such a lure to catch a 24-inch lai off Ahukini Landing of Kaua'i, and these leather-skinned leapers don't come much bigger.

Unexpected results often seem to occur in fishing when you do something you hadn't planned. Once when whipping for pāpio with bait, we discovered that we had left our spare casting weights at home. We dug around in the tackle bag and came up with a 1½-ounce silver-spoon lure. Fished as is, these lures had never been successful despite our experiments with approximately fifty different types. After removing the hook, we tied on the lure to be used solely as a casting weight. Behind the spoon we tied a 2-foot leader with a piece of shrimp bait on the hook. Three casts, three pāpio.

The flash and action of the spoon seemed to bring in fish from all over the reef, a fact observed in the past. Undoubtedly, they were attracted to the vibrating hunk of silver. You could see them dart back and forth under the spoon getting more and more agitated by the second. When we had tried spoons before, this attraction had proved frustrating because the pāpio never hit the spoon and eventually lost interest in watching it. These excited pāpio, however, discovered the shrimp when they tired of the whirligig in front of it.

For beginning whippers the difficulties of casting tiny weights are nearly overpowering, even on spinning tackle, the frictionless, backlashless wonder that turned the sport from a specialist's skill to anybody's game. Here are some tips to insure that you achieve all the distance you can expect after thirty years of experience.

Make sure you have enough line on the reel. As the amount of line on a spinning reel diminishes, the friction of line against spool lip increases dramatically and cuts down on distance. The spool should be filled to within an eighth of an inch of the beginning of the flare.

To achieve maximum distance with a spinning reel, the spool must be properly wound with line. To cut down on friction while casting, the line must be level and filled to the start of the curve of the spool lip.

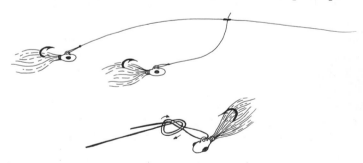

The double jig rig gives additional casting weight without limiting lure action. The second lure is attached to the line by a blood knot. The bottom picture shows how to tie a jig to the line with an end loop to give it a more erratic up-and-down action.

As shorelines become depleted of fish, whippers have taken to sea to cast from small boats. Fishing deep water at the outer edges of the reef can be miraculously successful for ulua.

Line should be wound on tightly. Usually, a small lure does not create enough drag in the water to provide the needed tension, especially because of the uneven jerking action of the rod. To get the needed tension, hold the rod with the right hand as far up on the foregrip as you can and let the line slide through the fingers as it is reeled. You can control the tension by regulating the pressure from the fingers.

Watch the spool lip for corrosion. A rough surface cuts distance and cuts lines.

Add extra weight by adding a second jig. The double-jig rig is made by tying a ⅛-ounce and a ¼-ounce lure to each end of a 2-foot leader. A loop is tied in the leader about one-third of the way from the heavier jig, and the line is tied to the loop. Since the lures are on separate leaders, both will jiggle enticingly when the rod is twitched.

Add extra weight by adding a wooden bobber. Tie a swivel to the line, then a short leader from the swivel to an egg-shaped bobber, then a longer leader from the swivel to the jig. The splashing float attracts fish (that's why some anglers paint them fluorescent orange) as well as helping to keep a hooked fish from diving into the rocks.

Note that none of these suggestions has anything to do with the actual muscles used in casting. The only way to get your timing right for distance is through practice, and the best way to practice is to go whipping.

# 12
# *Dunking*
## STILLFISHING WITH CAST BAIT

MOST HAWAIIAN 'ō'io, as well as many pāpio and kākū, are caught
by a method local anglers call dunking. Elsewhere in the world the
technique is referred to as stillfishing with a cast bait.

Dunking differs from slide-bait fishing in that the hook and
small bait are tied directly to the line and tossed out with the casting weight. It differs from whipping because the rig is left stationary on the bottom or only moved occasionally to a new position
nearby.

It's a much more relaxing art than either of the other two, since
the angler generally fishes from a sandy beach where he can stretch
out in the sun while his rod stays permanently in a holder. Well,
almost permanently. On two occasions I've had to resort to fins
and mask to find and retrieve rods that were pulled out of tipped
holders before I had the presence of mind to grab the rod on a
hard strike. Such are the drawbacks of sand spikes stuck in the un-
packed Hawaiian beach sand. One of these fish was still hooked
when I found the rod, and my family was treated to the hilarious
spectacle of a frogman trying to battle a fish with a 10-foot spinning rod while treading water. The reel was so full of sand from
being dragged along the bottom that it would neither crank, nor

yield line. The battle was, of course, no contest. Suffice it to say that the fish could swim better than I.

When I read in mainland magazines about fishing for the swift and powerful bonefish, I confess to being mystified. I don't recognize our 'ō'io in these tales of his Caribbean cousin. From comparisons of pictures, I can't tell the difference; they certainly do appear to be the same fish from the standpoint of physiology.

It is the personality that presents the problem. Our "gray ghosts" don't haunt the same places and aren't caught the same way, they don't act the same way when hooked, and there is even cause to believe that Pacific Ocean bonefish attain a bigger maximum size.

Atlantic bonefish swarm shallow-water flats in big schools that appear regularly with the incoming tide. Our 'ō'io is primarily a deep-water fish, coming into the surf to feed only just before dark or just at dawn.

Deep water? Some of the biggest 'ō'io are handlined up from depths of as much as several hundred feet. Don Andrews once returned from a bottom-fishing trip off Pololū Valley on the Big Island with a mixed bag of fish including 'paka, kākū, and a dozen or so mahimahi and ono caught trolling on the way back; but the fish that got most of the attention back at the dock were three 'ō'io, each close to 20 pounds. Any one of these three would have been a world record if caught on sporting tackle of the right weight class. All were pulled up from a hundred or more feet of water on handlines.

Don's comment about the kind of battle they waged would have surprised any bonefish expert except one from Hawai'i. Don said they jumped. Any Atlantic bonefish man would have winced at that statement, then probably smiled condescendingly before unraveling the tangled ignorance of misidentification by telling you the fish must really be a tarpon, milkfish, ladyfish, or other close relative, since everyone knows that bonefish *don't* jump.

Not only did Don's fish jump, but many of mine caught from shore while dunking have also. The first time it happened I was by myself and reluctant to tell anybody about the last-ditch leap my 10-pound 'ō'io made just before I brought him into the surf line. Who would believe me? As luck would have it, I mustered up the courage on a subsequent trip to describe it to the Lloyd Sextons. Within minutes one of the rods bent double, and as I set the

Three decades ago, the average Hawaiian bonefish catch was a 12-pound
fish. But that was long before this youngster was born and her 'ō'io is
now worth bragging about.

hook all three of us watched the fish clear the water completely in
a straight-up jump. I landed the fish and we verified its identity
before I released it.

On islands like Moloka'i and O'ahu that do have reefs, 'ō'io
can be caught by hunting them in the shallows in a modification
of the Bahamas style. The flats are not nearly so extensive, so the
fisherman must rely on finding a likely spot and working it in
hopes that a fish will come through before his patience ends. The
likely spots tend to be at the outer edges where channels in the
reef lead fish in from the sea. Here, dunking is the most efficient
method and baits may be shrimp or squid.

The most successful team of reef fishermen I've encountered used a very specialized technique. Their preferred bait was mantis
shrimp, which they gathered on the flats at low water while waiting for the tide to turn. To get to the offshore reef in the first
place they used small motor-driven skiffs which were hauled into
position by the bow line when the water got too shallow for the
motor. After the boats were anchored in position inside the reef
edge near a promising channel, they would wade to a chosen spot
with the baited hook and position the bait by hand—not by cast.
The best spot would be a shallow depression cleared of vegetation

by the action of mantis shrimp and with shrimp holes exposed. In theory it was this bottom feature the 'ō'io looked for.

The hand-carried casting weight was then stuck into one of the shrimp holes to hide it, and the bait was left lying completely exposed on the cleared sand where it would be an easy target for an 'ō'io ready to root with his nose for mantis shrimp. Of course, once the water rose high enough to bring 'ō'io into the shallows to feed, any new lines had to be cast into position. The fellow who showed me the technique had a 16 pounder to his credit.

The best fishing at many beaches seems to begin at the moment the sun turns red, and lasts until all light disappears. Chances are greater if the tide is coming in, and better still during the period following the full moon in what New England fishermen call "fishing the downside of the moon." 'Ō'io can be caught during the day in places remote enough to remain free of swimmers, but it is the beaches the swimmers like best that also attract 'ō'io to grub for small crabs in the tumbled sand along the surf line. 'Ō'io can even be caught at night. A school of big ones used to work the vast white sand stretches of Hāpuna Beach at about two o'clock in the morning.

Very few 'ō'io are caught on artificial lures in Hawai'i, which may surprise the Florida fisherman who stalks feeding bonefish with a fly rod and feather fluff ball, or a light spinning rod armed with flat skimmer jigs.

Hawai'i's 'ō'io will take a jig if worked right—that is, bounced along the sandy bottom—but this is a singularly inefficient operation since fish are not generally sighted; so the caster wears out his arm with repeated blind casts until finally an 'ō'io wanders by.

A bait lying on the bottom is just as effective and doesn't require the constant energy of casting. Since tiny lures are not used, light casting tackle is not needed and dunkers generally switch to 9- or 10-foot spinning rods and large spinning reels filled with lines testing at 15 pounds or more. Such tackle gives maximum casting distance and lifts the line above the incoming waves along the surf.

It is precisely the difference in type of tackle used and the depth of the water that results in the changed fighting tactics of the 'ō-'io, according to one piscatorial logician. An 'ō'io hooked on the light drag of a "fairy wand," such as that used by the Atlantic fisherman, has nothing to frustrate its powerful runs until its own blinding speed consumes its energy. Heavier spinning tackle capable of containing its power leaves it its strength, but the fish can't use it in the way its instincts determine. Thus the thwarted run turns into a centrifugal swing around a tethering point. With water under its keel deep enough to give the fish a start, this swing is just as likely to turn upward.

As to the monumental size of the Pacific clan, several IGFA records are held by 'ō'io, the Hawaiian kind, but this is not their chief claim to superior size since the all-tackle record, a 19 pounder, hails from Zululand in South Africa. Many bigger Pacific fish have been caught, among them several 25 pounders pulled from the lagoons at Christmas Island. Rumors drift by occasionally of 'ō'io as big as 30 pounds coming into the market, though these have been unsubstantiated with pictures or verifiable weights.

Ordinarily, I disregard rumors of outsized fish. Stories are too universally embellished in the retelling. If I have not seen the fish myself, or at least a photograph of it, I maintain a "healthy" scepticism. Thus, I have always raised an eyebrow over reports of unbelievably huge 'ō'io.

All but one, that is.

Hajime Nishimura of Moloka'i is a man I respect. If he tells me about a certain fish, I believe he has the species right and that the fish has not grown an ounce since its capture.

Hajime is a diver, and the story involves a netting trip he accompanied to use his underwater skills to clear the net of snags. When the time came to retrieve the net, the fishermen spotted the big gray shape of a fish trying to batter its way through the meshes of the gill net.

"We were all scared to go into the water because we were sure it was a shark," Hajime told me. Cautiously, Hajime eased over the side of the boat, slipping carefully into the water to begin an attempt to chase the "shark" away. Immediately, he relaxed when he identified it as an 'ō'io. True, it was bigger than any 'ō'io he had ever seen, but at least it wasn't a shark. He swam up behind the panicked fish, partly tangled in the net, and threw his arms around its neck, sticking his fingers into its gills to hold on.

He wrestled it up to the surface where his partners could give him a hand with it. Later, it weighed in at 27 pounds!

Not all of the giants that never made it to the IGFA-sanctioned roster were caught on commercial gear. Jack Ross tells of the time

one of his guests hooked a fish on spinning gear aboard his anchored boat after everyone else had set out to skin-dive near shore.
The fellow took a tremendously long time in bagging the fish and
finally needed Jack's help in getting it netted and boated. Being a
newcomer from the mainland whose only contact with Hawaiian
fish had been the trolling kind, Jack thought little of the catch,
remembering only that the fellow had called it an 'ō'io. Without
weighing it they consigned it to the frying pan and forgot about it
until Jack later discovered that an 'ō'io is a bonefish and that the
IGFA all-tackle record was a fish less than 40 inches long. Jack re-
called that the 'ō'io had stretched completely across the bottom of
his fish box and had even turned up its tail in the corner. As he
measured the bottom of the fish box Jack learned that the 'ō'io
had to have been at least 43 inches long. When telling the story
he now takes some consolation in the fact that identification was
not positive. But the only Hawaiian fish the 'ō'io resembles
enough to be confused with is the *awa* or milkfish, and this creature is a vegetarian requiring extremely refined techniques of baiting with seaweed or dough balls, which must be presented in the
most delicate manner to keep the fish from spooking.

In much of its habitat the bonefish is joined by the kākū, or
barracuda. The kākū is a perfect example of the type of fish which
creates entirely different impressions depending on the circumstances in which it is encountered. Trollers think little of them
since the kākū won't even break the heavy-duty rubber band on
an outrigger line trolled for marlin. Hooked on spinning tackle in
shallow water they can be nearly unstoppable. In Florida they are
feared because of their tendency to strike at any moving object
next to a boat including a paddle, a pushpole, or maybe even a
hand. Yet there is no record is Hawai'i of a kākū striking the paddling paw of a surfer stroking his board out to catch the next
wave. At least, no one has survived to complain.

Proponents of the barracuda as a game fish say that it has the
aerial ability of a mahimahi, the speed of an ono, and the bulldog
strength of a kāhala. Even if only half of that is true, they are
worth catching on tackle scaled down to their size.

On first glance the kākū's notorious teeth seem to be merely
scattered randomly throughout its mouth with no definite pattern
of purpose. These are none of the keen-edged, closely-set shearing
blades like those found in ono jaws, just pointed spikes that poke
out in irregular patches. Nature's intent is clear when you realize

that the long points are quick to penetrate with a minimum of jaw power. The kākū doesn't chew, its teeth are there to grab, hold on, and kill like daggers. This may be the key to the surprisingly small number of documented barracuda attacks. The kākū is interested only in creatures it can swallow with a minimum of chewing. Still, the spikes are sharp enough to rip up lure skirts; so wise jig fishermen hunting kākū use lures with tough nylon tails.

Any fisherman setting out for kākū needs a wire leader. An example of why, which also shows either their fearlessness or their stupidity, came when I was casting with shrimp bait in a sandy channel off Oʻahu. A fish struck cutting the leader instantly. I was sure it was a balloon fish, a regular nuisance in this manner, and became even more convinced when the action was repeated on several subsequent casts which suggested a whole school of the clipper jawed creatures. Switching to wire, I was surprised to hook a husky barracuda and, on examination, to discover that his throat was studded with a row of bright hooks, all mine. Neither the pain nor the inconvenience stopped his feeding for an instant.

Curiosity is another well-known personality trait of the kākū. He'll investigate anything that moves, even a wading fisherman. Such interest frightens the uninitiated because of the fish's fearsome reputation. Yet a Florida fisherman reports that he has seen barracudas refuse to attack needlefish (ʻahaʻaha) of the same size, even when the needlefish repeatedly bit the 'cuda.

Though kākū will take any dunked bait you can offer, their first choice is definitely something alive. A small live ʻoama (goatfish) or hahalalū (bigeye scad) is just about perfect for kākū, as well as pāpio, though neither bait is hardy enough to stay alive long and may not even survive the cast. This may not matter because they seem to be nearly as good used as fresh dead baits. Small live hīnālea are easy to catch and stay active long enough to attract big kākū.

Since dunking is basically a stationary operation once the cast is made, it pays to have a good reason to choose a spot. Kākū are very cooperative in this regard since they are generally spotted lolling just below the surface like sodden logs. Once located, the kākū is an easy target for a cast bait since it will investigate the splash rather than running in fear. A good procedure is to cast beyond the sighted fish and retrieve the bait very slowly along the bottom until the kākū moves toward it. His curiosity and appetite will force him to investigate.

Dead baits arouse the kākū's suspicion enough to cause him to exhibit a routine that can best be described as "tasting." The kā-kū picks up the bait with the very tips of its long pointed jaws and holds it until satisfied. Then it shifts the bait backwards one level to the clamping teeth, and this is probably the best time to strike if the angler wants a vigorous battle. A second or two later the bait will have been swallowed, and the hook may pierce a vital region eliminating much of the battle as well as the opportunity to release any unneeded fish.

This gentle grab of the bait at the very front of the mouth is the saving grace for the fisherman who is occasionally able to land kākū on very light nylon leaders with tiny hooks. Masa Matsushige, a *kama'āina* (native-born) who still dunks with conventional tackle instead of spinning gear, landed a 45-pound kākū which had been stealing his hooked fish as he tried for small bottom feeders. The kākū took a very small bait on a 15-pound monofilament leader. Masa was able to land it since the hook stabbed the fish in front of the teeth. And I once watched a 10-year-old lad snake a 15-pound leaper out of a Moloka'i fishpond on a tiny jig which snagged the kākū's jaw where it could not get at a 10-pound-test leader.

Its tolerance for a wide range of water temperature, including a preference for waters naturally heated on the flats or artificially heated by power plant discharges, makes the kākū one of the most available inshore game fish for the dunker. Indeed, some of the biggest live well within the city limits of Honolulu.

Deep-water dunking involves different problems from those encountered along the beaches or reefs. At times the bait must be perfectly positioned to be displayed where big fish can find it and small fish dare not try. A young fellow fishing off O'ahu's Iroquois Point found that the best way to do it involves no casting at all. Using a surf board, Wes Johnson would swim his baited line well offshore until he found the bit of bottom he liked best as seen through a face mask. With the bait positioned just the way he wanted it, he would swim back to his rod where it waited in its holder and get ready for action. In one two-day stretch when he was fourteen, Wes landed a 54-pound barracuda and a 30-pound ulua.

Some hook and line surfboarders don't even come back to shore to wait. They bring their tackle with them and present the bait to any fish they spot through face masks or specially mounted viewing plates built right into the board.

A rocky bottom will often hide the bait when the dunker relies on blind casting and luck is not with him. Though special hooks have been developed in Hawai'i to lessen the chances of catching their points in these coral obstructions, they still do hang up. Both the problems of the hidden bait and the snagged hook can be defeated by the dunker if he rigs a small cork on the leader an inch or two ahead of the hook and with just enough flotation to lift the bait off the bottom. Though special torpedo-shaped corks with central holes are made for the job, the fisherman can use any small bottle cork if he first pushes a hole through it with an ice pick. Once the central hole is made, the next step is to pull a loop of strong thread through the hole with a splicing needle of the kind used to join braided Dacron lines. When ready to tie up a leader, put the nylon leader through the loop and pull the loop back through the cork. No such special method is required for wire leaders; they can be pushed right through the ice-pick hole using their own stiffness. The cork will fit tightly around the leader so that it doesn't slide down onto the hook and get in the way. If the sinker is attached by a loop of line weaker than either the mainline or leader, the rig will not be lost when the sinker snags since the hook is always clear of the bottom. Only the lead weight itself will break free.

The cork has no noticeable effect on dunking for pāpio and kā-kū, though it may serve to make 'ō'io suspicious so that they

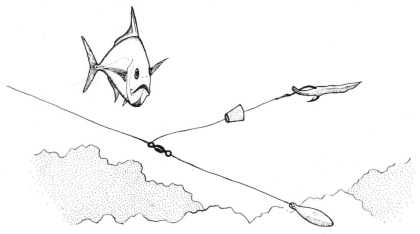

Threading a cork on the leader of a ''dunking'' rig raises the bait off the bottom to make it easily seen and less easily snagged.

avoid the bait. Since the latter frequent sandy bottoms anyway, there is little danger in losing rigs that lie right on the bottom.

One final comment on 'ō'io fishing is in order for the bonefish addicts around the world. Is great size a handicap on the reef? Could it be that feeding in thin water on tiny crustacea can't support the really big bonefish? If so, maybe there are offshore holes everywhere in the tropical world, not just in Hawai'i, where the retired giants live when they've grown too big to forage ashore with their offspring. Do you doubt it? It is true of the 'ō'io's shallow-water neighbors, the kākū and ulua, isn't it?

# 13
## *Shorefishing Baits*
### WHAT TO USE, HOW TO FIND IT

ABOUT A HALF DOZEN of the regulars were standing around the "moi hole" watching the surf churn against the black rock shoreline. Although rods and reels were in abundance, none of the boys was actively fishing. In fact, one of them had just remarked that there were a lot better ways to throw away money than by tossing hooks, sinkers, and swivels into a snag-filled cove after nonexistent moi. Another had blamed the poor fishing on the phase of the moon. "After all," he had said, "everybody knows the best time is when the moon is in the final quarter." A third had protested that they were all just lazy for having started late, and he was sure that if they had gotten there just at daybreak, they'd have been in time for the regular morning run of fish that swept up the coastline to explore each boiling opening in the rocks.

The big-tailed, rubbery-nosed fighting fish known as moi always schooled up at spots like this one as they searched for anything their ally, the rough water, pulled free from the rocks or dredged up out of the sand bottom.

This day, though, nobody had even had a touch despite the fact that all bait bags were well stocked with squid, shrimp, or succulent, wiggly strips of shiny aku belly. The latter is what many of the best of the moi fishermen had always chosen for waters like these, so charged with bubbles that only fish with X-ray vision could find food. Still, that's the way the moi like it, so they must be very adept at using their chin whiskers to sweep up food.

That's when a newcomer clambered down over the rocks with a shy smile for anyone who would return it. He reached into a small can to pull out a bait with an exaggerated care that made you know immediately that it was his only one. It took him nearly half a minute to get it exactly the way he wanted it on the hook. Then he stepped across the lava to the farthest rock out and expertly swept his flexing rod in an arc timed to drop this bait just short of the line of rock marking the other side of the cove. A turn or two of the handle tightened the slack and drew the bait toward the center of the returning backwash. Immediately, the rod vibrated with the kind of life that made every rock jockey there wish he could grab it.

"Keep him coming," one fellow said, so low that you knew he was living that fish as if it were his own, and he kept right on talking it in the way every unrepentant fishing fanatic does.

Let one moi get off and the school goes with it. That's why many of the moi fishermen like to use 20-foot-long poles with the line tied right to the tip. With it they would just haul a hooked fish right out of the water as soon as it hit so that there was no chance of scaring the rest of the school.

The newcomer timed the waves just right; just holding on when the water tried to draw the fish away, then hauling quick turns of line whenever the surf reversed back at the rocks. With a final wave-assisted sweep the moi flopped helplessly onto the rocks on his side and beat his sweeping V of a tail until his captor dropped him into the fish bag and unhooked him. With the same shy smile for all, and no more bait in his bucket, the successful fisherman worked his way back through the jungle of craggy 'a'ā and disappeared.

Lucky? Sure he was. His bait was in the right place at the right time. Just as important, it was the right bait. One type of bait will take fish when others don't on days when fish have just one food in mind. This fellow had learned that fish which feed in white water occasionally have their minds programmed for "sand turtles" and will accept nothing else. On another day it might just as well have been 'a'ama crab; on still another, perhaps, anything might have done just as well.

"Sand turtle" is a misnomer; the creature is actually a small type of sand crab about the size of the last joint of your thumb and with the general appearance of a fat beetle. Sand turtles burrow in the sand below the break of the wave and dash into dangerous territory in search of food scraps each time the waves stir the bottom with their rhythmic pounding.

Moi, pāpio, ʻoʻio, and any other type of fish willing to mix it up in the surf are set to grab an easy meal since the oval crabs don't have much mobility in the wash. The easiest way for the angler to catch this bait is to tie a squid head (not octopus) to a stick and force the latter into the wet sand a few feet shoreward of the breakers. Within five minutes any sand turtles in the area will have followed the scent through the suds to burrow under the squid head and partake of a leisurely meal in relative safety. They grab the tips of the tentacles and pull them into the loose sand where they feed without the danger of exposure. Though some sand turtles can be netted in the receding waves on the ocean side of the squid bait, the biggest are scooped from under it by digging the net into the top few inches of shifting sand as it liquifies in the sloshing surf.

The best baits are the females bursting with bright orange roe. Game fish attack both sexes from the underside and chew out the soft parts leaving just the shell on the hook of the slow striker. To beat this, the angler must choose a very sharp short shank hook (not an incurved ʻōʻio hook). The point is run through the shell from the underside near the tail and out the back. Then it is turned and forced back through the shell near the head so that the point is completely exposed where it protrudes from the underside. Hooked this way the point is always pulled toward the feeding fish. A hard upward sweep of the rod tip must come at the first nibble or the fish will leave no more than a flake of shell looking like a fingernail.

Another good crab bait is the black rock crab, or ʻaʻama. Despite the vast numbers seen scampering around on the glistening wet lava along the water line, the fisherman will find it difficult to catch these quick clingers. A man with a steady hand can usually get a few with a bamboo pole with a two-pronged fork at the end, formed from a pair of coconut leaf midribs. Across the tips is stretched a thin piece of nylon thread that can tangle in the eyestalk of a crab before he pulls in his eye. Once this eyestalk is withdrawn the crab won't extend it as long as the danger remains; so the pole wielder can pluck him off the rocks like a fruit from a mango tree. The more adept you are at sneaking up on crabs, the shorter the pole you'll need. Good crab stalkers can get away with a 6-foot wand.

A poor pole man might find it easier to use a longer one with a nylon thread dangling from the tip carrying a small hook. This hook is there only to hold a bit of bait, a piece of shrimp or squid, that will interest a crab long enough for the crabber to jiggle the tip and tangle the crab in loops of slack.

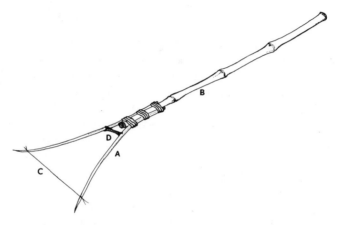

An 'a'ama crab catcher can be made by binding two strips from the midrib of a coconut palm leaf (A), to the end of a bamboo pole (B). A thin nylon thread (C) is then attached to the tips and held taut with a twig (D) as a spacer.

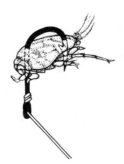

To keep nibblers from stealing a sand turtle, bait your hook as shown and strike at the slighest twitch on the line.

A live 'a'ama can be used whole, but this is not usually done unless the fisherman has been fortunate enough to catch a soft shell crab whose carapace has not yet hardened after shedding its shell. Even these are best used in small pieces. Leg meat makes a nice small bait if it can be removed whole. With a sharp knife and a little practice, anyone can get out a strip from the largest joint of each leg. Cut across the joints at the ends, then along the flatter edge of the leg and you can pry the shell open to withdraw the bait.

A fresh crab is more difficult to peel than one that has been dead 15 to 30 minutes, since the tissues don't seem to hang onto the shell so tenaciously after the wait. Like many other types of baits, the 'a'ama is more easily caught at night, when a bright light confuses it and roots it to the spot where it can be grabbed by hand.

As these examples show, shore fishermen in Hawai'i have always placed more faith in natural baits than artificial lures, a fact which is counter to the national trend. Maybe this is because so many different kinds are readily available to the man who knows how to catch them. In this and other chapters we have already described methods for getting sand turtles, 'a'ama crab, jumping jacks, and 'ōpae. Such common baits as shrimp and the true squid are readily purchased.

Sea worms, 'oama, hahalalū, and octopus are also excellent enticements for some species at some times. The sea worms, for example, are a favored bait for small fish at night, since the worms are visible in subdued light. Perhaps the simplest way to gather them is to break open dead detached coral boulders strewn along the bottoms of tide pools. The worms can be pulled from their tubes along the freshly broken surfaces. Worms should not be handled with the bare hands because they are covered with small bristles that irritate the skin. Any fragments of coral should be returned to their original site since they shelter other living organisms, even though the coral structure may be dead.

'Oama can be caught on hook and line. If you have ever seen a circle of fishermen with small cane poles standing in the calm shallows, they were almost certainly trying to catch these young *weke,* or goatfish. Weke of all sizes school up in large numbers and poke their barbels into the sand as they probe for food. Once chummed with tiny bits of shrimp, they will stay in one spot unless frightened by the movements of careless fishermen.

Hahalalū are the young of the bigeye scad, akule, and are most abundant during the August to November season when vast schools swarm inshore. They, too, can be chummed, though the best palu is not shrimp but any fish-based canned cat food mixed with sand to stretch the cloud of flavor down to the bottom. Schools of hahalalū sweep back and forth with a speed that makes them nearly invisible to all but the experienced eye. In a flash one has the bait and must be hooked instantly, or he's stolen the bit of shrimp and is gone.

When 'oama are not needed for live bait, they can be caught at night in shallow-water tide pools and then frozen until used. 'Oama can be spotted lying quietly on the bottom, seemingly "sleeping," if such a state can be said to exist among the finny species. Two men, one with a scoop net and the other with a gas lantern, can quickly scoop all they will need. The fellow with the light positions it behind his leg so that the shadow is a few inches in front of the sleeping 'oama. His partner puts the net down in the shadow directly in front of the fish and then scares it with his foot. Most of the time it will dart forward blindly into the net.

For the fisherman who would like an equal chance at 'ō'io or big pāpio, the best bait is a slice of octopus because it is high on the list of preferences of both species. Small reef fish tend to ignore the tough white strip, or quickly discover that their teeth aren't sharp enough to pull it off the hook. One slice of tentacle could make a bait that would last all day, even through the catching of several big fish. Indeed, it is so tough when fresh that it can be difficult to get onto a dull hook.

Skinning out an octopus tentacle takes patience and a very sharp knife because the white meat does not separate easily from the outer membrane and actually must be cut away rather than peeled off. If this skin is not removed, the outer layers tend to soak up water, making an unattractive bait puffed up with jelly-like sacs.

Finding an octopus during the daylight hours is usually done with the aid of a "look box," a wooden box open at the top so that you can see through its glass bottom. The "day squid," he'e, or common mud-flat octopus, is found in small reef holes and advertises its presence by surrounding the opening of its home with freshly turned coral bits and mollusk shells. Occasionally it adds some shiny man-made discard to the decor. When a spear is stuck into the hole the octopus usually will explore it by wrapping a tentacle or two around it, and then it can be quickly pulled from the hole. Watch out for the blast of water and ink when you grab him; he can squirt the black mixture 10 feet through the air if he is a big one.

An octopus must be grabbed by the body since he can shed his legs as a gecko drops its tail. Though the suckers which stick to your arms feel creepy, they can't hurt you. The beak at the center of the radiating circle of tentacles might; so try to avoid it. Most "squidders" slow the octopus down by forcing the body inside out. This is done by pulling backward on the mantle opening while pushing on the back of the body. Eventually, this will kill him, but initially, it just immobilizes him.

An old traditional method in Hawai'i for dispatching an octopus is to bite out its eye. This works very well because the central nervous system runs from eye to eye and can be severed at either end. It's a handy method when both hands are trying to hang on to a writhing octopus, a spear, and a drifting look box.

The octopus is most common from August to November when you can sometimes even find them wandering around on the reef outside their homes or just lying on a rock sunning themselves. During other months there may be fewer, but they tend to be bigger.

The night squid, or *pū-loa,* is a long, stringy, red free-swimming octopus that haunts the tide pools late at night. Less valued for food, less sought for bait, he's also a bit more dangerous to handle because he will bite if he can.

An old Hawaiian method used to catch octopuses in deep water is to rely on their curiosity about moving objects. Early fishermen used a lure made by tying a cowrie shell to one side of a stick balanced by a stone weight bound to the other. A pointed wooden spike was tied in at an angle at the base of the stick to complete the hook, and a few strands of palm frond were tied on to make a tail. This lure was lowered from a canoe on a line made from *olo-nā* fibers and then moved back and forth in front of any likely-looking spot. Any octopus seeing the moving lure would grab hold, after which a quick jerk on the line would set the hook for retrieval of the "squid."

Since the octopus does not dig its own hole but appropriates any cave left vacant, some *akamai* squidders have solved the housing problem for the octopus colony by placing pottery jugs in attractive places to be inspected every few days for harvesting of any transient octopuses.

Fishermen have been known to have so much fun catching bait that they just quit fishing.

## 14

# *Tackle: Choosing It, Making It*

RODS, REELS, LINES, LURES, SPLICES, KNOTS,
SWIVELS, SNAPS

### *Rods*

HOW MANY MISTAKES can a rod maker make in the making of one
rod? With the wide selection of fishing tackle available on the Hawaiian market, the question is an important one. An unsatisfactory
experience I've had with a trolling rod sent me for field-testing illustrates both the kinds of errors that slip by quality control spe-
cialists at mass-production tackle manufacturers and the qualities
to look for when sorting through the racks of rods in the sporting
goods supermarkets.

The buyer must judge his rod from at least three viewpoints:
suitability to his kind of fishing, quality of the components, and
excellence in workmanship. A low grade in any one of these areas
is grounds for rejecting the rod.

Suitability is what you look for first, and that doesn't mean just
not buying an aku pole to try for marlin. You must satisfy your
individual preferences on action. Two rods can be labeled "50-
pound class" for instance, but have markedly different flexibility.

Unlike a shore-fishing rod, the only job the trolling stick has is
to fight a fish, and you don't need to compromise on the fighting
action you like best. You may like a rod that flexes a lot and com-

pensates for quick changes in the fighting tactics the fish tries. Or you may choose a stiffer rod to give you a better "feel" for what the fish is doing as well as a little more lifting power.

You also have to worry just a bit about matching the rod to the type of line you use. If you like nylon monofilament, you'll want a stiffer stick to compensate for its stretch. An inelastic Dacron line may work better with a whippier blank.

How soft is soft and how stiff is stiff? A good power range runs anywhere from one-third to one-half "deflection." That means that when the rod is in its holder and a spring scale is tied to the line running out the tip guide, the pull needed to bend the tip at right angles to the butt should be between 17 and 25 pounds for a 50-pound-class rod. Which end of this range you choose is up to you.

Quality components are essential. You are wasting time and money if you don't get the best. This is where brand names help. The hardest part is to find out what company made the blank. Some quality names to watch for in glass rods are Fenwick, Garcia Conolon, and Harnell, but there are others.

Reel seats must be sturdy enough to support the pull of the harness against the fish; among the best is Varmac.

Poor-quality guides strip all the strength from the line. For trolling rods, get roller guides. For the heavy rods, the names to rely on are Mildrum and Fin-Nor. In the lighter outfits, choose AFTCO. More on the subject of guides later.

It was really the question of workmanship that made the rod sent for field-testing so unsatisfactory. Perhaps the best way of telling what to look for is to point out the seven mistakes this rod maker made.

First, the guides were not properly aligned. Any line that tried to wiggle its way from reel to tip would have looked like a *pūpule puhi* (crazy eel). They weren't even properly spaced. Under normal fighting power the line contacted the rod between the reel and the first or "stripping" guide. The line should be able to run from reel to guides to tip without ever touching the rod, even under full power.

Second, the reel seat was not properly aligned, either. This is difficult to judge unless you mount a reel on the rod and note whether the guides are perpendicular to the reel crossbars. Since the screw-in lock on a trolling rod keeps the rod from twisting, this mistake cannot be corrected without removing part of the reel seat and reglueing it.

Third, the foregrip hadn't been completely glued on. It was loose in places and eventually tore free while fighting a fish. You can determine whether this is a problem by holding the butt in one hand and giving the foregrip a gentle twist.

Fourth, the fancy-grained finish on the butt was poorly applied and chipped off from the gentle touch of a rubber-lined rod holder.

Fifth, the guides did not have underwraps so they worked loose after a few fish.

The sixth mistake is admittedly esoteric and is only really a factor on light rods like the 20-pound-class wand I was testing. Because of the way a rod blank is made, by wrapping glass around a tapered center mandrel, it will develop its own best and most natural bend. Thus the rod has a curve that is visible to the naked eye by sighting along the blank. The guides should always be installed on the side *opposite* the bend. Otherwise, the rod will twist under pressure causing the guides to strain against their wraps.

The seventh mistake was either the result of poor packing which may have strained the rod in shipping, or a defect in the blank itself. Either could have been discovered by close inspection to determine any deviation from a smooth straight surface. The last 6 inches of the rod broke off when the line snapped free from the outrigger pin.

After you've bought the rod, avoiding all of the pitfalls, watch the wrappings carefully after each use. The one place nearly every rod maker skimps is on the number of varnish coatings on the wraps (the glass blank itself needs no other coating than its bonding resin) because each layer of varnish must dry and this delays production. The rollers should be oiled after every use, and the screw locking nut on the reel seat should be turned free, then the grooves oiled.

Before turning from trolling rods to casting rods, let's take an in-depth look at the subject of guides.

The typical tourist from Kansas is usually flabbergasted when he gets his first look at a big-game trolling rod.

"Hey, Mabel, look'a here at this fish pole. It's a pool cue with a lot of chrome-plated pulleys tied onto it. Say fella, how come you use those fancy wheel things?"

The answer to the malihini's question is friction. How much friction? When a marlin hits, it is not unusual for the distance between boat and fish to open at the rate of 30 miles per hour or more. This means that 44 feet of line is racing across each guide each second. On a one-thirty rod with a drag set at 40 pounds, that dry Dacron line is cutting down on the guides with enough pressure to bend that pool cue our mystified tourist mentioned.

No matter how smooth ring guides are, they will chafe the line somewhat on the heavy outfits under these conditions. Though ring guides will suffice on 50-pound-class rods and under, the heavy rods need the freewheeling rollers.

On 30 and 50 rigs, a roller tip and roller stripping guide will take most of the strain if your budget can't, with less expensive ring guides in between. The stripping guide must be double roller, one wheel above, the other below, because the trolling reel sits so high off the rod that the line will tend to bear on the top roller before the rod flexes.

Tungsten carbide rings are the most durable, even though their dull gray surfaces are the least attractive. Any softer metal will groove quickly. Rods in the 6-, 12-, or 20-pound class are fine with rings since the friction problem is minimal because of the lessened tension, and the wheels would be too small to bother with anyway.

Light "whipping" rods also endure guide problems. The first place the manufacturer chooses to cut down on costs is in the number and quality of the rings. All hardware must be as corrosion proof as possible or the warm Hawaiian saltwater will etch it into a filelike surface that whittles the line out of existence. Carbide rings have not proved practical for the giant thin spinning guides required for their flexibility. Hard chromed stainless steel seems to have provided the best solution so far with carbide as the best possible tip ring.

The development of ceramic guides threatens to make all other kinds obsolete. With hardness and smoothness unattainable with any kind of metal or metal alloy ring, the ceramic guides come closest to perfection at an affordable price.

How many guides is enough? It depends a bit on the action. The best all around "whipping" rod is a 7-foot, one-piece stick with a light action tip and a two-handed butt. From the front of the reel seat to the delicate tip is a span of 66 inches with seven guides spaced at distances, measured from the tip, of 4, 8, 13½,

20, 27½, 35, and 43½ inches. These measurements are included here as much for the man who buys his tackle as for the man who makes it. By contrast, an excellent 10-foot "dunking" rod may also have just seven guides spaced over its 10-foot length from tip to reel seat. These guides would lie at 7, 15, 24, 34, 46, 59½, and 73½ inches.

The bigger rod would almost certainly be a two-piece blank ferruled not quite in the center but with a joint leaving a 6-foot lighter section for better casting. Such a take-apart feature is valuable for packing rods over long distances.

A two-hand butt on the "whipping" rod? It distributes the casting load over both wrists as well as providing a little more leverage when braced against the body while fighting a fish. The butt also enables the angler to stow the rod in a sand spike.

What length and action are best for shore casting in Hawai'i?

When you are standing with both feet planted at the edge of the surf of a promising shoreline, and both hands on the butt of a long surf rod, trying your hardest to put a bait in the path of a hungry ulua or 'ō'io, the best spots always seem to be just outside casting range. That channel mouth is still 20 feet beyond your longest toss; that sandy patch can't be reached even with a running start. At such moments of frustration some fishermen decide to buy a new rod. Maybe one that is longer; or perhaps one with more "action."

It is not unusual to see fishermen who have pursued this line of logic as far as surf rods 14 feet long. But there is an imbalance somewhere in the equation relating length of cast to length of rod. With a 13-foot rod I cannot cast farther than my fishing partner, Ken Ozaki, does with his 9-footer, even though I am half a foot taller and 40 pounds heavier. He can cast all day with little effort, while I huff and puff to keep up.

Experienced distance casters, the kind who go for measured world records in casting tournaments, will tell you that the biggest fisherman in the world doesn't need a rod longer than 10½ feet to crank out a cast of 400 feet on a conventional reel using 36-pound-test line and a 4-ounce sinker. If he is willing to drop to 25-pound-test, he can beat 500 feet with the same rod and reel. With an 11½-foot spinning rod, a 2-ounce weight and a reel capable of holding 600 yards of 20-pound line, a fisherman might hope to toss the lead over 500 feet. Such a reel is so big that its weight makes it very impractical for steady fishing.

The point to be made is that the gigantic rods of 13, 14, and even 15 feet so often seen on the Hawaiian fishing grounds are not needed. The distances above are based on actual recorded casts on regulation fishing tackle by practicing surf casters.

In action the answer then? Do you need a rod that coils and uncoils like a vaulter's pole? Yes, action is the answer, but not in the way many frustrated casters think. Many fishermen think that the more the rod flexes, the longer the cast. In actual fact, the *reverse* is true.

Here is the test one champion tournament caster uses. He supports the rod in a horizontal position by the butt only, with one nail under the reel seat and one above the butt. He marks the spot where the tip is unflexed, then marks a second spot where the tip moves with a 3-pound weight. The difference between the two points is the "deflection."

For a rod used to cast 2- or 3-ounce weights, deflection should not exceed 24 inches and is best at around 22. Rods used with larger weights should deflect no more than 20 inches.

Since casting is only one function the rod must fill, the angler might choose a slightly different rod than the tournament caster uses.

### Making Your Own Rod

You can double your fishing fun with the pride that comes from fighting a fish on a rod you made yourself. Since fiberglass took over from split bamboo as a construction material, putting together an excellent quality rod has become almost easy. Making a fishing rod means merely assembling a collection of ready-made parts and saving the money you would have to pay for workmanship in a custom-made one.

Here is how to make a trolling rod, the most difficult type. The parts needed are: a blank, roller top, a set of five guides, a foregrip, a wooden (not metal) spacing collar, a reel seat, wooden butt, and slotted gimbal butt cap. You'll also need several spools of nylon or silk winding thread, color preserver, varnish, ferrule cement, and epoxy resin glue.

Total cost varies depending on the materials and the pound-class of the rod. By mail order you might save a bit of money, but many stores in Hawai'i have all the parts.

Start with the butt, which can be ready made or turned on a lathe from hardwood stock such as hickory or ash. One end must be turned to a diameter that will allow it to fit snugly inside the reel seat for about 3 inches. The other is tapered to accept the gimbal cap. Glue the gimbal cap to the end with epoxy and secure it in position with a stainless screw. Glue the reel seat to the butt with ferrule cement, making sure to line up the reel housings with the cross slot of the gimbal.

Several types of reel seats are available. Trolling rods require one that locks the blank into a fixed position. Such a seat comes in two pieces: a female section which attaches to the butt and holds the reel, and a male section which is glued to the blank.

Before the male section can be glued to the blank it must be fitted with the wooden collar which has a center hole of the exact diameter as the fat part of the blank. Some rod companies make blanks with expanded ends to fit perfectly into the reel seat. Otherwise, you need the collar to fill the gap between the blank and the reel seat. A heavy-duty epoxy glue such as Marine-Tex is your best bet. After checking to make sure the collar is the right size both for the blank and the seat, glue it to the blank first, then to the seat.

Sight along the blank to see if there is any natural curve to it; there usually is. Before the glue dries, align the blank so that the curve points away from the side the reel is on.

Now glue on the foregrip. You can buy a one-piece cork grip or build it up in sections from cork rings. Newer grips are being made from tubes of rubber; some excellent rods have grips made from tight windings of rope. The grip should be at least 6 inches long.

When the glue is set on the rest of the rod, you are ready to wrap the guides. Spacing is important. A good plan for the stan-

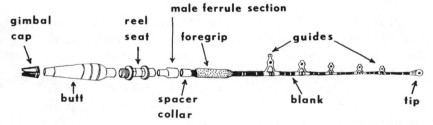

The basic components of a trolling rod are the same as for all rods, though individual parts may be designed differently. The spacer collar is needed only when the end of the rod blank is too thin to fit snugly in the male ferrule of the reel seat.

dard 30-pound and heavier rods is a guide spacing of 4½, 12, 22, 34, and 47 inches from the tip, measured to the center of each guide.

To control the tension of the winding thread, spool it on to a small star drag reel attached to another rod. Then run it through the first guide of that rod. Now you've got a rod winder as good as any sold. By adjusting the drag on the reel you can get exactly the tension you need on the winding thread.

Put five wrappings on the rod having lengths 1 inch more than the total length of each guide from end to end of the feet. Finish each wrap by winding the last few turns over a loose loop of thread. Then insert the end of the winding through the loop and pull it back under the windings for a neat finish. So far you have only the underwraps.

Wind on the guides one at a time by first taping one foot of the guide to the rod in the correct position before winding on the other foot. In each case wind the wrapping by starting beyond the foot and working toward the ring for a binding that won't slip.

When the wrappings are completed, coat the thread with three layers of "color preserver" allowing each layer to dry completely before the next. If you try to varnish the thread without using the preserver, you will immediately destroy the color of the windings. Coat the wrappings with at least three layers of polyurethane varnish.

Attach the tip with ferrule cement, the kind that softens when heated. It makes it easier to get the tip off again if it needs to be replaced or realigned.

Now go out and fight a fish.

### Reels

Gradually the angler gained line as the strong fish began to tire at last. He did not know that each turn of the nylon line choking down on the reel spool took him one step closer to the death, not of the fish, but of the reel itself.

"Hey, I'm having a devil of a time cranking this handle," he called, as he began to realize there was something wrong with the equipment. "It seems to be binding."

A few more turns, then pop! Another reel blown apart from the tension of a stretched line.

"Hell, the reel's quit. I gotta handline him in. Look at that buggah! He's big. That's the biggest mahimahi I ever saw. If he has another run in him we don't stand a chance.''

As though heeding the fisherman's words, the speckled golden beauty turned and shot away from the boat on a run nearly as strong as his striking charge. The rod tip jerked down and the fisherman jerked forward from the strain. Then, with a crack like a rifle shot, the line snapped and whipped its end back into the angler's face. The reel had landed a small marlin the week before, and the pressure bound into each tight wrap of the nylon monofilament line had worked against the side plates for 7 days.

This unfortunate fisherman had decided not to spend the extra money for a trolling reel with a one-piece spool turned from a solid block of metal. He learned that there was no such thing as an inexpensive reel by losing a $15 lure, a pair of half-dollar hooks, $3 worth of wire, a $2 snap swivel, and some $34 worth of mahimahi flesh at the market value of the time—all of $55 lost when the mahimahi broke that line. He lost enough to buy a reel that would have landed the fish.

Spool failure is the most dramatic problem that can befall a trolling reel, but not the only one. Many fish are lost when the drag overheats and seizes up on a strong fish. Star drags have been standard features on trolling reels for several decades. By turning a star-shaped wheel mounted just inside the crank, the fisherman can change the amount of holding power of the reel. He can adjust the braking strength so that the reel will give line when a fish pulls harder than the breaking strength of the line. That way the fish is forced to tire itself by constantly pulling against a small but steady strain that eventually exceeds its own ability to resist.

Despite the fact that these reels have accounted for many IGFA records, the star drag has its faults. It works by the transmission of pressure through a series of metal washers alternating with fiber or leather ones. Because of the relatively small surface area of the washers, heat can build up inside the drag and cause the fiber washers to stick to the metal ones eliminating the slipping effect between the turning surfaces. This can also happen just from prolonged use.

If the reel is inspected regularly, cleaned and lubricated properly, and the washers are replaced after hard use, there is little chance of this happening. The metal washers must be polished occasionally to remove all of the corrosion that will otherwise cause them to chew up the fiber washers and eventually bond right to the sticky surface. The washers can eventually disintegrate completely.

Few fishermen have the time and patience to do this frequently with every reel they own, hence the development of the lever-action luxury reels. Instead of the star wheel, they have a large lever that activates twin floating discs inside the reel with surfaces as wide as the side plates themselves. The Penn International 130, for example, boasts a drag surface of 25 square inches. The position of the lever can be seen at a glance, so the fellow fighting the fish knows exactly how much drag is on the line at any instant. Unbreakable pinion and spool shafts, all one-piece, enable the angler to use even stretchy nylon lines without danger.

Trolling reels should not be flushed off with a hose; this just forces the salt deeper into the mechanism. Unless the salt water itself has been driven into the reel by inundation during fishing, it is best removed by wiping with a wet rag or sponge full of fresh water. Reels should be protected from being splashed with salt water during fishing. If they do get dunked or catch a heavy wave, they should be pulled apart and dried out, then sprayed internally with a water-displacing lubricant. No lubricant should ever get on the drag surfaces, of course, or the line will alternate between slipping too easily and seizing up during each pump of the rod.

Taking the drag apart is easy; getting it back together again is the tough job. The would-be reel mechanic is wise to keep his owner's manual handy to find out what to do with all of the leftovers.

Spinning tackle presents simpler problems because the mechanism on the best reels is surprisingly easy to take apart and maintain. Many of the early, whirling "coffee grinders" tended to explode into a shower of springs and screws under the pressure of even small saltwater fish, since they were primarily designed for catching miniature inland fish. The first of the seagoing fixed-spool reels were just giant adaptations of their dainty fresh-water prototypes. Line guides on the bails cut through about as fast as it takes a power saw to go through a piece of pine. Spools snapped in half from the coiled tension of the only kind of line that can be used on such reels, solid monofilament nylon. They never seemed to carry enough line to handle any decent Hawaiian fish, and the line itself had to be too light anyway.

Now spinning reels are big, strong, corrosion resistant, and simple. Efficient gear trains have replaced the boxes of tiny wheels that shed their teeth like chips from a lathe. Helical gear systems in the best reels rely on two gears in an arrangement so simple it is surprising they weren't the first design tried. Carbide line rollers last the life of the reel if kept lubricated before and after each use. Spool capacity runs as high as 400 yards of 30-pound-test line on the biggest practical models, and a range of sizes is available to match any type of fishing imaginable. A good match for a 7-foot whipping rod is a reel that will take 150 yards of 10-pound-test; for the 10-foot dunking rod, a reel able to pack at least 300 yards of 20-pound-test is best. The most dangerous place for corrosion is the spool flange, so this should be washed after every trip with a hundred feet or so of line stripped so that the fresh water can get deeper into the spool.

### Lines

The differing needs of trollers and casters have been met by the development of two lines which are different in both construction and composition. Trollers choose braided Dacron; casters pick nylon monofilament.

Braided Dacron is smaller in diameter for lines of the same strength, lies well on a revolving spool reel, has a minimum of stretch, and can be woven to very fine tolerances to satisfy fishermen in hopes of setting IGFA records. All are advantages to the troller.

Since monofilament is an extruded line, its strength can vary over a much wider range, so that a spool labeled "50-pound-test" can mean anything from 35 to 60. On the other hand, its springy coils and hard surface make it the only choice for casting with a spinning reel, and its translucence makes it the psychological favorite for all kinds of shore casting because it suggests invisibility (which is not quite as complete as the typical observer might believe). Even Hawaiian fishermen who use "conventional," revolving-spool casting tackle have switched to mono despite the problem of an increased tendency to backlash and spin loops into the spool edges where they eventually foul with the internal workings of the reel. The problem is tolerable because the hard smoothness makes slide baiting easier.

Some of these characteristics of solid mono appeal to the troller. He can splice a piece of heavy monofilament into the end of his Dacron braid and have the best qualities of both. This section of hard-surfaced line resists chafing as it is drawn through the water better than the many stranded string. With improvements in reel construction, the so-called memory of the nylon is less of a problem. This is the aforementioned tendency of stretchy lines to exert multiplying pressure on the reel spool as they fight to return to their original elongation. Some experts are predicting that the improved technology of extruded lines will eventually result in a product capable of eliminating all competition both offshore and on.

Still, braided Dacron is the line you will see most often trailing from the outriggers and flatrods of the sportfishing fleet. All Dacron is made by DuPont and nobody else. DuPont sells the fibers to line manufacturers who then use their own methods of weaving and treating lines. Since Dacron tends to be a very dry line that causes more friction than other types, the final step in the process of making lines is frequently some attempt at lubrication. One method is to coat the finished product with Teflon; another is to run the fibers through a bath of waxes and oils as the line is being braided. The latter has the advantage of causing fewer fibers to be broken in the weaving process from the abrasion of Dacron strand against strand as they are worked together. The result is a more uniform strength.

In Hawai'i fishermen choose hollow Dacron instead of line braided around a core. This is partly because the coreless lines are easier to splice and partly because the core usually breaks while fighting a fish, thus decreasing the line strength. The latter happens because the core is composed of straight filaments, while the outer covering is the braid which cinches down on the core as it tightens. Thus the core is literally pulled apart.

Tapered lines are sparking interest among Island fishermen because they increase reel capacity without presenting any serious disadvantages. A reel capable of holding 500 yards of 80-pound-test is first loaded with 250 yards of 30, 250 yards of 50, and then finished off with 200 or more yards of 80-pound. All sections would be spliced with a needle for a total of 700 or more yards of line instead of the intended 500 of 80. The theory is that a big sprinting fish now has an extra 200 yards of line to contend with. Through boat handling, the fisherman should be able to get back all of the 30-pound and most of the 50. Then, when the tough toe-to-toe fighting comes, the angler can finish the fight at full strength. The alternative to the tapered line can be to watch the reel get cleaned by a "screamer" before much can be done about it.

No fisherman can take maximum advantage of his line unless he is fully aware of all of its characteristics, including the amount of pressure he can put on it while fighting a fish. The latter can be determined by tying one end to a stationary object and then pulling against the line with an upward sweep of the rod tip. Though a quick tug may break the line, no steady pull transmitted through the tip of a rod matched to the line will do it. A 50-pound rod may break 20-pound line, but a smooth upward pump of a 50-pound rod on a 50-pound line cannot break a 50-pound line regardless of how strong the angler is.

Many shore fishermen discover the difficulty of breaking a line that gets stuck on the bottom. The angler who takes the line in his hands to pull on it is asking for deep and painful cuts in the creases of his palm and fingers. The only safe way to break off is to wrap the line in a spiral around a cloth-covered forearm and walk backwards. Wraps must be spaced far enough apart so that they cannot bind on each other and cut.

According to one old kama'āina fisherman, it was the development of the line that made fishing possible, and the line remains the angler's most important weapon.

### Lures

It is a tradition in Hawai'i for the fisherman to make his own lures. Pride of craftsmanship has continued into a time when plastics technology has replaced the bone-and-shell culture with rainbow-hued trolling lures, but even these have had their origin in Hawaiian waters, so that people around the world who want to use them must turn to Hawaiian fishing lore for their answers.

Plastic trolling plugs, the kind known around the world as Konaheads, are simple to make, though the process is time consuming. It takes one to make one; you have to have a lure from which to make a mold before you can make your own first lure. Such a mold can then be used to turn out replicas endlessly.

The best mold rubber developed at this time is a white thick liquid known as Silastic, which hardens after thorough mixing with a catalyst. A pint of Silastic makes a mold for one marlin lure or two mahimahi lures, so don't mix up more than you can use.

Take the lure you wish to copy, remove its skirt, and polish the whole lure with rubbing compound to make a clean smooth surface. Get out all nicks and scratches, or they will be part of every lure your mold makes. If a deep cut means you'll need to alter the shape to polish it away, fill it with a hard-drying putty.

Sand the blunt back end until it is perfectly smooth and flat. Now file a ⅛-inch notch at the exact top of the skirt flange. When the mold is finished, this notch will have formed a little nub of rubber to help you position the mirrors inside so that they will always face the sides.

Now cut a 2-inch piece of $\frac{3}{16}$-inch copper automotive fuel line pipe and file one end to the same angle as the scoop on the front end of the lure. When matched with the leader tube this short piece of pipe should continue along the same line as though it were a part of the original tube. Whittle a wooden peg to fit tightly inside the tubing to hold the added section of pipe in place. The added section makes a receptacle in the finished mold to hold the tubing in position while the lure hardens around it.

Rub the lure surface with automotive wax to make a parting film so that the rubber will release after the mold is cured. Cut a piece of two-sided tape in a circle the same size as the back of the lure and use it to stick the base of the lure to the bottom of a frozen orange juice can. The paper cans are more easily removed from around the finished mold after it has cured. Metal cans are extremely difficult to get off. If the can is not tall enough to extend up to the top of the pipe, tape another can on so that the outer mold is long enough.

Two sizes of cans are available. For the most economical use of the rubber, pick the smallest can that will do the job leaving a half inch or so around the fattest part of the lure.

Mix enough rubber with catalyst to fill the can to the top of the pipe. Pour the rubber in slowly so that air bubbles won't be trapped below any ridges in the lure. Let the mold harden completely. Don't try to rush the process even if it takes a day or so. (It should be hard enough that it cannot be scratched by a finger nail.) When the mold is completely cured, peel off the can from the outside.

You almost certainly will not be able to get the lure out of the inside of the mold if the ridges are deep or the lure itself is markedly concave. That is to be expected. Take a sharp knife and cut the mold from the flat back end of the lure straight down about half way. Now the lure can be worked out with the fingers.

Let the inside of the mold cure thoroughly before using it.

The most popular lures are made with mirror strips inside to reflect bright flashes of light in all directions as the lure charges along. These can be cut from any flat mirror with a simple glass cutter. The edges should be smoothed with  emery cloth or they will start cracks in the plastic as it hardens. Some anglers replace the strips with pieces of colored vinyl tile, others with strips of wood that were wrapped with reflective aluminum tape. Still others make a mold that produces a fish-head-shaped insert, and a final group of anglers choose solid color lures, completely opaque, and use no insert at all.

Cut a piece of copper pipe about 2 inches longer than the total length of the plug head, in other words, the same length as the mold. Cut a piece of two-sided carpet tape about 2 inches long and wrap it around the pipe to hold the mirrors. They will stick to the tape instantly and be held firmly in position. The mirrors should be positioned back-to-back, with the reflective sides facing out, of course.

For eyes, glue a pair of buttons to the mirrors. A small piece of double-sided tape does this job instantly as well.

Slip the tube into the mold with the end passing into the receptacle at the bottom. Then line the mirrors up with the rubber nub at the top. Wrap the mold with masking tape to hold the crack shut. Don't apply pressure during the wrapping or it will distort the mold and change the shape of the lure. The tape will not stick to the rubber, so it must be wrapped in a spiral making it stick to itself.

Into a waxed-paper cup pour enough casting resin to fill the mold. Now put in several drops of clear resin tint of your favorite color. Blue and yellow are popular. Add a few drops of catalyst for each ounce of resin in the cup by following the directions on the can. Mix thoroughly for several minutes with a disposable wooden coffee stirrer.

Fill the mold with the mixture and *be patient.* Your lure may take anywhere from 2 to 20 hours to cure completely. Don't get excited and try to rush things. Leave the lure in the mold until it is completely hard.

Your first reaction when you take off the tape and pull out the lure will be disappointment. That "thing" you've made is covered with an uneven sticky surface. No matter how long you let it air-cure, it will never get completely dry.

Your next step is to use a sharp knife to scrape the gummy coating off. Quick strokes with the knife will get the job done in a few minutes. The roughened surface can be polished after the pipe is sawed off close to the lure on both ends and filed smooth with a half-round file. Be careful when filing not to alter the shape of the scoop or you will change the lure's action.

Polish the lure with several grades of "wet" sandpaper starting with 200, then 400, then 600 grit. A final polish with rubbing compound will give it a glossy sheen.

The tail is built up from an inner skirt and an outer one. Two schools of thought offer two opinions on the shape of this colorful kicker. One says the skirt should be sparse and tapered to present as little chance as possible of its getting in the way of a hook point on the strike. The other says the skirt should be full and cut off square so that the blunt end enlarges the bubble created when the lure is pulled under and thus increases the amount of popping noise made when it breaks water. I favor the sparse-tapered skirt because I have caught fish on lures that have had no skirt at all. We hooked a 40-pound mahimahi on a lure that had been completely stripped by an ono. Unusual to be sure, and certainly not the recommended practice.

The inner skirt is most often cut from red inner tube rubber, or failing that, red upholstery plastic. Freddy Rice points out that red is the color of excitement in the sea. Squids and small fish throw off red hues when disturbed. Aku flush deep pink along their silver flanks.

The outer skirt is a pair of tapered pennants of silverflake plastic auto seat cover material. One or two hooks are hung on the leader after it is run through the center of the lure to arm it. IGFA rulings require that the trailing hook must have some part buried in the skirt, even if only the eye. The front hook can be moved up an inch or two to comply with the ruling by drilling out some of the back end of the lure so that the crimped collar is inside the head of the lure.

Putting two hooks on a lure is not done for the purpose of catching two fish at a time, of course, but this does happen occasionally. One notable instance occurred on the *Coreene C II* out of Honolulu with Captain Toots Tsutahara. While the crew was working a mahimahi school, a big bull took off on a run with one of the marlin plugs being trolled from an outrigger. Evidently the fish still held the lure in its mouth instead of letting it slide away along the leader, as most lures do when a fish is hooked. A second mahimahi tried to take the lure away from the first and hooked

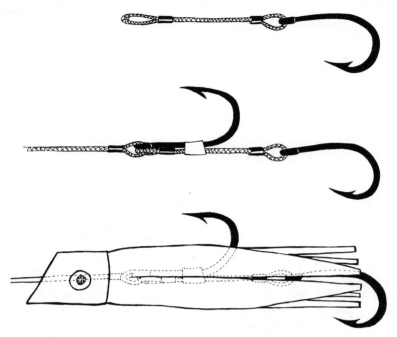

A trolling plug may be armed with tandem hooks without ruining its action. The trailing hook is rigged on its own short leader *(top)*, then attached to the main leader with the same loop that holds the first hook *(middle)*. A small piece of surgical tubing on the shank of the first hook restricts the trailing leader to keep it from tangling. Rubber bands may be used instead. The hooks are pulled up under the lure skirt *(bottom)* when in use.

himself on the other barb. The anglerette, Bonita Feingold, successfully battled both fish to gaff, one a 30 pounder, the other a 20.

Actually, the second hook is there to increase the chances of getting a solid hookup on any strike. Trolling strikes can be so fast and violent that one point is just pushed out of the way without taking hold of anything. Occasionally, though, a lure will have better action with one large hook than with two hooks.

Amidst all of the worry about just the right action, an unlikely event will happen that makes the fisherman wonder if any of it makes sense at all. Murray Heminger, Jr. was aboard the *Pao Pao*, which was sitting dead in the water with no fuel and a spent battery. A lure that had been reeled in was just hanging in the water next to the drifting boat, while efforts were made to get the boat

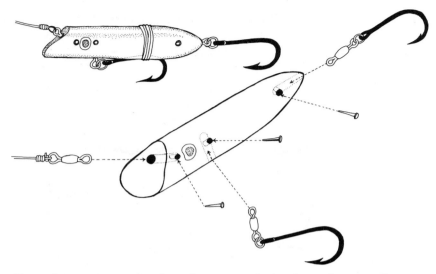

To make your own taperina, shape an 8-inch piece of strong, buoyant wood (Philippine mahogany is good), 1¼ inch in diameter, as shown. Attachment points are made by drilling three holes wide enough to take barrel swivels. The swivels are pinned in place with brass nails.

started. A 310-pound marlin hooked itself on the lure and was fought to gaff with no help from the boat at all.

A few kama'aina trollers steadfastly ignore the plastic trolling plugs. Their wooden "taperinas" have been catching fish for three decades or more and they see no reason to switch. A pair of mystified Hilo fishermen who followed taperina expert Mateo Alcoran around one day would hasten to agree. As they went completely fishless they had to endure the sight of Mateo boating ono after ono—a total of six in two hours, all on the mysterious wooden "stick" with two hooks.

One way to make them would be, of course, to screw two hooks and a leader eye into a stick of wood. On a big fish, the hooks might pull out. A better alternative is to drill holes into the lure in the appropriate spots and of a diameter large enough to admit a strong two-way swivel, such as the Sampo ball-bearing swivels used for trolling. The swivel is pinned into place by driving in a brass nail from the side. I find it most convenient to drill a small hole in from the side on the path that the pin is intended to take. It makes the difficult job of positioning the retaining pin much easier. The leader hole should be positioned one-third of the way

down from the top of the scoop. The swivel hole should be angled
into the lure perpendicular to the angle of the scoop. The wood
chosen for the lure should be a light but strong wood like Philippine mahogany. The body should be tapered slightly for its entire
length. When constructed carefully, such a lure will not spin out
at any speed under 10 knots.

### Splices and Knots

Getting it together is half of fishing; keeping it together, the
other half. Great volumes have been written on the art of bending
lines into joints that won't come apart, but the techniques used
along the Hawaiian waterfront have been refined to a select few.

Offshore trollers who used braided lines must be experts with

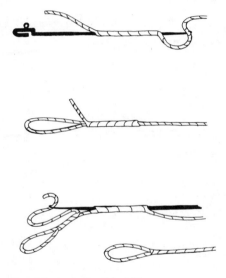

How to make a spliced loop in braided line:

*Top.* With end of line toward you, insert the splicing needle about 6
inches from the end. Thread the needle about 3 inches up through the
hollow center of the line, then out. Now catch the line with the hook.

*Middle.* Pull the line back through the hollow center and detach the
needle. Hold the loop with the thumb and forefinger of your left hand
and work back the outside covering of the line with your right hand. This
outside covering should literally be turned inside out.

*Bottom.* Slide the loop open as large as you wish. To form a double
line at the end of a trolling line, you may want a loop from 15 to 30 feet
long. Starting 1 inch from the end of the loop, insert needle in line and
pull the loose end back through. Smooth it out and trim loose ends.

the splicing needle. The latter is generally packed with the line
and comes as a bonus at the time of purchase. Needle work is relatively simple and can be learned in an instant by following the
steps shown in the accompanying diagrams. The two-line splice is
smooth, nearly indetectable, and just as strong as the line itself.
The loop is the first step in making a double line for the fisherman who wants to take maximum advantage of the 15 to 30 feet
of extra strength the IGFA allows. Since a trolling line may be

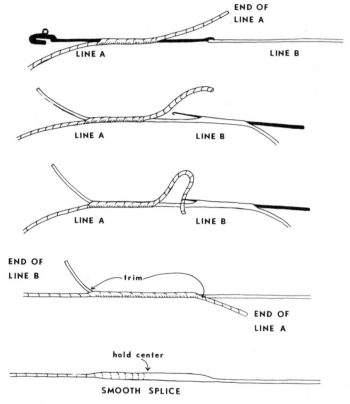

How to splice two sections of braided line:

Insert needle from left to right in line *A* about 4 inches from end for a
length of about 2 inches. Hook end of line *B* and pull it back through
the hollow center of line *A*, then unhook the needle. From right to left,
insert needle in line *B* and thread it through the center for about 2 inches. Hook loose end of line *A* and pull it back through the center of
line *B*. Work the splice together by pulling loose ends. Trim line ends
flush with splice.

doubled back for its last 15 feet on tackle rated at 50-pound-test or lighter and 30 feet on heavier tackle, a loop is formed and opened to as long as the length of the doubled section which is allowed. Then the swivel is knotted on the end using the Bimini hitch.

Despite the fact that the latter is not the strongest of knots, it is simple to tie and untie, while its lack of strength is no real handicap in conjunction with double lines because the knot is tied at a place where the line is twice as strong to begin with.

For the troller who eschews the double line as unnecessary, the spliced loop is still made but is opened only a few inches, just enough to finish it with a Bimini hitch.

To join braid and monofilament the angler can make an excellent smooth splice if he has patience. This joint is a local invention used nowhere else in the world. After rounding off the end of the monofilament line to smooth out any rough edges that might catch, the mono is forced up inside the hollow braid for the length of about 12 inches. The end of the braid where the mono exits is whipped with dental floss starting about 3 inches away. Whipping is done by alternating half-hitches with turns around the line. This splice works like the "Chinese finger catch," the woven toy tube which refuses to release your fingers as long as you try to pull them apart. One of its most important uses is for the angler who does not like to use long wire leaders because of the difficulty they present at gaffing time. This splice allows the troller to introduce a heavy piece of monofilament, such as 300-pound-test, into the 130-pound braid to make up, say, 20 feet of the leader which is then finished off with a swivel, snap closure, and

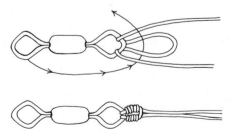

The Bimini hitch is a strong, simple, and versatile joint for connecting a swivel to a double line. First form a loop in the double. Pass it through the eye of the swivel. Then pass the swivel through the loop five or six times. The hitch can be easily taken apart by reversing the steps.

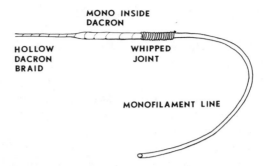

A strong smooth splice for joining hollow braided line to heavy monofilament can be made by first rounding off one end of the mono and inserting it inside the Dacron for a length of approximately 12 inches. The end of the Dacron is then whipped with alternating half-hitches and turns around the line.

The improved clinch knot is a universal method for tying monofilament to any type of ring, whether on a swivel or hook.

another 10 feet of wire for a total length of 30 feet. This monofilament section of leader can be reeled right up into the guides and onto the reel so that the fish can be drawn into gaffing range without requiring anyone to handle the wire. For the small boat angler willing to get by with 5 or 6 feet of wire and the rest heavy mono, this means he will be able to gaff the fish himself while holding it at the boat with the rod. Heavy mono resists the abrasion of the flanks of the fish well enough so that no more than a few feet of wire are needed. Indeed, some fishermen have eliminated the wire entirely.

Shore fishermen who work exclusively with monofilament line must know how to knot it to a hook eye with an improved clinch knot or a smooth snell, and they need to be able to tie two strands of the same size together with a blood knot. Those anglers who believe in beefing up the end of the line by tying on a section of heavier monofilament as a "shock" line need to master one of several knots available for joining lines of different diameters.

Among these are the "shocker" knot and the "improved blood knot."

The best end loop for monofilament is the simplest. Other fancier knots, such as "perfection loop," have been developed, but they actually make a weaker joint. Any angler wishing to test the relative strengths of two different knots need only tie them both in the same section of line, then pull until the weaker one breaks.

Piano wire leaders require round-nosed pliers and the ability to make a haywire twist finished off with a half-dozen right-angle turns. Without the twist the loop collapses under pressure of a

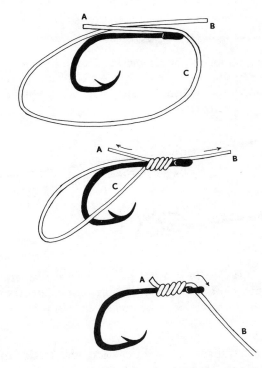

For a professional hook snell, first cut the leader to about 4 inches longer than you will need. Both ends (A and B) must be free to work with. Hold the ends along the hook shank (as shown) with the thumb and forefinger of your left hand (top). Starting at the eye of the hook, wrap section C around the shank in a tight coil for at least eight turns. Pull end B through the coil until loop C disappears. Tighten the knot by pulling firmly on both ends, A and B (middle). Finish the snell by passing end B through the hook eye (bottom).

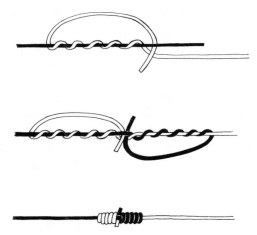

The steps in tying a blood knot are shown. This knot is used to join lines of similar diameter. The ends are clipped off close to the knot. One end may be left long as a second attachment leader for a hook or lure (see the diagram of the double jig rig).

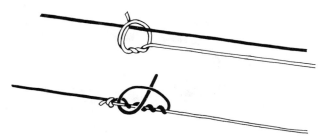

A "shocker knot" is used to join two pieces of monofilament of differing diameters. Whippers use it to attach a short section of heavy line to the end of their light casting line. The steps can easily be seen from the diagram.

strong fish as the square turns slide along the leader to choke the hook or swivel ring. Always leave an extra 2-inch piece of wire end left over so that it can be turned back on itself to break off. When piano wire is cut with wire snippers it leaves a sharp edge. A smooth break leaves no sharp edge.

Cable wire under 200-pound-test is best crimped with one or more sleeves to hold a loop. Heavier cable should be spliced for maximum insurance against sleeve failure. The steps are simple. First the sleeve is slid down over the leader, then the end is separated for 2 inches into two bunches containing three and four

wires each. These are bent toward each other and woven back together, a process much simpler than it looks since the wires lie together well. At this point, even without the sleeve, the loop has
the strength to hold. The sleeve just finishes it off so that the
rough edges neither unravel nor catch on anything in use.

### Swivels and Snaps

Nothing twists more easily than a piece of wet string. That's a fact
of life every fisherman must consider and find a way to counter.

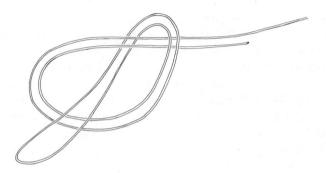

The best end loop for a leader is often the simplest. It does not have the
strength of the more complicated knots, but it can be tied much faster
and is quite serviceable.

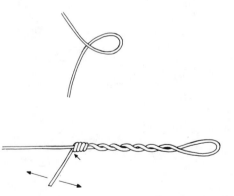

For piano wire, the haywire twist is the basic bend. Note that the free
end is not twisted around the main section, but each is twisted around
the other. To do this, start your loop as shown at the top. Break off the
extra wire by bending it back against the last coil. This gives a smooth,
snag-free end.

No matter how well an active trolling lure tracks, it will revolve more often in one direction than the other. Without some method of combatting the twisting effect thus created, the line rapidly begins to imitate the twirled strips of colored crepe paper that decorate children's parties.

The answer on the offshore grounds is the ball-bearing swivel. It is the most expensive of the twist relief devices yet invented, but it is compact, strong, and nearly frictionless. Ordinary barrel swivels are almost useless for trolling because the drag of the lure jams the loops tight against the barrel so that the device acts like one welded piece. By contrast, the ball-bearing swivel halves turn against each other with ease under pressure, and the casing is so well formed that it does not admit water, hence there is very little chance for corrosion. Such swivels come in a variety of sizes and rated strengths; the angler is cautioned to pick one with a liberal margin for error. The one disadvantage of such swivels is their tendency to break at the stem where the welded ring is attached, but this happens only to the smaller sizes. Though split rings are available on ball-bearing swivels, smart trollers always choose the welded rings since the split rings will pull open on heavy fish.

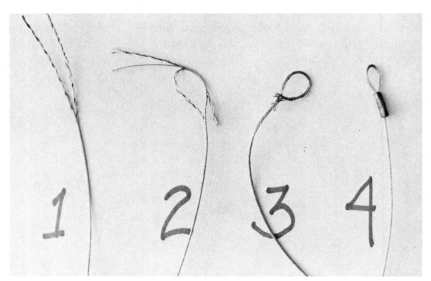

Four steps to a strong endloop in a cable leader: *(1)* Unravel a few inches, *(2)* twist the raveled sections back together again following the natural lay of the cable twist until *(3)* the loop is complete; *(4)* slide a sleeve over the raw ends and crimp it tight to keep the loop from working loose.

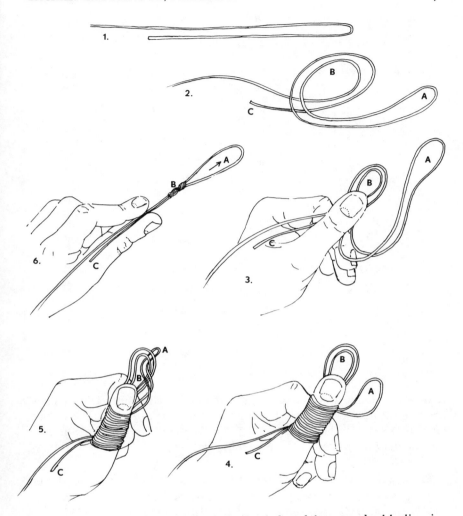

The Spider hitch makes a strong, easily tied end loop or double line in monofilament. Start by doubling the line the regulation length *(1)*. The IGFA allows 30 feet on 80- and 130-pound class lines and 15 feet for lighter tests. *(2)* Form a small loop. *(3)* Grasp this small loop tightly between thumb and forefinger, being sure to extend the thumb beyond the forefinger as far as possible to make the next step easier. *(4)* Wrap loop *A* ten turns around the thumb and loop *B*, starting closer to the base of the thumb and working upward. *(5)* Pass the long loop through the small one and pull it until you feel tension on the section of line being held between the thumb and forefinger. Pull the turns off the thumb one at a time. *(6)* Tighten the knot with a strong steady pull. Then clip the loose end off close to the knot.

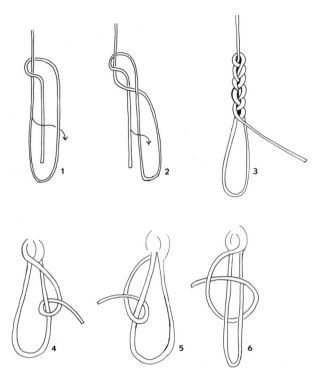

A braided double works well in light monofilament lines. The braid is done exactly like a hair braid for at least 12 inches *(1, 2, 3)*. It is finished off with a series of half-hitches *(4, 5, 6)*. The end can then be whipped with dental floss to keep it from working free.

Eventually all mechanical creatures break down, and the ball-bearing swivel is no exception to the law of built-in obsolescence. The first clue will be a visual twist in a braided line, which is readily apparent as the line is reeled in. A monofilament line so twisted tends to try to wrap itself around the rod tip or embrace each guide. An angler using mono who suspects that his bearings have given up at last to corrosion can check the line by grasping it at two points about 3 feet apart and pulling them together to form a loop of slack. Any malfunction of the swivel will be seen immediately as the loop whips around itself in a haywire twist. If the fisherman turns the swivel in his fingers, he can feel it catch on a bit of roughness. That's the time to discard it.

Hawaiian trollers have adopted three different types of connectors with which to hang leaders on the swivel at the end of the

line—each connector having its own special place. The most popular for heavy cable leaders is the "ice tong" snap since it is small,
strong, and smooth with no place for a tangle to occur. It cannot
be used with small-diameter leaders because they eventually find
the crack in the loop and pull free.

With light wire, an interlocking snap is the one that will hold
best. But the top choice for offshore bait fishermen who drag live
aku is the "pigtail." It is the bulkiest and most visible of the connectors, but it is also the strongest and will hold the smooth

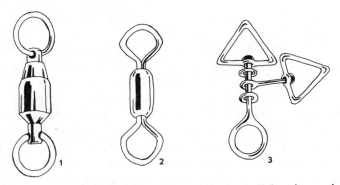

The three common types of swivels are: *(1)* the ball bearing swivel used
in trolling, *(2)* the barrel swivel for shore casting, and *(3)* the crossline
swivel used in bottom fishing.

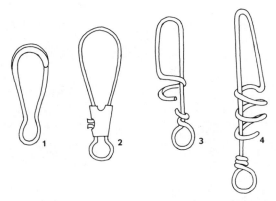

The four most popular connectors are: *(1)* ice tong snap for heavy cable
leaders, *(2)* interlocking snap for light wire, *(3)* the simple pigtail for
slide-bait fishing, and *(4)* the complex pigtail used as a universal link
anywhere its superior strength is needed.

single-strand wire without letting it get away. It can be a devilish device to have on the line in a tangle, however.

For slide-bait fishing the one-loop pigtail has replaced the split ring as the first choice. The dunker generally uses a simple barrel swivel or three-way swivel and has no use for a snap. Neither type chosen by the dunker does much to relieve twists, since the friction coefficient for each is so high, but the angler is not generally bothered by the twisting problem. His major interest is in having a functioning joint for binding line to leader and sinker. Because of that simple need a single welded ring would probably do the job as well as anything, but for the aesthetic pleasures of the sport most fishermen make fancier choices.

The whipper has little use for snaps and swivels since he is actually better off without them. They detract from the finesse of little lures and light lines. Still, the whipper who works with plugs or wire leaders may have need of a convenient way to change lures. In such a case a tiny interlocking snap is the best solution. No swivel is needed with it, nor should one be anywhere on the line because it will only make a fish suspicious.

Offshore bottom fishermen choose crossline swivels to tie up any rigs that won't be using spreaders. Here again, the twisting problem is not much relieved by the device; it just gives convenient attachment points.

# 15
# *The Territory*

## HAWAI'I, MAUI, MOLOKA'I, O'AHU, KAUA'I

THE INSHORE REEF is a closed system. Unlike the immense shelves of the major continental landmasses, the Hawaiian reef is not refreshed at regular intervals by new sea creatures, spawned in safety elsewhere, whose changing season prods them to replace those that have moved on. When the inshore fisherman has exhausted what is there today, he cannot hope to find a new supply tomorrow. The reader would be assisted in no way by a detailed list of top shore-fishing locations around the islands. Before this information could be used by many people, fishing pressure would have reduced them to no better than most other spots. For example, when a new road opened to a formerly remote point in South Kona, the ulua disappeared within three months. A general rule of thumb for shore fishermen: the harder a place is to get to, the more likely it will have fish.

The offshore fishery is an open system replenished regularly by fish that migrate through the enormous pattern of currents spanning a large portion of the globe. Only a small fraction of these fish come in contact with sport fishermen. No diminishing effect could possibly result from the miniscule efforts mounted in the islands to catch these fish.

Some general comments follow about both types of fishing that visitors might expect to encounter as they travel through the islands. Travelers have their best chance of catching fish during a short stay in any place by chartering professional offshore fishing captains. Charter boat facilities exist at nearly all the major islands; though these are thought of primarily as facilities for tourists, many residents charter regularly on their own home islands.

A common attitude articulated by one kama'āina on why he charters: "I'm part of a small group of good friends who hire a boat once a month and split expenses. We plot and plan all month trying to figure just what day will be best and where we are going to fish. We use our own tackle and compete with each other to see who will catch the most. This gives us a real sense of being fishermen, and not just customers. We've found a boat and crew we like and have become 'regulars,' so we get special considerations and feel very much a part of the operation. But most importantly, we get a dozen trips a year at less than it would cost any of us to own a boat, with none of the worry."

### Hawai'i (the Big Island)

Inshore fishing is best along the lee coast from 'Upolu Point in the north to South Point. Few sandy beaches exist and the reef is very narrow, where it exists at all, since the island is geologically the youngest of the chain. In the southernmost regions steep-cliffed shorelines can be fished only by slide-baiting. Almost everywhere else the best sport is had by whipping. The coastline from South Point to Cape Kumukahi is largely undeveloped and produces good fishing for those who can get off the road in a four-wheel drive vehicle to probe likely spots. This coastline is generally very rough from mid-morning until late afternoon, so the most comfortable fishing comes with an early start at the first light of dawn. The Hāmākua coastline, which completes the rough triangular shape of the island, is difficult to fish because the waters are generally rough, the shorelines steep, and the waters dirty—filled with cane trash and runoff silt. Like many places in the islands, there are remote spots with the right combination of circumstances along each of the three coasts, but their locations are well-guarded secrets. Even the promise of lucrative guide fees is not enough to prompt the regulars into taking visiting fishermen to the glory holes.

Offshore trollers can hire boats out of Kawaihae, Kailua-Kona, Keauhou Bay, Hilo, and, in certain seasons, from a point near

Waiōhinu for fishing the waters off South Point. At Kawaihae the fishing is generally for mahimahi and ono. Occasionally, wind conditions allow big boats to get around 'Upolu Point to troll for ulua. Kona boats fish from Keāhole Light to Miloli'i with two-day charters possible for the long run to the productive waters off South Point. At Kona the emphasis is on the Pacific blue marlin and 'ahi, but other fish are also caught regularly as well. At South Point the catch is primarily 'ahi, ono, mahimahi, rainbow runner, ulua, and black marlin, as well as the Pacific blue marlin for which the island is famous. Hilo boaters work the coastline toward Cape Kumukahi for mahimahi and ono, but occasional marlin and 'ahi are also caught.

Since deep waters are very close to shore, bottom fishing off the Big Island is as good as at any of the major islands.

The 'Alenuihāhā Channel between Hawai'i and Maui is usually among the roughest stretches of water in the world. Boats which must brave the elements on regular trips between islands for tournaments or dry-docking have found that the secret of a smoother trip is to follow in the flattened wake of an interisland barge if they are fast enough to keep up.

### Maui, Kaho'olawe, and Lāna'i

Inshore fishing for small game fish can be excellent along Maui's sandy beaches on both sides of the saddle connecting West Maui and East Maui. Fringing reefs are wide along the western coastline, so pāpio and 'ō'io are in good supply. The eastern half is surrounded by steep-cliffed shorelines that make access to the water very difficult.

Offshore trollers operate out of Lahaina and fish the waters between the southwestern shore and the offshore islands of Kaho-'olawe and Lāna'i. Anglers who can locate the remains of a wrecked ship off the northeast coast of Lāna'i, will find ono and ulua. The lee edge of Lāna'i sets up the kind of eddies that produce marlin and 'ahi. When the US Navy allows fishing around Kaho-'olawe, its fringing reefs are productive for trollers along the drop-offs with the eastern shore being especially hot at times. The tiny island of Molokini in the Alalākeiki Channel has been the scene of good action. Boats willing to circle the island and troll the north shore occasionally have fantastic luck with small mahimahi. During one five-day stretch a Maui boat landed nearly 200 of these "cane knife" size fish.

### Moloka'i

Inshore fishermen will find that the reefs that edge the southern length of the island provide the best whipping in Hawai'i. From Hālawa Valley on the eastern tip all the way around to Pāpōhaku Beach along the western coast there are many stretches of productive shoreline, much of it to the west of Kaunakakai being accessible only by four-wheel drive. The sea cliffs of the north coast make fishing difficult, but several spots can be reached. Visiting fishermen should not overlook the possibilities for catching big barracuda in the many fish ponds along the south coast. At one time Moloka'i was the site of approximately seventy such protected stretches of water cut off from the ocean by man-made dikes. The ponds were used for mullet culture and many have broken down from disuse. Those that are still operational have become infested with barracuda which swim in through the gates when very small and then grow to 40 or 50 pounds.

Offshore fishermen are equally blessed, though no charter facilities are available at this writing, and anglers who wish to fish the famed Penguin Banks must charter boats in Honolulu, then weather the sometimes rugged trip across the Moloka'i Channel. The Banks are actually an underwater extension of the island itself, and stretch as far as a point south of O'ahu's Diamond Head. Wave action, perhaps at some time in the past when the region was much shallower or even above the water's surface, has cut it flat at a level depth of roughly 25 fathoms with nearly straight sides that drop into the seemingly bottomless depths. Trollers work back and forth across the banks for small fish and then out over the drop-offs for marlin and 'ahi. The best catches are often made off 'Īlio Point at the northwest tip of the island where the northward-directed current passing through Kaiwi Channel meets the western current running the length of the rough north coast. Bottom fishing is often exceptional along the 50- to 60-fathom line that skirts the edge of the Banks, and many Honolulu boats make the trip just to catch bottom fish.

### O'ahu

Inshore fishing along O'ahu's southern coast has almost disappeared, a tragic decline from a time when it could probably have been matched by few other shallow reef areas of the world. Too many of the after-effects of escalating population growth have combined to destroy what once was an extremely rich reef fauna.

A similar tragedy has befallen most of the traditional good fishing spots along the windward coast including "Bamboo Ridge," once the site of an annual migration of ulua; the moi holes at Makapu'u Point; the 'ō'io grounds at Waimānalo Bay; the pāpio playground at Kane'ohe Bay; and the many reef spots along the remainder of the coastline which once teemed with big pāpio waiting for whippers and dunkers. Some big fish are still caught by knowledgeable fishermen in hidden sections from Kahuku Point to Ka'ena Point, and an occasional good catch can still be made at Barbers Point, but the O'ahu shore fisherman has had to pack his bags for the neighbor islands to find the type of fishing he once took for granted.

Offshore fishermen have their pick of a large fleet of fishing boats berthed at Honolulu's Kewalo Basin. Many of these boats head to Penguin Banks for mahimahi, ono, and small tunas. Others choose to fish the Wai'anae Coast, another productive lee area, for marlin and 'ahi. Small boat fishermen trail their skiffs to ramps all over the island to be near waters carrying the latest run. Pōka'ī Bay in the center of the Wai'anae Coast is frequently the gathering point for these fishermen of the "mosquito fleet." Ka'ena Point has produced many big fish because of its eddying current pattern. Cornelius Choy's 1,805-pound marlin was caught off Mākaha, then followed a week later by a 711 pounder caught off the Kahe power plant. Other good spots on the Wai'anae Coast are Kepuhi Point and Barbers Point, fishing grounds which are several hours trolling to the south. Bottom fishermen unwilling to make the trip to Penguin Banks have found good holes off Mākua as well as other spots. Boats that turn east from Kewalo Basin find sport off Diamond Head, Koko Head, Hanauma Bay, and Rabbit Island, then on into the waters influenced by Moloka'i.

### Kaua'i

Inshore fishermen can find good sport off Hanalei where a guide service for reef fishermen is available, but big fish can be caught all around the island. Among Kaua'i's credits is a former all-tackle world record bonefish weighing slightly over 19 pounds. Many beach and reef areas exist around the island except for an inaccessible strip along the Nā Pali coast.

Offshore trollers will find boats at Port Allen, Nāwiliwili Harbor, and Līhu'e. Trolling for 'ahi can be unbeatable during the spring run starting in late April or early May and lasting into June.

As an example of what is available then, one boat landed eight 'ahi over 200 pounds each during one three-day weekend in 1970. A former world record 'ahi was a Kaua'i fish, and a 1,008-pound marlin was caught off Waimea on the southwestern side of the island. Trollers willing to make the run from Port Allen to the offshore island of Ni'ihau occasionally have excellent sport with many kinds of big fish including 'ahi, ulua, ono, and sharks. One boat picked up twenty-eight ono in two days of fishing, nineteen on the first day. The spring run of 'ahi is generally encountered off the east side of the island between Hanalei and Anahola, but it sometimes fools the experts with all action starting up along the southern coast. Many excellent bottom-fishing areas exist around the island and stretch toward Ni'ihau.

# 16
# Sport Fish

BILLFISH, TUNAS, JACKS, DOLPHIN FISH,
AMBERJACK, SNAPPERS, WAHOO, THREADFIN,
GOATFISH, MILKFISH, BARRACUDA, BONEFISH—
AND BAIT FISH

THOUGH MUCH INFORMATION about Hawai'i's sport and food fish
is abundantly distributed throughout the entire book, in this
chapter we will add some additional facts about many of the species of interest to hook and line fishermen. Several excellent practical guides have been published on the physiology and identifying
characteristics of Hawaiian species, and no attempt will be made in
this chapter to duplicate such efforts. To assist any novice fisherman who wishes to search the literature of marine biology for detailed accounts of the physical structure of the fishes mentioned in
this book, we are including in this section the Hawaiian names,
scientific names, and whatever English counterparts exist.

### The Billfishes

Three species of marlin *(a'u)* exist in Hawaiian waters: the Pacific
blue *(Makaira nigricans)*, black *(Istiompax marlina)*, and striped
*(Tetrapterus audax)*. Confusion over the different species has been
rampant because each has been known by many colloquial names,
such as black, red, white, and silver marlin as well as swordfish
and adopted Japanese terms like *natagi*.

In addition, since all can be of the same color at some time before or after death and all have bars (''stripes'' really refer to hori-

zontal markings when applied to fish) of some degree of intensity while alive, there is difficulty in telling them apart.

Striped marlin have the slenderest bills, highest dorsal fins, straight and highly visible lateral lines, and pectoral fins that can be pulled flat against the flanks. Black marlin have short wide bills, low dorsal fins, humped heads that give the impression of carrying much of the body weight forward on the "shoulder," and, generally, rigid pectoral fins which remain straight out on big fish, requiring them to be broken before they can be pulled flat. In cross section these pectorals are shaped like airplane wings, thicker in front and tapering to a sharp trailing edge. The Pacific blue has a heavier bill than the striped and shows no lateral line at all. If the skin is lifted to expose the pores along the buried lateral line, the pattern seen is very irregular. Unlike the black, the blue has pectoral fins that are hinged and will flatten against the flanks.

The small "natagi" marlin, which show up in schools averaging 30 to 70 pounds per fish during the winter season, are baby striped marlin migrating through the chain. They return in the fall with more muscle.

Striped marlin make up the bulk of the commercial catch, blues the major portion of the sportfishing bag. It is possible that sportfishing methods that work well on the blues are ignored by most stripers.

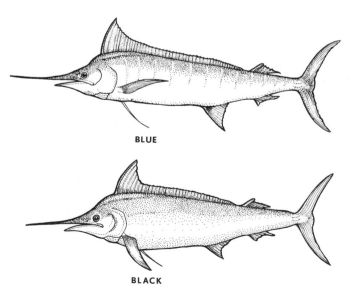

BLUE

BLACK

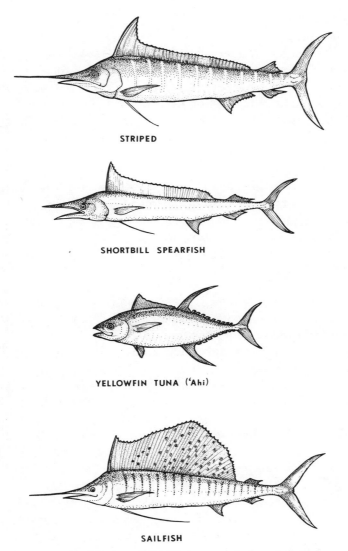

STRIPED

SHORTBILL SPEARFISH

YELLOWFIN TUNA ('Ahi)

SAILFISH

Hawai'i's most prized game fish. These are the catches that count for points in the Hawaiian International Billfish Tournament.

Some blues are in Hawaiian waters all year, but the greatest concentrations migrate through during the summer months. Black marlin tend to live near landmasses and are practically unknown in the open temperate seas. Though they have been caught in Hawaiian waters all year around, they are relatively rare sportfishing catches on plugs. According to Freddy Rice's records, the two months when blacks are most prevalent at South Point are April and October.

Male blue marlin generally outnumber females in catch statistics by approximately three to one. Whether this is their ratio of relative abundance or whether males are more susceptible to standard fishing methods has not yet been determined. This is an answer fishermen would dearly love to know since the females generally outweigh the males. A rule of thumb on size is that a fish weighing more than 300 pounds is nearly always female.

Attempts to catalog the stomach contents of captured marlin, to discover their feeding habits, have been hampered by the fact that billfish often evert their stomachs during the battle. Such food as remains in the stomach has been subject to rapid digestive processes that render small food items unidentifiable within a few hours. Small tunas are the normal food in most years, but at times when blue marlin are especially abundant, their stomachs also contain the young pelagic stages of weke, surgeonfish, squirrelfish, butterflyfish, and triggerfish, most of which are in the 2- to 3-inch size range, according to records gathered by John Naughton of the National Marine Fisheries Service.

The most notable marlin catch in Hawaiian waters was the largest marlin ever taken on rod and reel anywhere in the world, the 1,805-pound blue caught aboard Cornelius Choy's *Coreene C* on June 11, 1970, by a team of malihini anglers who took turns working on the fish and thus disqualified it as an IGFA record.

Two other billfishes are rarely caught in Hawai'i, the sailfish, or *a'u-lepe (Istiophorus platypterus)* and the shortbill spearfish *(Tetrapterus angustirostris)*. Since both have very prominent dorsal fins that run the entire length of the back, they are occasionally confused with each other. The a'u-lepe has a sail which is twice the height of the body and a long slender bill. The sail on the spearfish is rarely higher than the body width, and the bill is almost entirely absent.

For some reason not yet clear, the sailfish goes through periods of relative abundance. During the summer of 1972, for example, several sailfish were caught off the Kona Coast every week, though a half dozen per year is the general rule. That summer Zander Budge caught two just a week apart, despite the fact that he had never even seen one caught before in his entire career.

Freddy Rice suggests that the sailfish is primarily a night feeder in Hawai'i and that the best month to catch them is May. Sails are

Sailfish are rare in Hawai'i, but when they do strike, they are exceptional sport on light trolling gear.

such acrobatic leapers when hooked that in the confusion of a double strike on Monte Richards' boat one sailfish speared the other in the fight and broke off its bill. Though they are generally caught only on small live baits in other waters, Raymond Yamasaki caught a 100 pounder that was so committed to the taste of plastic that it struck four times on three different lures before finally hooking up.

The long slender spearfish is rare in Hawai'i and nearly nonexistent elsewhere. Since it rarely exceeds 50 pounds, its tendency to strike at the small feathers trolled for aku on light tackle makes its capture a sporting proposition.

The all-out battle of the Pacific blue marlin has one very negative aspect: they exhaust their oxygen reserve and are often unable to recover even if released; so most blue marlin are generally brought to port after capture.

It is well known that marlin use their bills as killing weapons, slashing and clubbing their quarry to stun them long enough for the less agile billfish to catch the quicker bait fish. But there is also evidence that they use them as spears.

Whether the billfish use their spears in any undersea, titanic dueling battles is perhaps debatable, but the fact that billfish do attack each other is unquestionable; and the loser can count on being eaten. A billfish caught by singer Danny Kaleikini during the 1976 HIBT had a whole broadbill swordfish in its belly.

Occasionally, a billfish caught on a live bait is "stunned" by the experience, according to Australia's Peter Goadby. Once hooked, the billfish is sluggish, not really alert to what is happening. There may be quite a time interval during which the fish doesn't seem to realize he is in danger, or is unable to respond to it. Quick crews can gaff such fish in minutes.

This rarely happens to a billfish hooked on a lure because he must first work himself into a fever pitch just to chase the lure down in the first place. Don Walker witnessed an example of this heightened emotion. While trolling on his private boat *Lualani,* he spotted a dark shape trailing one of his lures. With a flash of electric blues, the fish struck—and missed. It settled back to its trailing behavior, as dark as a shadow. Again, like a lightning slash at midnight, it streaked in on the lure in full color, and missed again. Don swears this happened seven times, and believe me, when he talks about it he swears a lot.

Caught between the choice of losing the fish by pulling in the lure to see what was wrong with the hooks, and losing the fish because the rig was malfunctioning, Don remained a stunned spectator to the mental and physical preparation the fish goes through as it readies itself for attack. Perhaps this fireworks display is just what many call it, "feeding colors"; but of what evolutionary value could a bugle call signaling "charge" be in a world of stalk and pounce?

### The Tunas

Nine different tunalike fishes are found in Hawaiian waters, though only four are caught regularly. The complete list includes the yellowfin tuna, or *'ahi (Thunnus albacares)*; bigeye tuna, or *po'o-nui (Thunnus obesus)*; skipjack tuna, or *aku (Euthynnus [ = Katsuwonus] pelamis)*; Pacific bonito, or *kawakawa (Euthynnus affinis)*; Japanese mackerel *(Scomber japonicus)*; frigate mackerel, or *keokeo (Auxis thazard)*; striped bonito *(Sarda orientalis)*; bluefin tuna *(Thunnus thynnus orientalis)*; and albacore, or *'ahi pāhala (Thunnus alalunga)*. Only the first four of these figure prominently in the sportfishing catch.

Yellowfin and bigeye are so similar in appearance that little attempt is made to distinguish between them, and both are generally lumped together as "'ahi." As a result, the bigeye *(also called po'o-nui)* may be more or less common than the yellowfin caught by surface means, but it usually does exceed the yellowfin in total volume as part of the commercial catch made by longline fishermen.

Commercial fisherman Bob Leslie says that the bigeye catch is greatest in the fall and winter months when the water is colder. At this time the longliners switch to "deep" lines.

Surface catches of bigeye by trollers are rare, according to Freddy Rice, but when a school does come up it is likely to provide action for several days until the water condition that brought the fish up returns to normal.

Kona fishermen have begun to learn how to "fish the porpoise" in order to catch tuna. California fishermen have long known that porpoise and 'ahi feed together, but this fact has only recently become helpful to Hawai'i's anglers. Experiments by Butch Chee, Bart Miller, Johnny Honl, Bobby Brown, and others have resulted in new evidence on how to "read" porpoise activity to find 'ahi and marlin.

Fishing the porpoise is one of the most exciting fishing adventures an angler can ever experience. Contemplate this scene.

The vast ocean is a biological desert until you encounter this living drama so intense that you will never live long enough to forget *any* detail. A storm of black birds as dense as the funnel of a tornado sweeps in a screaming swirl, spiraling down to the wave tops with a cacophony that dims the din of a thundering engine into silence. Striped silver torpedoes slash across the surface packed so tight their propelling tails slap each other's faces; but these aku are the targets. Porpoises charge around the edge of the melee, herding the aku with the tense control of sheep dogs, content to nip at the skipjacks trying to escape. Below are the rolling golden flashes of 200-pound tuna. It is an exploding mass of continuous turmoil like the sun. And when its energy is gone and its fragments disappear, you realize that your every muscle hurts from the knots you've tied them in so long, and you are completely wet without ever having felt a wave.

Whereas lures drawn through the porpoise school before feeding action begins would draw no interest from the accompanying 'ahi, once the porpoises give the signal, the tuna and marlin take everything in sight. This regimentation is complete as long as the intelligent porpoises are in control, but occasionally an 'ahi or marlin goes berserk at the sight of all of the food packed in the middle of the activity and bashes in to break up the ball of aku. The predators scatter in all directions as each tries to grab a few more bait fish before the action stops. It is at that moment that a trolled bait is most likely to be hit.

Trolling is not always the best way to fish porpoises, however. For a sure strike, you must use an 'ōpelu bait. The trick is to position your boat ahead of the moving school and stop. To a 12/0 hook you've fastened a whole 'ōpelu on a nylon leader. The bait is put on a ti leaf with a handful of chopped 'ōpelu pieces. The leaf is folded over to hold the pieces then placed on a round stone. Five or six turns of line are wrapped around the rock to hold the ti leaf and bait on, and a slip knot is formed in the line. The stone is dropped overboard to plummet to 20 fathoms before the line is jerked to open the knot. Almost at the instant the package opens the 'ahi strike the bait.

One major difficulty in trying to pull a tuna out of such a melee is the tendency for others to contact the line and break it off.

Tunas, in general, have better eyesight than many other species, evidenced by their preference for lures rigged on clear monofilament leaders rather than on wire. Studies by NMFS marine biologist E. L. Nakamura suggest that the yellowfins have the sharpest eyesight of the whole clan. This could very well be an evolved necessity since feeding 'ahi swim rapidly at speeds between 3 and 10 miles per hour and may have only a fraction of a second to spot and choose a bait. This sharp eyesight may also account for the early Hawaiians' careful selection of lures for different light conditions.

Tuna are more able to spot a defect in a lure or bait, and handliners find that sometimes they must use live baits rather than dead ones for this reason. Many trollers admit that only their very best lures work for big 'ahi; the tuna reject lures that catch marlin, mahimahi, and ono, but the most productive lures for all species are the ones 'ahi accept only as a minimum standard.

All tunas are exceptionally powerful fish. Though not spectacular fighters, since they rarely perform on the surface, tuna wear out the strongest anglers by their unstoppable runs. Tuna power comes from at least three different anatomical characteristics: structure, circulation, and muscle network. The end of the backbone is firmly welded to the tail forming a single unit that cannot be flexed. Most other fish have a hinged joint held rigid by muscle. Since the tuna bone structure itself guarantees rigidity, the power of the muscles is transferred to the tail undiminished. Horizontal keels on the caudal peduncle contribute to the efficiency of the application of the muscle power. A British designer has reportedly incorporated such keels into a new freighter reputed to crank out more speed on less fuel.

The deep plum-red tissue along the backbone represents a dense network of vessels that keep the muscles gorged with blood. This exchange of blood supplies oxygen to and withdraws fatiguing wastes from the muscles at an extremely rapid rate. The rich tissue also helps to maintain body temperature above that of the surrounding sea water.

The rotund but streamlined shape of the tunas incorporates lacings of tough muscle from snout to tail fork, muscle kept in fighting trim by constant exercise since tuna must swim through life without ever stopping.

At normal cruising speeds of roughly 10 miles per hour, the tunas open and close their mouths regularly to breathe by pumping water across their gills. For short bursts at high escape velocities they clamp their mouths shut to complete their streamlining, and this is the factor that leads to their demise at the end of a line. If the angler keeps pressure on the tuna so that he continues to swim hard with his mouth shut, he cannot pull in enough oxygen and tires.

Though the all-tackle record is a fish of only 296 pounds, many

Hawaiian 'ahi have been caught which were bigger, including a 310-pound fish reported by Dudley Lewis as having been caught on June 17, 1973, by five anglers who took turns on the rod, thus disqualifying it in the eyes of the IGFA.

In recent years the "jet" lure is stealing the headlines from the traditional Kona plugs, especially because of its success with 'ahi. These jets look more like the nozzle from a shower head than they do a fish catcher. Were it not for the four or more holes that run lengthwise through the head, you'd be tempted to dismiss this metal and plastic attractor as just an oversize jig with a rounder shape. Some anglers say the water rushing through the openings creates a sound, others that it gives the plastic tails extra action, still others that it sets up a bubble stream that arouses the 'ahi's curiosity. Detractors say the holes just help sell the lure, but that's when they've stopped working.

Plug fishermen say that jets are not better attractors than the plastic Kona plugs, despite the fact they seem to bring more fish to the weighing scale. They just have a higher ratio of hookups to strikes since they run straight and are easily overtaken by a pursuing fish.

Night fishing for tuna is a thrilling sport practiced at a few selected spots along the windward shores of the islands. During November and December a great migration of several different kinds of tuna enters Hawaiian waters and moves along the ledges of the Hāmākua Coast at night. Commercial fishing boats leave from Hilo Harbor to intercept the schools at a ledge off Pepe'ekeo between 12 and 16 miles offshore.

When a fisherman locates the bank he wants to fish, he lets out a sea anchor, a great parachute to drag in the water and slow his drift. Then he rigs up lights to shine on the water around the boat. Perhaps he'll also suspend a submersible light underwater so that the sea surface around the boat glows.

Light in the water at night attracts many kinds of sea creatures, but to help stimulate action, the fisherman will also usually chum with pieces of whatever low-value fish flesh he can get. To this pool of light laced with food the squid come first, and by their presence add to the hypnotizing effect the angler is creating to draw the attention of tuna sliding along far below.

The fisherman baits a line with an 'ōpelu, a chunk of fish, or a whole squid caught from the school surrounding the boat. He lowers his bait to 20 or 25 fathoms, then baits other lines dropped to perhaps 10 fathoms. Now he watches his depth recorder, paying particular attention to the black marks being traced out by the stylus on the moving roll of paper indicating "objects" between the boat and the bottom.

Soon he sees the black line of fish gathering down in the depths far below the boat. He watches it drift upward on the paper drum until it reaches 20 fathoms, and just at that moment his deepline races out with the strike of a fish, which turns and lunges for the bottom, dragging the mass of black marks back down with him.

If this fish gets off, the school stays with him and the whole process of waiting begins again. Few fish are lost, though, because the angler relies on the sure-hooking properties of the rolled-point ulua-style hooks. Steadily, he works the fish back to the surface. Since he is a commercial fisherman, he is hauling a handline, but there is no reason why a sport fisherman could not be doing it with rod and reel.

The school comes back up with the hooked fish, and as they reach the level of the other lines, all lines are struck at once. For the rest of the night the school is pumped up and down like an elevator, while the fishermen work themselves to exhaustion filling the fish boxes.

The fish? Usually, they are what the Hilo anglers call bluefins. These are not really bluefin tuna, however, but bigeye tuna, the kind with the scientific name *Thunnus obesus*. They look very much like the yellowfins, complete to the gilt edges of their back and belly streamers, but as their name bigeye implies, their eyes are larger than those of the common yellowfin. As a matter of fact, as the *obesus* of their scientific name suggests, they are also chunkier than the yellowfin.

The "bluefins" grow to nearly 400 pounds, but the largest the Hilo anglers get are just over 200 with the normal run averaging 50 pounds. Sometimes the school contains yellowfins as well, and surprisingly, also albacore. The albies and bigeye are satisfied with squid baits, but the yellowfin want ʻōpelu.

The albacore are surprising not only because they are very rare in Hawaiʻi's waters, but because they are so big. Albies of 80 pounds are frequently caught with some topping 90. The current all-tackle world record is less than 75 pounds.

The timing of the run, of course, is a Christmas bonus for Hilo fishermen. It is precisely that season when fish prices are at their highest.

The kawakawa can be differentiated from its cousin, the aku, by its lack of side stripes and the presence of belly spots (near the youngster's left hand). This 15-pound fish was an unclaimed world record for 20-pound-class tackle.

Perhaps there are similar spots that can be reached readily from other Hawai'i ports where tuna can also be taken at night, and it is just a matter of time before enterprising fishermen find them.

### The Jacks

Ulua seem to need very little excuse to start up a new family branch. Throughout the world there exist perhaps as many as a hundred different types, some seemingly identical to others except for a difference in the number of scales on a chest patch or the number of scutes in the anterior portion of the lateral line.

Approximately fourteen species are referred to as ulua. Many are so close in appearance that fishermen pay very little attention to specific names other than black, blue, white, yellow, or long-fin. All are similar enough in habits and habitat that an ulua fisherman never really knows what type he has hooked until the battle is finally over.

The black includes *Caranx sexfasciatus, Caranx lugubris, Caranx helvolus,* and *Uraspis reversa;* the last two are deep-water species with white mouths, and the first two are among the biggest inshore fish found in the world. White uluas include *Carangoides ajax, Carangoides equula, Carangoides ferdau, Carangoides gym-nostethoides,* and *Caranx ignoblis (pāʻūʻū).* The first of these is a jack that may not be found anywhere else in the world, and the last is the one that most resembles the jack crevalle of the tropical Atlantic.

Yellow ulua include *Gnathanodon speciosus (paʻopaʻo)* and *Caranx cheilio.* The former has pronounced vertical bars when first caught, and the latter has a thick-lipped profile. The blue ulua, *Caranx melampygus (ʻōmilu)* is one of the commonest types on the near-shore reefs. Its hide is covered with dark spots against a neon blue background. This fish also tends to turn black as it gets older and moves into deep water to live. We've caught ʻōmilu of 10 pounds that had very large black patches covering most of their back.

Two long-finned ulua *(ulua kihikihi* or *kagami ulua)* complete the list. Depending upon which authority describes the fish, *Alectis ciliaris* has several extended rays in the dorsal and anal fins and *Alectis indica* has just one in each. Much more communication is needed among tropical scientists around the world to determine which species are actually the same, though now classed as differ-ent. For example, Frederick H. Berry, biologist with the U.S. Fish and Wildlife Service, has claimed that *Carangoides ajax* is just the mature form of *Alectis ciliaris,* perhaps with its streamers rubbed off from hard use.

Ulua are the toughest opponents the surf caster will find any-where in the world. No angler who has ever caught a healthy ulua on sporting tackle will disagree with its description as the toughest fighting fish of its size, partly because of its power and the rest because of its ability to get down into the rocks to break line. The ulua never jumps; it is master in the water and keeps the fight on its own battleground.

Many ulua are excellent food fishes, unlike other large jack crevalles found elsewhere. Among exceptional catches are the 134-pound fish caught by L. A. Perry off Barbers Point on Oʻahu and a 127 pounder caught by Peter Kelin, Jr., off Diamond Head. Ulua undoubtedly grow even bigger than these. For several months divers off Kawaihae reported seeing a pair of enormous ulua at the same spot each day. Professional diver Dave Norquist told me of his first encounter with them.

"I was circling a coral head looking for small fish for an aquari-um collection when I came face to face with an ulua with a head so thick his eyes were 18 inches apart. He looked as though he could swallow my own head with one bite. I've never been afraid of an ulua before, but I backed off and swam back to the boat immediately, never taking my eyes off the fish as he followed me up."

A month later, an unidentified troller weighed in a 200-pound ulua at Eddie Laau's icehouse in Kawaihae. The other fish is still out there.

An interesting recent discovery about the ulua may prove valuable to fishermen and others who care about their protection and propagation. Biologist Rick Grigg of the Hawaii Institute of Marine Biology (HIMB) reported that the results of surveying the waters adjacent to sugar mill discharges along the Hāmākua Coast of the Big Island indicated that ulua were more abundant in the immediate vicinity of the mills. Whether the sugar cane debris was beneficial to the fish or just discouraging to the fisherman has not yet been determined.

### The Dolphin Fish

The lucky angler who has watched a school of mahimahi dancing across the wave tops in pursuit of flyingfish that fill the air like flung silver will never see greater natural beauty. The gourmet who dines on mahimahi steak risks spoiling himself for any other dish.

The dolphin fish *(Coryphaena hippurus)* is excitingly beautiful because it can change colors rapidly. When it first strikes a lure it is a bright blue and silver flash as it leaps from the water in a graceful arch with its head shaking in anger. Then it switches to golden yellow with neon blue spots as it tires and is drawn to the boat. The sail that runs the length of its back is an olive green ribbon flecked with blue spots.

Fish of 20 pounds are average and 50 pounders turn up each week. The IGFA record of 85 pounds was beaten by an 86 pounder caught by a Hilo commercial fisherman, though it did not qualify for official sanction. The 80-pound-class record of 75½ pounds was beaten by a 78½-pound fish caught off Haleiwa, O'ahu, by Mark Chun, who didn't realize how special his fish was until after it was eaten; too late to apply for recognition.

Recent studies indicate that mahimahi are blessed with a rapid growth rate averaging nearly 5 pounds per month during maturational peaks.

### The Wahoo

Hawai'i's *ono* may be a close but poor relative of the wahoo strains found in other waters. Though ono are powerful fish that sometimes leap to grab a trolled lure, they don't perform the acrobatic antics reported about their Florida and Baja California cousins during the fight.

All IGFA record wahoo in line classes testing 20 or more pounds are fish that exceed 115 pounds, yet it has been several decades since a Hawaiian angler has seen one of this size. The largest of recent years was a 90 pounder caught near Kaua'i, but few fish caught are over 75 and the average is near 30 pounds.

Ono are solitary fish in Hawaiian waters; double strikes are rare. They do school up on occasion, and quadruple strikes are sometimes reported, especially when the fish have teamed with mahimahi and 'ahi around a drifting object. The lonely nature of this sharp-toothed sea wolf is contrary to reports of large stationary schools encountered off Baja.

The Hawaiian name advertises the fish as "delicious," but only if great care is taken to be sure the meat is only lightly touched by the fire and not dried out. Indeed, ono has been receiving special attention of late as a sashimi fish.

The origin of the word "wahoo" is not universally agreed on by etymologists, but a very plausible account was given to me by the noted angling authority George C. Thomas III—and it involves a Hawaiian derivation.

Despite the fact the the wahoo has worldwide distribution in tropical seas, both Atlantic and Pacific, it was first discovered in the Pacific. The first recorded wahoo catch occurred in 1769. This wahoo was caught on a strip of pork rind by a crew member of Captain James Cook's *Endeavour* at the Tuamotu Islands near Tahiti. A Swedish naturalist, Dr. D. C. Solander, was aboard ship and recorded the biological details of the fish from the scientist's viewpoint. Being the first scientist to give an account of the fish, Solander earned the honor of having the scientific name of the wahoo include his own. To all scientists from that time on the wahoo was *Acanthocybium solandri.*

Further explorations showed that the fish was very plentiful around the island of O'ahu, a regular port of call for later voyagers, so that the Hawaiians' ono became known as the "O'ahu fish." Maps of the time, which are still in existence, indicate that a very common spelling of the word "O'ahu" was "Wahoo."

Stories differ on why they are called wahoo. Maybe it's just the way you feel when you've boated a good one.

Thus it is easy to see why an Atlantic civilization might first learn of a fish from the Pacific, despite the fact that it was also found in the Atlantic, and adopt the name commonly used by Europeans exploring the Pacific. In any event, the actual Hawaiian name is not wahoo, but ono.

### The Amberjacks

Two species of elongated jacks occur in Hawaiian waters, the greater amberjack, or *kāhala (Seriola dumerili)* and the rainbow runner, or *kamanu (Elagatis bipinnulata,* Hawaiian salmon). Kāhala and kamanu are rarely caught by trolling, but Hawaiian fish caught this way have held IGFA records. The all-tackle kāhala record was a Kona fish of 120 pounds and the top kamanu is a Kaua'i fish just 1 ounce shy of 31 pounds, boated by Hobie Goodale.

Generally, both fish stay deep and cannot be enticed up to the surface, even by such methods as baiting with a live fish which have proved successful elsewhere. Occasionally, for no discernible reason, kāhala come into shallow water where they are taken by surf casters. On one occasion, while trolling out of Kawaihae Harbor with all lines set, Paul Christenson of Kukuihaele had a triple kāhala strike, then picked up another pair after circling back. All five fish were caught inside the buoys in water less than 60 feet deep.

One of the two or three largest kamanu ever caught in the world was a 32-pound fish caught by a Kohala fisherman who chose not to enter it in the IGFA records, though all sporting requirements for 80-pound-test line had been satisfied.

Bohdan Bartko, operator of a miniature submarine used for research off the water of Makapu'u, O'ahu, reports encounters with big kāhala at depths of 100 fathoms. These fish take advantage of the lights on the front of the sub to assist them in feeding. They hunt back and forth through the light beams, then dart to the bottom to pull small creatures out of the sand; the latter may have been startled into immobility by the bright and unexpected lights.

A visit to Kona by twenty-five of the world's top outdoor writers in January 1976 was saved by a 113-pound kāhala, one of the only fish caught during their visit. It was taken by what has become a very successful method. A live aku was rigged and towed on the surface for marlin. The aku was then allowed to sound in 90 fathoms of water, a very productive depth for kāhala. The aku was snatched immediately as it came within range. Freddy Rice told me later that the method works about half the time. "The other half, you've got to reel in all that line for nothing."

Though live bait is always best, the kāhala and kamanu can be taken on whole akule and whole 'ōpelu. The hook is imbedded in the back just behind the head and low enough to catch the backbone. Then it is drifted along the bottom.

The kamanu gets its name "Hawaiian salmon" because of an interesting similarity in Hawaiian words. There is no s in the Hawaiian language, so English words were often changed to Hawaiian equivalents by replacing the s with a k. All Hawaiian words also had to end in vowels, so a name like *Samuel* was transcribed as *Kamuela,* and a word like *salmon* was changed to *kamono.* The strong similarity between *kamanu* and *kamono* led to the former being called the Hawaiian salmon, to differentiate it from the true salmon.

### The Snappers

Though the snappers are very important commercially in Hawai'i, commanding a high price at market, only one member of the family is important as a sport fish. Most of the snappers are caught in such deep water that the physical circumstances of their capture render them unable to put up much resistance. Only the *uku,* or gray snapper *(Aprion virescens)* is capable of putting up a struggle from hookup to boating. This species is not the same as that known as gray snapper in other waters.

Deep-water red snappers include two different fish which have been called *'ula'ula.* To distinguish between them, modern anglers call *Etelis carbunculus* by the Japanese name *onaga* because of the extended rays in its caudal fin. *Etelis marshi* is another bright red snapper which comes from the same waters, but is distinguishable by its short tail and broader head. Onaga have been caught from depths exceeding 200 fathoms. Boh Bartko's submarine explorations have encountered onaga only along rough and broken bottoms.

Other snappers include the *'ōpakapaka (Pristipomoides microlepis,* usually referred to as *'paka);* the *kalekale (Pristipomoides sieboldii* and *Rooseveltia brighami* have both been referred to by this Hawaiian name at times); and two snappers introduced from Tahiti during the mid-1950s which are increasing in commercial importance, the striped snapper, or *ta'ape (Lutjanus kasmira)* and the black-tailed snapper, or *to'au (Lutjanus fulvus).*

### The Goatfishes

This family contains many small reef fish whose size would keep them from being of much importance to sport fishermen except for the fact that they can be taken in shallow water on very light spinning tackle.

The *weke* and *weke-pueo (Mulloidichthys flavolineatus* and *Upeneus arge)* can be caught in sandy-bottomed channels on the lightest spinning tackle made. They attain a weight of several pounds and are capable of a spirited fight. Weke are very adept at stealing the bait, which is usually a small piece of shrimp, unless small hooks, numbers 6 or 8 limerick style, are used. Even then, the angler must be ready to strike quickly or the weke will have the bait and be gone. Weke-pueo tend to be much greedier than the rest of the family and more easily hooked. A 20- to 30-inch leader of very light monofilament is needed, 6-pound-test or less, to fool the weke's sharp eyes. Weke are very responsive to tide changes and often will mill in great schools without feeding until the right conditions are met. An incoming tide during the last few hours before dark can be very productive. Anglers are occasionally surprised to hear the weke emit a pathetic croaking noise as it is being removed from the hook, which may account for its use by early Hawaiians in sacrificial ceremonies.

Three red-colored goatfish appear in inshore waters and are difficult to distinguish from each other at times because the colors are variable according to the bottom conditions above which the fish are feeding. These are the *malu (Parupeneus pleurostigma),* the *moano (Parupeneus multifasciatus),* and the *kūmū (Parupeneus porphyreus).* Each will show an interest in an active jig, swimming along next to it and occasionally striking it, though most of the time they will veer off, to come back for another look on the next cast. They are easily caught on a strip of squid bait. A large red deep-bodied fish which was almost certainly one of these three species was caught aboard *Spooky Luki* while trolling near shore. We could not positively differentiate which species it was, but it weighed a colossal 5 pounds, far bigger than the typical fish caught, which weigh under a pound. This giant goatfish took a standard aku feather.

The *weke-'ula (Mulloidichthys vanicolensis)* is a deep-water fish caught on sandy bottoms. Though many anglers report catching them in as little as 10 fathoms, University of Hawaii scientists have netted them at depths of 46 to 52 fathoms. These fish were more likely the species *Mulloidichthys pflugeri,* which are also known as weke-'ula. The deeper-water weke appear to be primarily night feeders.

### The Threadfin

The *moi (Polydoctylus sexfilis)* is the only member of its family that appears in Hawaiian waters, though three of its cousins are found in the south Pacific inshore waters. One possible point of confusion over identity is the name threadfin, which is often used by mainland biologists to describe the long-finned ulua. The term threadfin, as applied to the moi, refers to the filaments that protrude from the lower part of the pectoral fins near the back of the lower jaw and appear much like whiskers. This species is very much in its decline along Hawai'i's shorelines as its habitat is destroyed and it is relentlessly hunted by fishermen of all kinds: pole, throw net, trawler, and gill net. Further, most do not achieve maturity since they are preyed on by larger fish and unthinking humans while in the small *moi-li'i* stage, at which time they are found in shallow-water tide pools.

For the past two years the Hawaii Institute of Marine Biology, financed by state and Sea Grant funds, has taken a special interest in the moi, with an eye toward spawning and culturing the *moi-li'i,* the fingerlings, in hatcheries.

Saltwater fish do not spawn readily in captivity, and experiments at aquaculture with most species have depended on being able to capture fingerlings in the wild. With some species, fish culturists have been fortunate enough to be able to stimulate spawning in captivity through hormone injections.

With this in mind, the moi has proved to be even more remarkable in captivity than anyone could have hoped. The moi will spawn spontaneously in captivity with no hormonal injections needed.

The predictability of its spawning cycle at sea has been its undoing as a wild creature. Anglers have quickly learned that the six months from May on are the times the moi school up and crowd rough shorelines during the last quarter phase of the monthly moon cycle. Thus the fishermen catch the moi at the worst possible moment, during the time the fish is trying to produce the next generation. This same spawning predictability has proved to be a boon for the HIMB fish culturists because it makes the gathering of the eggs much simpler.

Dr. Robert May of HIMB, leader of the moi culture project, has found that the moi are not disturbed by small enclosures (what shore fisherman has not seen large schools of moi-li'i thriving in shallow tide pools trapped on rocky ledges at low tide?). The hatchery moi have been raised in small ponds and cubical cages ranging from 3 to 10 feet along one side.

In the wild, moi feed on any crustaceans the surf pulls loose from the rocks or drives out of the sand. In captivity scientists are raising moi on a heat-treated mixture of fish meal and the common plant called *koa haole*. The moi is an efficient user of food and can gain a pound of weight while being fed less than 2 pounds of food.

The captive moi have grown rapidly, reaching two-thirds of a pound in ten months. By keeping the moi in water warmed to 82 degrees Fahrenheit (slightly warmer than in the wild) and at 35 parts per thousand salinity (slightly less than sea water), scientists have accelerated the growth, but there is no economic way yet known to maintain the best environment, according to Dr. May.

Moi weighing more than 6 pounds would be extremely unusual, but a western Pacific relative known as the giant threadfin (moi are called striped threadfin) can grow to 200 pounds. Such a fish would be more than ten times the size of the biggest Hawaiian moi ever recorded.

At times moi travel in enormous schools. We once encountered such an assemblage while torching at night in O'ahu's Maunalua Bay. Fish surrounded us as far as we could see by lantern light in all directions. According to the Pukui-Elbert *Hawaiian Dictionary*, such a school was considered an omen of disaster for Hawaiian chiefs.

### The Bonefish

Many fishermen consider the '*ō'io (Albula vulpes)* to be the greatest inshore game fish in the world. This is another Hawaiian fish that is in decline because of increasing population and fishing pressure. All 'ō'io should be returned to the ocean except those that are injured when caught. Though the Hawaiian name 'ō'io has several meanings, one pertains to "a procession of ghosts." Any fisherman who has ever seen a school of 'ō'io appear magically in shallow water can recognize the symbolism that has caused mainland fishermen to dub the 'ō'io "the gray ghost."

### The Needlefish

Like a polished samurai sword slashing through the air, the long narrow assassin sliced into the bait. Its flat sides flashed a ribbon of light, mirror bright. A second later the sea surface lay undisturbed as the angler tightened every body muscle to hold his impatience in check while the long fish worked the mutilated bait back over its slender boney jaws and into the recesses of its mouth. When he was sure that his hook could track a path into yielding flesh, the angler swept his rod tip up and watched the water ex-

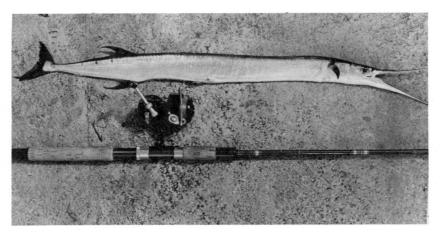

The jumpingest sport fish of all is the ʻahaʻaha.

plode. Beating its tail with a whirring sound audible above the stillness of the cove, the yard-long fish gouged a path across the surface ten times his own length, then dipped below the ripples to gather strength for more violence.

His inability to rid himself of the hook by slashing at the leader with the needles lining his jaws drove him to new heights of frenzy. He tumbled cartwheels in the air and threw his body into double and triple reflex curves. Before he finally gave up, he provided as much action as any fisherman could ever want, but no one would have ever called this creature a game fish, and no record book will ever care much about how large his species grows.

As spectacular as is the sport of catching ʻahaʻaha, few people pursue it. Many of the strikes that "whippers" have, as they ply their light spinning rods in action along the shorelines of Hawaiʻi, are from needlefish, but few of these creatures are caught, because the angler's reflex action works against him. If the bait is not swallowed, the hook will not penetrate because the needlefish grabs the bait with thin boney jaws that allow no hook point to pierce them.

Several different species of needlefish inhabit Hawaiian waters. Trollers often encounter them offshore. They are always very willing to investigate a trolled lure but will only very rarely strike. Somehow, they seem to be able to tell the difference between an artificial and a natural bait. On a recent trolling trip one of our aku lines started singing, and we were able to haul in a needlefish that had obviously raced in front of the lure after looking it over—the lure caught him in the middle of the back.

The offshore needlefish are very fond of flyingfish and can get up into the air after them when they are in hot pursuit. Trollers who watch for the telltale sign of flyingfish bursting in the distance are usually hoping that the silver flashes will mean mahimahi, but the *mālolo* are just as likely to have taken to the air because needlefish are on the prowl.

The inshore fisherman who wants explosive action on very light spinning tackle has a few tricks to learn. The best rig is a very light torpedo-shaped weight with a 20-inch leader trailing along behind. At the end of the leader should be a small hook with shrimp or squid bait. Needlefish have two characteristics that need understanding when this rig is fished. First, they are attracted by a moving bait, and second, they always stay near the surface; they rarely go deep to grab a bait. The bait should be tossed out and reeled very slowly. When the fish strikes, all movement must stop. The casting weight must be so light that it does not pull hard on the bait in the fish's mouth.

This fish is edible, though it has bones of a strange greenish color that cause a marked drop in appetite for anyone who isn't expecting it.

The name needlefish may come from the needlelike teeth on its bill but probably results from the pointed snout, a potentially dangerous weapon. There are substantiated stories of anglers who have been seriously injured by needlefish that have jumped toward a bright light at night and struck the fisherman standing nearby. Captain William Gray, in charge of collecting sea creatures for the Miami Seaquarium, was injured by a needlefish whose bill penetrated completely through his leg under just such circumstances.

### The Milkfish

For a fish with such an unglamorous English name, the *awa* *(Chanos chanos)* is a spectacular fighter, displaying a penchant for repeated jumps and capable of attaining a size that makes him a very worthy opponent. Awa can grow as long as 5 feet and weigh as much as 50 pounds.

My first sight of a school of awa playing near shore startled me so much that I could barely cast my jig to the dozen or so fish that all looked to be 4 or more feet long. Repeated casts right in front of their noses were completely ignored. It was only later that I discovered they were vegetarians and could not be caught by standard methods. One successful procedure is to palu them with handfuls of stale bread crumbs until they start feeding, then to float a hook with a bread ball right on the surface. This is done by threading a small cork on a light wire leader and drifting it to the fish with a friendly current. The bread ball must lie at the surface and cannot move unnaturally or the fish will avoid it. Once an awa is hooked, it must be played with a very light line since the mouth tissue is weak and the hook will not hold well on the frequent violent jumps.

Awa can often be found offshore of sugar mills where they feed along the surface on the vegetation mixed in with the cane trash. They disappear at the sight of an approaching boat, but will return to the surface if the engine is shut off and the crew chums with bread.

### The Ladyfish

Just as there are no salmon in Hawai'i, even though there is a fish local people call salmon, there is no tarpon in Hawai'i despite the existence of a fish occasionally referred to as a tarpon. In fact, until recently, no real tarpon was ever caught in the Pacific Ocean, which may explain the species' scientific name, *Megalops atlanticus*. The *atlanticus* part speaks for itself; the *Megalops* refers to the extremely large eye of this herring family fish.

Hawai'i's "tarpon" is actually *Elops hawaiiensis*, better known locally as the *awa-'aua* and on the mainland as the ladyfish or tenpounder. It is actually quite similar in appearance and behavior to the true tarpon in that it is a silvery, herring-like fish found in shallow sandy waters and capable of frequent frantic leaps when hooked. Unfortunately, it is now quite rare, possibly due to the change in quality of near-shore waters.

Both names for the awa-'aua used on the mainland are misleading. The "ladyfish" is certainly no lady when it comes to a fight, and this "tenpounder" almost never gets as big as 10 pounds. The typical awa-'aua averages perhaps 2 pounds and a 6 pounder would be bragging size. When it is caught, it is usually by a whipper tossing small jigs for pāpio on a sandy or muddy flat.

The awa-'aua will take a shrimp bait, but it seems to prefer a moving target. Few will be caught on a dunked bait, except, perhaps, just after the cast when the bait has only just begun to settle to the bottom.

In a way, it is strange that the awa-'aua should be declining in numbers throughout its normal range. As a food fish it is nearly inedible. The quality of the meat is barely passable, and it has so many bones that it must be fixed for fishcake by first kneading out the bones, just like its very close cousin, the 'ō'io. Not only that, it is one of the most primitive fish in Hawai'i; its history begins with the earliest prehistoric fishes. That would indicate that the species has tremendous survival powers supposedly making it able to withstand most environmental changes.

Unfortunately, it is one of those few fish of Hawai'i that depend on the very fragile estuarine areas for its environment. It is these stream mouths and shallow bays that often are the first habitats affected by the poisonous effluents of an affluent civilization.

Because of its Hawaiian name, awa-'aua, it is often confused with another very close relative, the awa, or milkfish. This is another spectacular leaper and another herring family fish. It gets much bigger than the ladyfish and has a rounder cross section as opposed to the flat flanks of the awa-'aua.

If you were to guess that the ladyfish looked more like a big anchovy, or nehu, you would not be far wrong. In addition to the milkfish, bonefish, and tarpon, this little lady is also related to the nehu.

### The Barracudas

Two barracudas inhabit Hawaiian waters, the *kākū*, or great barracuda *(Sphyraena barracuda)*, and the smaller *kawele'ā*, or Japanese barracuda *(Sphyraena helleri)*. The kākū may be the one nearshore species which is no less common now than it has ever been in Hawaiian waters. Indeed, it may actually be on the increase in populous areas.

### The Bait Fish

Though no fish, including yellowfin tuna approaching 300 pounds, are exempt from the menu of some other Hawaiian predator, several species occur in Hawaiian waters that are usually thought of only as bait fish, rather than food fish. These include the *mālolo*, or flyingfish *(Parexocoetus brachypterus* and others); *'aha'aha*, or needlefish *(Strongylura gigantea* and others); *nehu*, or anchovy *(Stolephorus purpureus); pīhā (Spratelloides gracilis);* *'iao,* or silversides *(Pranesus insularum); iheihe,* or halfbeak *(Euleptorhamphus viridis); 'ōmaka,* or blue runner *(Caranx mate);* *'ōpelu,* or mackerel scad or cigar minnow *(Decapterus pinnulatus);* *akule,* or bigeye scad *(Selar crumenophthalmus);* and *āholehole,* or mountain bass *(Kuhlia sandvicensis).*

Nehu are an extremely important bait in the commercial skip-jack tuna industry, for reasons that should be of great interest to sport fishermen. A description follows. Techniques commercial fishermen use may be adaptable to the sporting fraternity's needs.

Nehu are a small silvery member of the anchovy family rarely growing more than a few inches long. Commercial aku fishermen net them in sheltered bays and inlets, store them in live wells in the holds of their sampans, and scatter them as a living chum whenever a school of aku is encountered. The whole operation relies entirely on the ability of these live nehu to hold the school. Not just any kind of live bait will do the job. According to NMFS biologist Heeny Yuen, in a 1974 paper entitled "Desired Characteristics of a Bait for Skipjack Tuna," the nehu is really

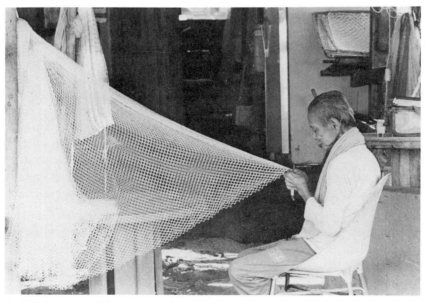

Bait fish are readily gathered with throw nets, the making of which is an art still practiced by veteran fishermen.

special. Heeny says that the bait must be attractive, but not so attractive that the aku just eat the chum and pay no attention to the jigs and baited hooks.

Furthermore, the chum cannot just scatter and swim away wildly, or the aku will go with them. Nehu cluster around the boat for protection when released. This habit of "initially diving, then fleeing toward the surface" proves especially enticing to aku, according to Yuen.

As any troller knows, jigging a lure through an aku school, causing it to dart forward in jerks, means more hooked fish. Yuen says that bait fish with "quick, short darting movements will excite skipjack tuna" much more than the steady swimming baits do. Chalk up another plus for nehu. Yuen notes that slow-swimming baits are sometimes totally ignored by aku even though they represent an easy meal. But there is another side to every coin; the bait cannot be so quick and elusive that it takes the aku out of hooking range. The nehu passes that test, too.

In other words, when aku feed they depend primarily on their sight rather than any other sense, and the bait fish must look right and act right. For the actual baiting of aku, then, the nehu can't be beat.

Nehu cannot be raised in captivity and must be caught immediately prior to use. An estimated 40 percent of the aku fisherman's time is spent in catching these bait fish with nearly 300,000 pounds of nehu being required annually to support the current fleet of sixteen aku sampans. Mortality is high in the bait wells, and the aku boats are limited to a range of about 20 miles. Traveling beyond this range abuses the bait to such an extent that a large percentage dies, making the increased range coverage inefficient.

The NMFS has experimented with the northern anchovy (most popular bait fish of the eastern Pacific tuna industry), the threadfin shad, topminnow, and tilapia. The northern anchovies must be imported from California in live shipments. When originally caught, roughly half the anchovies die almost immediately, and shipments are not sent until they have been held for a few days to eliminate the weak ones. Even so, a 1,600-pound shipment loses roughly one-third in transit.

Threadfin shad could be raised here, though attempts to establish them have not been successful. They spawn in fresh water

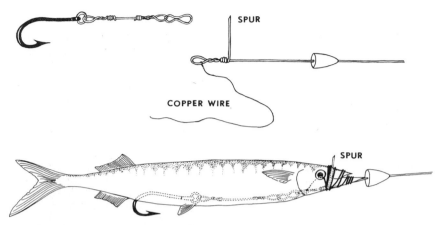

The best way to rig an iheihe for trolling is with this two-piece internal rig. The ice tong snap is fed through the body with a bait needle, beginning at the vent and emerging at the gill opening, where it is then attached to the main leader, outside the fish's body. The leader spur is forced up through the head from the bottom and carries the towing strain. The thin copper wire is fed through the eye and wrapped around the head as shown. The beak is broken off just ahead of the mouth. The lead weight, shown on the leader, is optional. A striking fish is hooked instantly with no dropback.

several times a year, but cultivation would require a large amount of land. Their flat reflective bodies make them great aku attractors.

Topminnows are hardier than nehu but not as attractive to aku. They have been in Hawai'i since 1905 when they were established to control mosquitos, and they have become abundant. Inexpensive pond culture makes them economically attractive.

Tilapia are easy to raise and very hardy. They tend not to be as attractive as nehu since they are not a silvery fish, but they have proved successful as a supplement to chumming with nehu.

Nehu are a great bait for many of the inshore game fish and will take pāpio, kākū, 'ōmaka—even akule and weke. They don't need to be used alive and can be frozen after being caught, then stored for future outings. They make a good bait either dunked, or whipped slowly.

The iheihe, also known as the ballyhoo and halfbeak, are among the best possible trolling baits because of their exceptional durability, even after being frozen and stored for as long as six months.

Though these long, skinny silver fish can regularly be seen dur-

World-renowned as the "ballyhoo," the iheihe is a top trolling bait for mahimahi and ono.

ing the day flying across the surface, they are most easily captured at night. Iheihe are attracted by lights and will congregate in quiet harbors and bays at night under the influence of the lights surrounding the harbor, or the glow of a suspended gas lantern. Once the bait fish drift into the pool of light, they can be caught by a throw net or scooped up quickly by the deft use of a large hand net.

A second successful fishing method is to attach a light to the side of a boat where it can shine directly on the water. As the boat moves slowly across the surface, iheihe, mālolo, and ʻahaʻaha dart into the lighted area, then dart back out. A fast man with a net can get many of these. They are edible, though dry and boney.

A stationary light from a drifting boat will also attract akule. These excellent bait fish are then caught on small white flies.

# 17
# *Some Lessons from History*
## THE LONG EVOLUTION OF HAWAIIAN FISHING

It is probable that the Hawaiians of Captain James Cook's time knew more about the fishes of their islands than is known today.

Gosline and Brock,
*Handbook of Hawaiian Fishes*

HAWAIIAN FISHING, in the years before Captain James Cook started the process that was eventually to change everything except the balmy breezes and the volcanic eruptions, was a strange mixture of science and superstition. In that respect it differed little from most other pursuits in the rest of the world of the time.

When a Hawaiian fisherman's fund of knowledge and expertise led him to expect success at a certain place and time, and there was none, he was as ready as many people are even today to assume that other forces, unknowable ones, were working against him. What evolved was a mystical system based on the *kapu* and designed to bring good luck or ward off bad.

It is easy for more "enlightened" people of the present to view these kapus with humor, but they served their purpose in binding the fisherman to a tradition that fulfilled his life and provided for his family.

Some kapus were designed to conserve natural resources. For example, 'ōpelu, small mackerel scad which provide food for nearly every other pelagic fish, were kapu half the year, and when this ban on catching them was lifted, another immediately went into effect to protect aku for the remaining six months.

If a section of coastline became depleted from overfishing, all fishing was banned until the balance was restored. It was worth a man's life to defy the kapu even if he were starving.

One such kapu changed history, according to one possible version of the events of 1779. After landing at Kealakekua Bay on the Big Island and wearing out his welcome among the Hawaiians, Cook headed north along the coast while the natives who had honored his visit with weeks of feasting returned to their homes. The *ali'i* (chiefs) placed a kapu on the bay to allow the fish population to recover from the heavy fishing pressure that had kept the throngs fed while they had indulged their curiosity over this deity, the god Lono who had come to visit them as predicted in legend.

Cook's ship broke a mast at the Māhukona wind line during one of the heavy February storms that pour out of the 'Alenuihāhā Channel. He returned to the only safe harbor he knew, Kealakekua Bay, for repairs. By breaking the kapu, he planted the seeds of suspicion among the Hawaiians that he might not be the god they had thought he was. Cook was killed when he set out to recover a boat stolen by Hawaiians who no longer feared him as a god.

Luck played a great part in the fisherman's theories about fishing, even as it does today. Whereas a modern angler might accept poor or good luck as a chance phenomenon no different from the success encountered in rolling dice, a Hawaiian angler believed he could control it by ritual. He never told anyone except his family that he was going fishing. If someone asked his plans, he was just going for a walk. No one was to wish him good luck, else bad luck would surely follow.

No time was spent on idle chatter once the fisherman set out, and he could count on bad luck if he forgot something and had to return home to get it. Once on his fishing canoe, the paddlers were not to look back at the fisherman as he sat in the stern and he, in turn, was not to call back to anyone on shore.

While he was gone, his family was not to involve itself in discord or strife. They were to conduct themselves in peace and harmony, and could neither gossip nor sleep. Everyone was expected to be trying hard, even if he were just waiting at home for the catch.

Each fisherman had a *kū'ula,* a stone object he believed to represent a fish god, and he kept it near his favorite fishing spot.

When a good catch was made, he paid tribute to the kūʻula by offering it the first fish caught. This fish had been marked with a notch in the fin or tail so that it could be told from the others.

Lures themselves were assumed to have luck, and many tales are told of famous lucky lures passed from fisherman to fisherman in one family. Some lures were so famous as to be known by specific names, and tales are recorded of battles over special lures that had been stolen.

Ancient Hawaiians paid a great deal of attention to lure color and always examined the stomach contents of the first fish caught to decide what color lure to choose. Such lures were made of bone or shell. The mother-of-pearl shells, called *pā,* imitated the opalescent glow of the nehu, mālolo, ʻōpelu, akule, or ʻoʻama that the fish were eating.

Since large shells were not common near the major islands, some fishermen sailed as far as Midway to get shells for the big lures.

Fishermen believed that to catch something that lived in the sea the lure should be made from something taken out of the sea. The only exception was in the use of hooks made of bone—human bone. A successful fisherman knew that his body would be recycled after death and that his bones, at least, would continue to go fishing long after his spirit had departed.

Since a good deal of handwork was involved in grinding and shaping lures (their hooks had to be drilled and lashed with *olonā* fiber), a lot of work went into getting ready for a fishing trip, but none of this work could be done after dark if the angler wanted good luck.

Once a school of fish was found, there was to be no talking. Anyone who forgot was reminded with a crack on the head with the nearest solid object, usually a paddle. If the fish were aku, the paddlers splashed water with their hands to add to the commotion as though there were many baitfish trying to escape. This technique survives today on the most modern tuna boats, which spray water around the boat for the same reason, or, as some commercial fishermen explain it, "to hide the fishermen from the schools of fish below."

Bottom fishing rivaled aku fishing for the angler's attention, depending on the season. Research at the fishing village of Lapakahi on the Māhukona coast suggests that early anglers had already developed the skills needed to hook fish in water 1,200 feet deep.

In an early successful attempt at aquaculture, Hawaiian fishermen of North Kohala established a special oyster bed off Pololū Valley. At regular intervals the oysters were brought to the surface where the edges of their shells were chipped. After being returned to their original positions on the bottom, the oysters grew thicker shells to counteract the effect of the damage. When, at last, the shells were thick enough, the fishermen carved them into lures. Examples of these shells are on exhibit at the Kamuela Museum, a private museum owned by Albert Solomon, who told me the story of the Pololū shell beds.

Among the equipment pioneered by the earliest Polynesian fishermen and refined through the years is the incurved hook known now as the *tankichi* hook. Originally, such hooks were made from shell with the point continuing around in a circle so that it was directed toward the shank. In the days before barbs were added as a means of securing the hook so that it could not be shaken free from the fish's jaw, the incurved point was an essential trap. The fisherman could keep his line down on the bottom until every hook had been taken and did not have to worry about losing the fish already caught. Indeed, a fisherman who wished to keep secret the identity of his favorite spot would drift away from it with the hooked fish before pulling up his line so that no one else could discover the exact spot where the fish had been caught. An added feature of this design is that the point is protected from coral snags by the shank, even though it remains in a good position to grab the jaw bone of a fish as it turns to run with the bait.

The occasional marlin was caught when it became entangled in

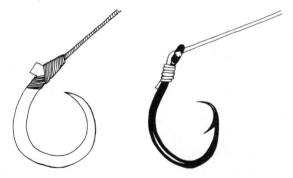

The modern metal hook *(right)* retains the basic shape of the original shell hook of the early Polynesians.

a bottom fisherman's line, but few people fished especially for them. Indeed, they were not even recognized for their true identity by most people and were referred to simply as swordfish as late as the mid-1940s.

The careful balance between man and nature maintained by the early fishermen and their life style disappeared as a result of new forces brought into play by the increased demands on the environment of a more acquistive civilization.

By 1937 resolutions were being introduced in governmental bodies to establish commissions to study causes of depletion of fish life in Hawaiian waters surrounding the Territory of Hawai'i.

By 1940 an irate group of sport fishermen were organizing to combat the menace of the commercial fishing fleet of Japanese sampans which, local anglers claimed, was ruining Hawaiian waters for sportfishing. The sport fishermen numbered approximately 2,000; the registered commercial sampan fleet totaled 32.

During World War II, fishing came to a halt as beaches were closed to all except the military. Not until early 1943 were fishermen finally able to secure permits to fish the beaches. According to newspaper reports, permits were issued only to American citizens and citizens of countries with which the U.S. was not at war to reduce the possibility of any assistance Hawai'i's Japanese population might be supposed to provide to Japan. As an interesting lesson in the division of military powers, shore fishing was turned over to the jurisdiction of the Army, boat fishing (restricted to within 2 miles of shore) became the province of the Navy, and *hukilau* (seine) fishing was jointly controlled by Army and Navy.

Many mainland fishermen first discovered the delights of Pacific trolling during the early 1940s, as they found themselves stopping in Hawai'i for "rest and recreation." Stan Blum, an Illinois angler, set down in a letter his Pacific piscatorial adventures while enrolled in Uncle Sam's Navy.

"I fished from Pearl Harbor to Guam, to Kwajelein, to Majuro, to Ulithe in those days on everything from a motor whaleboat to a sea-going tug, and even on the battle-wagon *North Carolina* trolling into Panama Bay until I got chased when they had to catapult the seaplanes. Our favorite fishing boat in Hawai'i was a torpedo retriever with two fishing chairs. It operated out of the submarine base at Pearl Harbor. I got a 404-pound silver marlin which was a record at the time, but which the IGFA now have replaced with the Pacific blue. We caught many ono, striped marlin, 'ahi, and mahimahi. I carried my own 15/0 and 12/0 rigs all over the Pacific as well as all the hooks, leaders, lures, and smaller tackle needed to get right down to business every time an admiral invited me aboard.''

These enlisted tourists went home and told tales of the glorious islands, and these stories helped bring the flood tide of people which washed up the bases of the dormant volcanoes in a multicolored wave that threatens never to recede.

Even so, by 1948 offshore fishing still had not developed to a point where it was a substantial tourist attraction. A fishing columnist writing in the *Honolulu Advertiser* that year claimed that exploitation of big-game fishing off Hawai'i was ''impossible because (1) the larger breeds of game fish such as tuna, marlin and sailfish do not exist or stay here in sufficient numbers to warrant attracting big-game fishermen, and (2) the local fishermen have not learned the habits of the big fish and don't know how to fish for them.''

Inshore, the lazy few who cannot see beyond the next few moments capitalized on any technological advance that might bring a quick ocean harvest regardless of any long-range consequences. Hawai'i has seen such appallingly destructive methods as dynamiting, poisoning underwater caves with bleach, breaking apart of coral heads after they have been surrounded by a net to catch any fish that have sought refuge inside from the spearguns, and deep-sea dredging for sand and coral that has devastated many acres of bottom now unable to support any kind of life. Though dynamiting was ruled illegal in 1945, arrests were still being made as late as 1951 despite the obvious difficulties inherent in hiding an explosion set off at the end of the Hilo breakwater. As insane as the other destructive practices mentioned are, and despite the fact that poisoning with chlorine bleach is also illegal, they are still being done in Hawai'i.

Simultaneously, an explosion in shore fishing was detonated by the development of spinning tackle. This easy style of fishing allowed the novice to cast within minutes of buying the inexpensive equipment, without that abomination that had always plagued beginners, the backlash. The simultaneous introduction of translucent monofilament lines and powerfully springy fiberglass rods put anyone within easy reach of shore fish. This equipment allowed the tiniest of lures to be cast, the very size lure most capable of catching inshore fish. Spinning clubs bloomed, and the schools of

Whipping, in the days before spinning tackle tripled the sportfisherman's reach, was practiced with a 20-foot-long rod and an equal length of line.

'ō'io, pāpio and moi disappeared under the onslaught or discovered more devious ways to exist.

In the early 1950s, charter fishermen were learning how to exploit the offshore grounds for the big game that many people did not even know existed. Two charter boats were in operation at the wooden wharf and cargo shed at Kailua-Kona. George Parker on the *Mona H* and Henry Ahuna Chee on the *Malia* began attracting international attention for their claims of IGFA record fish caught in the calm Kona lee. By 1957 the Kona fleet had grown to seven vessels. The simultaneous development of reliable outboard motors and fiberglass skiffs meant that the offshore grounds became the playground of marauding bands of "mosquitos" like the Kona Mauka Trollers and Kawaihae Trolling Club, ready to put their stingers into any big fish willing to fight.

In 1959 Peter Fithian convinced the local anglers of the value of an international tournament, and the fledgling "Kona Billfish Tournament," contested between a few handfuls of local boats of all sizes, grew into the "Hawaiian International Billfish Tournament," a five-day battle between a fleet of big cruisers carrying teams from all over the world. The HIBT has become so popular that entries have been limited at about seventy teams, just to be able to process the prize catches at the end of each day.

The reef fauna was always noticeable for its many "holes," filled in other areas by such fish as the snappers and groupers. Many attempts have been made in the past to introduce species to fill the gaps. Some of these have been such ridiculous efforts as the planting of king salmon in 1876, of the striped bass in 1922, and the California anchovy in 1932.

In 1958 the Hawai'i Division of Fish and Game brought in a shipment of live fish from the Marquesas Islands which included 2,591 assorted groupers and snappers including 2,435 ta'ape (striped snapper, *Lutjanus kasmira*). Within nineteen days the ta'ape had traveled 52 miles from its Kane'ohe Bay release point, and by August 1960 small ta'ape had been found off the Big Island. The ta'ape has become so well established that as much as 132 pounds of these snappers have been caught by handliners on one trip. Two other species released in the 1950s have also become established, the toau (black-tailed snapper, *Lutjanus fulvus*) and the *roi* (spotted grouper, *Cephalopholis argus*).

But all fish and all people, whether malihini or kama'āina, are caught in a vicious cycle. Hawai'i's environmental bounty attracts people; too large a population destroys the environmental bounty.

By 1969 Honolulu was dumping 50 million gallons of raw sewage a day into the ocean off Sand Island. Human waste was reported off Waikīkī and had already begun to wash ashore in the Portlock area. These facts were duly reported in Honolulu newspapers. The steady barrage of excrement, garbage, dirt, and silt into island waters was by that time already destroying the coral. Unre-

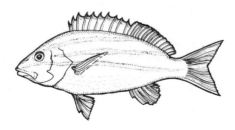

TA'APE

The ta'ape, or blue-lined snapper, is the most successful of the food fish introduced to Hawai'i's waters.

moved (and unremovable) chemicals in the sewage stimulate the growth of vegetation in the water causing algal blooms that kill the coral.

The potential occupancy of Waikīkī by 1973 was approximately 55,000 persons. This number, equal to 90 percent of the population of the entire Big Island at that time, was being housed on seven-tenths of a square mile of land.

In 1967, as an example of what might yet be recoverable of reef populations in densely "civilized" areas, Hanauma Bay on Oʻahu was designated a marine conservation district, and all harvesting of ocean life was ordered to a halt. This bay, though only a twenty-minute drive from Waikīkī via a superhighway, is far enough from the tide of sewage and development that a miraculous transformation has occurred. A seriously depleted fauna recovered within a year to become a marvel and, eventually, the closest approximation to what might have been in the days when Cook met the Hawaiians—a modern kapu with an ancient precedent.

To appreciate how well the Polynesians knew the sea, one need only recall that they sailed on voyages across the Pacific nearly a thousand years before Columbus, with few aids other than the stars. Equally important, by the time of Cook's landing, the Hawaiian Islands supported an estimated population of 300,000 people existing largely on seafood. Sir Peter Buck, former director of the Bishop Museum, stated in his fascinating book *Arts and Crafts of Hawaii* that "fishing was the most varied and extensive food-procuring occupation of the Hawaiians." It is possible that the Hawaiian population, at the time it discovered Captain Cook on the horizon, consumed more locally produced seafood of every kind on a daily basis than does the present population.

It was their knowledge of the sea and of how to use it effectively that resulted in a balanced harvest that produced a sustaining ecological system. Every man knew how essential it was to use the life of the sea wisely, because every person profited or hungered. It is with the belief in that principle that some of this knowledge is being passed on to you.

# Appendix
# *What Do I Do with It Now?*

## NOW THAT YOU'VE CAUGHT IT,
## HERE'S HOW TO EAT IT

THOUGH MANY SAGES have referred to Hawai'i as the melting pot of the Pacific, they have failed to mention that the vessel intended is a cooking pot. Kama'āinas readily borrow ideas from their neighbors regardless of ethnic origin, and popular fish dishes in Hawai'i can be traced to every locale in the world. Here is a sampling of fish recipes selected by Tsugi Kaiama, Dorothy Chow, Setsui Hamada, Julia Kimura, and Shirley Rizzuto.

### Smoked Fish a la Sid Weinrich

| | |
|---|---|
| 10 pounds of sliced fillet of ono, aku, kawakawa, marlin or 'ahi | dash of Aji-no-moto (monosodium glutamate) |
| ½ cup Hawaiian salt | 2 cloves garlic, smashed |
| ¾ cup sugar (brown sugar or raw sugar provide an interesting flavor) | 2 tablespoons ground red pepper |
| | 3 cups water |

Dissolve ingredients in water. Marinate the fish for at least 3 hours in refrigerator. Wash the fillets off very carefully in cold water. Sun dry in screened enclosure for 2 to 3 hours.

Smoke at low heat (electric smokers work well with the above brine) until as dry and hard as you prefer. Smoked fish keeps well in the refrigerator for several weeks. If frozen, it keeps well for up to a year. Serve at room temperature, or heated.

### Charcoal-broiled Sesame Fish

6 skinned fish
½ cup melted butter or vegetable
  oil
½ cup sesame seeds

4 tablespoons lemon juice
1 teaspoon salt
dash of pepper

Clean and dry the fish. Place in a well-greased, hinged wire grill. Combine the remaining ingredients and baste the fish. Cook about 4 inches from moderately hot coals for 8 minutes. Baste, turn, and cook other side until fish flakes easily.

### Mahimahi with Sesame Seeds

1 cup flour
2 teaspoons salt
dash of pepper
2 pounds fish fillets
2 eggs, beaten with 2 tablespoons
  water

1 cup sesame seeds
¼ pound butter
3 bananas
3 lemons

Combine flour, salt, and pepper. Dip fillets into the seasoned flour, then use tongs to dip it into the beaten eggs, then into the sesame seeds. Heat butter in a large skillet and fry fish until golden brown on both sides. Drain on absorbent paper and keep hot in the oven.

Halve the bananas lengthwise, then cut each half into two. Roll in the remaining seeds. Sauté quickly in the same skillet and arrange on platter with the fish. Serve with lemon slices.

You may substitute chopped nuts, macadamia or almonds, if there are no sesame seeds handy.

### Mahimahi with Nut Sauce

2 pounds fillets
1 teaspoon salt
flour
5 tablespoons butter
1 cup chicken broth
¼ cup wine vinegar
1 teaspoon fresh ginger root, minced

1 cup brown sugar
3 tablespoons shoyu
2 tablespoons cornstarch
½ cup chopped nuts (macadamia,
  almonds, or unsalted peanuts)

Season fish with salt and dredge with flour. Melt butter in a large skillet and sauté fish until golden. Remove to the oven and keep warm, taking care not to let it dry out.

Combine remaining ingredients, except the nuts, in a saucepan and heat. Simmer 10 minutes or until hot and thick. Pour sauce over the fish and sprinkle nuts over all.

### Baked Kawakawa

Remove the head, tail, and innards, then split the fish in half from the back to tail bone. Remove the center bone and make deep slits into the flesh every 2 inches across the fillet.

Place a piece of garlic into each slit, then rub Hawaiian salt into the slits and over the fish according to your taste. Let stand for 10 to 15 minutes.

Place the fish in a baking pan, skin side down, and pour ¼ cup vegetable oil over it. Bake, uncovered, at 325 degrees (F.) for 45 minutes. Serve with lemon wedges and shoyu.

## Broiled Fish Teriyaki

6 fish steaks or fish fillets
1 cup shoyu
⅓ cup sugar
1 clove garlic, minced

1 slice fresh ginger root, minced
2 tablespoons sake or sherry, optional

Marinate the fish for 2 hours in the teriyaki sauce made from the shoyu, sugar, garlic, ginger, and sake. Drain. Broil it in a pan, not on a grill, about 3 to 4 inches from the heat source. Baste once or twice, and do not turn the fish over. Serve when fish flakes readily.

## Charcoal-broiled Mahimahi

For a 1-pound fillet, leave the skin on and cut the fillet into liberal pieces sliced at an angle against the grain. Put the fillets into wire grills that clamp together at the handle.

A proper fire is important. The coals should be medium low and not burned down to ashes.

Make a sauce using ½ pound butter, 2 tablespoons lemon or lime juice, and a dash of vermouth. Brush or pour it on the fish and roast over the coals, skin side down first. Cook according to thickness of fish and heat of fire, about 5 minutes on first side, then turn and baste, finishing with skin side down. Use a spatula to remove the meat from the skin which will probably stick to the wire.

Pour any remaining sauce over the fish, and garnish with lemon before serving.

## Broiled Fish Steaks

Use mahimahi, ono, swordfish, 'ahi or any deep-sea large fish that can be filleted.

Season fillets with salt and pepper. Lay the slices on a flat baking sheet or on heavy foil. Spread mayonnaise over steaks (like buttering bread) and broil them until golden brown puffs appear. Turn steaks, spread with mayonnaise, and broil the same way. Serve hot with lemon slices, soy sauce, or just plain.

This recipe is especially good for dry types of fish meat because the mayonnaise will make it moist.

## Lemon Shoyu Broiled Fish

3 pounds whole 'paka, moi, or
   mullet
½ cup butter, melted

2 tablespoons shoyu
1 tablespoon lemon juice
1 teaspoon sake

Prepare fish for broiling. Cut three to five crosswise slashes through the fish to the bone. Combine remaining ingredients to make sauce.

Broil fish 10 to 12 minutes, turn and broil another 10 minutes. Baste with sauce during broiling and serve hot with remaining sauce. Serves 6.

## Raw Fish (Sashimi)

1 pound raw fish
1½ teaspoon fresh or dried ginger
    root, grated
¾ cup shoyu

1 cup watercress tips or shredded
    lettuce, or ¾ cup thinly sliced
    daikon and cucumber

Use fish with firm flesh and few small bones, such as tuna, red snapper, or sea bass. Remove all skin and dark meat. Cut diagonally into strips 2 inches long, ¾ inch wide and ⅛ inch thick. Chill. Arrange slices on a bed shredded or sliced vegetables before serving.

For dipping, make a sauce of the shoyu and ginger, with a bit of dried mustard for added zing.

## Raw Fish (I'a Maka)

½ pound raw 'ō'io
3 tablespoons green onion with
    tops, finely chopped
1½ teaspoon salted roasted *kukui*
    nuts (*'inamona*)

6 tablespoons *limu-kohu, limu
līpoa.* or *limu līimpe'epe'e*
(seaweeds)
1 cup ice water
1 tablespoon ice cream salt

Scale and clean fish, cut crosswise into several pieces and sprinkle with salt. Chill several hours.

Rinse fish, taking off excess salt, but do not wash thoroughly. Cut into small pieces and remove skin and bones. Mash flesh with fingers and add ice water gradually. Add all other ingredients and mix thoroughly. Serve immediately with an ice cube in the center of each serving.

## Poke

Poke is a Hawaiian raw, salted fish dish served at lu'aus and eaten with poi, or as a beer chaser. Most Hawaiians prefer to use uhu (parrotfish), mahimahi, aku, 'ahi, or ono, but any fleshy fish can be used.

Remove bones and cut the fish into inch-square cubes. Sprinkle cubes with Hawaiian salt and work all the pieces with your fingers to get them evenly salted. This can be done in advance and refrigerated.

Before serving, mix the salted fish with *limu kohu* (seaweed), roasted and crushed *kukui* nuts or sesame seeds, and chili peppers, chopped fine.

## Fish Cake Pūpū

1 red kamaboko, sliced and cut
    lengthwise (kamaboko is fish
    cake.)
8 fresh shrimps, chopped into
    ½-inch pieces

1 cup flour
¼ cup cornstarch
½ teaspoon salt
4 teaspoons baking powder
1 cup water

Mix all ingredients together in a bowl. Heat some oil in a saucepan for deep frying and drop mixture in by tablespoonfuls. Cook until done.

### Fish with Coconut Sauce

1 ½- to 2-pound piece of white fish
2 cups milk
2 cups grated coconut

Place fish in a baking pan and rub it with salt. Make a coconut cream by combining the milk and grated coconut, bringing it to the scalding point, cooling it, then squeezing it through cheesecloth.

Pour the coconut cream over the fish and bake at 325 degrees (F.) for 20 minutes per pound. Baste often with sauce during baking.

### Mullet in Coconut Milk ('Ama'ama me wai niu)

1- to 1¼-pound mullet or white fish
¼ teaspoon salt
water
1 coconut or 1 cup shredded packaged coconut
½ cup milk

Scale and clean the fish and cut crosswise into individual servings. Place in a pan and add salt and water to a depth of ½ inch. Cover and simmer until fairly tender but not overcooked.

Grate coconut or grind in grinder. Heat the milk, pour it over the coconut, and let stand about 15 minutes. Squeeze it through a poi cloth or two thicknesses of cheesecloth, squeezing out as much liquid as possible. Add this milk to the fish and bring liquid to boiling point. Serve immediately.

### Portuguese Pickled Fish

2 pounds fresh, firm fish
1½ cups vinegar
2 cloves garlic
2 teaspoons salt
6 whole cloves
¼ teaspoon thyme
6 small red peppers
⅛ teaspoon sage
1 bay leaf
¼ cup olive oil

Clean fish and combine with other ingredients. Let it stand for 16 hours. Cook in a pan for 10 or 15 minutes. Drain the fish and fry it whole or in slices, in hot oil, until evenly brown. Serve hot.

Squid may also be prepared in this manner.

### Poached Hawaiian Salmon in Dill Sauce

8 ounces Hawaiian salmon
  (kamanu)
½ onion, diced
fish stock
¼ lemon, wedged
½ onion, wedged
parsley and fresh dill to taste

Poach the salmon in the fish stock with the parsley, dill leaves, lemon and onion wedges.

Sauté diced onion in butter until translucent. Make a paste ball by adding flour and finely chopped dill leaves. Add fish stock to make a sauce to whatever thickness you desire.

Serve the salmon with the sauce over it and add a few sprinkles of parsley and dill on top for color.

### Fried Fish Korean-style (Kun Saingsen)

6 slices fish, ¼ inch thick
2 tablespoons white sesame seed, browned and pulverized (method follows)
3 tablespoons shoyu

1½ tablespoon oil or fat
1 tablespoon sesame or salad oil
⅓ cup green onion with tops, finely chopped
1/16 teaspoon black pepper

Use any firm fish with few small bones. Dip slices into a mixture of shoyu, oil, sesame seeds, onions, and black pepper. Heat oil or fat, and fry fish until thoroughly cooked and golden brown. Serve hot with Red Pepper Sauce (recipe follows).

To pulverize sesame seeds, clean and dry seeds in the sun or in a warm place. Put in a frying pan, heat and stir constantly until they crackle. Crush in a bowl with a wooden masher.

Red Pepper Sauce:
2 teaspoons sesame or salad oil
¼ teaspoon ground red pepper, fresh or dried
1 teaspoon sugar
1 teaspoon white sesame seed, browned and pulverized
1 small clove garlic, chopped fine

2 tablespoons green onion with tops, chopped fine
2 teaspoons ginger root, fresh or preserved, chopped fine
⅛ cup shoyu
¼ cup water

Combine all ingredients. Pour over the browned fish (may also be used on meat) and simmer a minute or two. Serve hot and garnish with more green onion and sesame seed.

### Fried Barracuda or Pāpio

After removing the skin and center bone, slice the fish into ½-inch-thick pieces on a slant. Salt lightly, roll in flour, then dip into slightly beaten eggs seasoned with more salt, pepper, chopped parsley, and a pinch of Aji-no-moto (monosodium glutamate). Fry in a skillet until golden brown. Keep the dish warm in the oven if necessary before serving.

### Steaming Fish

You do not need a fancy fish-shaped steamer to steam fish. A wide pot with a tight fitting lid, such as a Dutch oven or roaster, will work just as well.

Add a few inches of boiling water to the bottom of the pan. Place a rack large enough to hold the fish platter in the pot. If you do not have a rack that will fit, set the platter directly into the pot, with the water at a depth three-quarters the height of the platter.

Cover the pan tightly. Keep water just at boiling point. Do not allow the water to boil down during steaming. Watch it carefully, and add water when necessary to maintain the proper level.

## Steamed Fish with Cabbage Root

1½-pound mullet, red snapper, or
   ulua
1 tablespoon sliced ginger root,
   fresh or preserved
½ cup shoyu

1 green onion with top, finely
   chopped
2 tablespoons peanut or salad oil
⅔ roll salted mustard cabbage
   root (optional)

Clean the fish without removing the head and tail and place in a serving dish. Pour the shoyu and oil over the fish.

Wash the cabbage root and chop fine. Wash, peel, and cut the ginger root into strips ¾ inch long and ¹⁄₁₆ inch thick. Sprinkle cabbage root, ginger, and green onion over the fish. Steam 15 minutes or until tender. Serve hot.

## Steamed Fish with Mushrooms

1 pound fish
3 dried mushrooms
2 tablespoons shredded ginger
2¼ tablespoons green onion,
   minced

1 teaspoon cornstarch
1 teaspoon sugar
½ teaspoon salt
3 tablespoons shoyu
2 teaspoons sherry

Soak mushrooms in warm water until they expand, and clean. Squeeze dry and shred.

Clean fish and rub with a mixture of the cornstarch, sugar, salt, shoyu, and sherry. Place on a platter and garnish with shredded ginger, green onions, and mushrooms. Steam for 20 minutes.

## Steamed Uhu, Mullet, or Pō'ou

When steaming a fish weighing more than 10 pounds, salt the cavities lightly and place in a baking pan lined with heavy foil. Pour about ¼ cup peanut or vegetable oil over the fish, and cover the pan with a foil tent, but do not let it touch the fish.

Bake at 350 degrees (F.), 1 hour for a large fish, and 45 minutes for one under 5 pounds.

Make a sauce by boiling ¼ cup peanut oil with ¼ cup shoyu, juice from a 2-inch piece of ginger root and a pinch of Aji-no-moto (monosodium glutamate). Chop green onions and sprinkle generously over the baked fish. Pour sauce over all just before serving.

## Fish Baked in Ti Leaves

Use any piece of fish large enough for baking.
Rub the fish inside out with a mixture of onion juice, lemon juice, and butter.

Wrap it in ti leaves and tie securely so that no moisture can get in. Place it in a baking pan with a little water covering the pan bottom. Bake at 375 degrees (F.) for 45 minutes or more, depending on the size of the fish. Discard the leaves when serving.

Corn husks or aluminum foil may be substituted for ti leaves if individual pieces of fish are to be baked. When removing the husks from the cobs, keep the stems and sheaves intact. Place one slice of fish in each husk. Wrap carefully and tie tips of leaves together. Place in a pan containing just enough water to cover the bottom and bake as for ti leaves.

Wrapped fish may also be steamed for 1½ hours instead of baked.

## Fish Baked in Ti Leaves (I'a Lāwalu)

| | |
|---|---|
| 1½-pound slices or 2½-pound whole fish (butterfish, kūmū, mullet, moi, moano) | 1½ tablespoons Hawaiian salt ti leaves or corn husks |

Scale and clean a whole fish. Wrap it in several ti leaves tying the ends together with string or thin strips of the ti leaf stem. If individual pieces of fish are being used, split the ti lengthwise into two pieces and wrap the fish in one piece. Wrap the other piece around the fish in the opposite direction, tying with thin stem or string.

Put the tied fish into a moderate oven and bake 1 to 1½ hours, depending on the size of the fish if whole, or 30 to 45 minutes for individual servings.

For additional flavor, place a piece of bacon, one bay leaf, and onion and green pepper slices on each piece of fish before tying it up.

## Parrotfish in Ti Leaves

| | |
|---|---|
| 10 ounces fresh fish, whole, half or fillet | ½ tomato, diced |
| ¾ cup green onion in 1-inch pieces | ½ green pepper, chopped |
| ½ cup shoyu | 1 clove garlic, minced |
| ¼ cup sugar | 1-inch piece of ginger, sliced |
| | 2 ti leaves |

Combine tomato, pepper, and onion. Make a sauce of shoyu, ginger, garlic, and sugar.

Place fish in the ti leaves. Top with the tomato mixture and cover with the sauce. Wrap leaves around the fish and place in the top of a double boiler or steamer. Steam 12 to 15 minutes or until the fish is tender.

## Fish Balls Soup

| | |
|---|---|
| 4 slices 'paka fillet | 1 onion, sliced |
| 1 egg | 3 cloves garlic, crushed |
| 4 tablespoons minced green onion tops | ¼ teaspoon Aji-no-moto (monosodium glutamate) |
| 2 tablespoons flour | salt and pepper to taste |

Prepare fish so that it is free of bones and skin, and chop fine. Add onion leaves, egg, flour, and salt, and pepper. Shape mixture into small balls and set aside.

Sauté garlic in fat until golden brown; add onion, Aji and 7 cups of water. When water is boiling, drop balls one by one into soup and cook until done.

Season with salt and pepper and serve hot.

## ‘Ō‘io Tempura

| | |
|---|---|
| 3 cups ‘ō‘io | 6 tablespoons sugar |
| 1 cup cornstarch | 3 eggs |
| 5 teaspoons salt | 2 cups water |
| 3 teaspoons Aji-no-moto (monosodium glutamate) | |

Age ‘ō‘io in the refrigerator for 3 days. Scrape meat off bones with a spoon; you'll get about 1 cup per pound, so you'll need at least a 3-pound fish.

Combine the salt, Aji, cornstarch, and sugar with the water. Add to the scraped ‘ō‘io and knead until well blended. Add beaten eggs last. Drop by teaspoonfuls into hot fat until brown and crisp.

For extra flavor, add some minced fresh shrimp to the ‘ō‘io.

This can also be pan fried. Make patties and fry in ¼ to ½ inch of oil.

# *Glossary*
## SOME OF HAWAI'I'S FISH AND REEF ANIMALS

| Hawaiian or Other Local Name | Common English Name | Scientific Name |
|---|---|---|
| 'a'ama | black crab | *Grapsus grapsus* |
| 'a'awa | wrasse | *Bodianus bilunulatus* |
| 'aha | needlefish | *Strongylura* spp. |
| 'aha'aha | juvenile needlefish | *Strongylura* spp. |
| 'ahi | yellowfin tuna<br>bigeye tuna | *Thunnus albacares*<br>*Thunnus obesus* |
| 'ahi pāhala | albacore | *Thunnus alalunga* |
| āholehole | mountain bass | *Kuhlia sandvicensis* |
| aku | skipjack tuna | *Euthynnus (=Katsuwonus) pelamis* |
| akule | bigeye scad | *Selar (=Trachurops) crumenophthalmus* |
| 'ama'ama | mullet (pond) | *Mugil cephalus* |
| a'u | Pacific blue marlin | *Makaira nigricans* |
| a'u | black marlin | *Istiompax marlina* |
| a'u | striped marlin | *Tetrapterus audax* |

| Hawaiian or Other Local Name | Common English Name | Scientific Name |
|---|---|---|
| a'u | shortbill spearfish | *Tetrapterus angustirostris* |
| a'u-kū | broadbill swordfish | *Xiphias gladius* |
| a'u-lepe | sailfish | *Istiophorus platypterus* |
| awa | milkfish | *Chanos chanos* |
| awa-'aua | ladyfish | *Elops hawaiiensis* |
| 'āweoweo | bigeye | *Priacanthus cruentatus* |
| hahalalū | juvenile bigeye scad | *Selar (=Trachurops) crumenophthalmus* |
| hāpu'u | deep-sea grouper | *Epinephelus quernus* |
| he'e | octopus ("day squid") | *Polypus* sp. |
| hīnālea | wrasse | numerous species of the family Labridae (*Thalassoma* spp., *Coris* spp., etc.) |
| humuhumu | triggerfish | numerous species of the family Balistidae |
| 'iao | silversides | *Pranesus insularum* |
| iheihe | halfbeak | numerous species of the family Hemiramphidae |
| ika (Japanese) | squid | |
| kāhala | amberjack | *Seriola dumerili* |
| kākū | barracuda | *Sphyraena* sp. |
| kala | unicornfish | *Naso unicornis* |
| kalekale | snapper | *Pristipomoides sieboldi* |
| kamanu | rainbow runner | *Elagatis bipinnulata* |
| kawakawa | Pacific bonito | *Euthynnus affinis* |
| kawele'ā | Japanese barracuda | *Sphyraena helleri* |
| keokeo | frigate mackerel | *Auxis thazard* |
| kūmū | red goatfish | *Parupeneus porphyreus* |
| lai | leatherback | *Scomberoides sanctipetri* |
| mahimahi | dolphin fish | *Coryphaena hippurus* |
| mako (Maori) | mako shark, sharp-nosed mackerel shark | *Isurus oxyrinchus* |
| mālolo | flyingfish | numerous species of the family Exocoetidae |

| Hawaiian or Other Local Name | Common English Name | Scientific Name |
|---|---|---|
| malu | goatfish | *Parupeneus pleurostigma* |
| mamo | damselfish | *Abudefduf abdominalis* |
| manini | convict tang surgeonfish | *Acanthurus sandvicensis* |
| manō | shark | *Squalus fernandinus* and many other species |
| menpachi or mempachi (Japanese) | red squirrelfish | several species of the genus *Myripristis* |
| moano | red goatfish | *Parupeneus multifasciatus* |
| moi | threadfin | *Polydoctylus sexfilis* |
| moi-li'i | juvenile threadfin | *Polydoctylus sexfilis* |
| nabeta (Japanese) | | *Hemipteronotus umbrilatus* |
| natagi (Japanese) | juvenile striped marlin | *Tetrapterus audax* |
| nehu | anchovy | *Stolephorus purpureus* |
| nohu | scorpionfish | *Scorpaenopsis gibbosa* or *S. cacopsis* |
| 'oama | juvenile goatfish | *Mulloidichthys flavolineatus* |
| 'ō'io | bonefish | *Albula vulpes* |
| oi oi | tiny Pacific bonito (kawakawa) | *Euthynnus affinis* |
| 'ōmaka | blue runner jack | *Caranx mate* |
| 'ōmilu | blue crevalle or jack | *Caranx melampygus* |
| onaga (Japanese) | red snapper | *Etelis carbunculus* |
| ono | wahoo | *Acanthocybium solandri* |
| 'ōpae-lōlō | brackish water shrimp | *Penaeus marginatus* |
| 'ōpakapaka or 'paka | snapper | *Pristipomoides microlepis* |
| 'ōpelu | mackerel scad | *Decapterus pinnulatus* |
| otadi (Japanese) | subpopulation of aku (skipjack tuna) | |
| pāo'o kauila | blenny | *Exallias brevis* |
| pa'opa'o | yellow jack | *Gnathanodon speciosus* |
| pāpio | juvenile jack (ulua) | *Caranx* spp. |

| Hawaiian or Other Local Name | Common English Name | Scientific Name |
|---|---|---|
| pā'ū'ū | white jack | *Caranx ignoblis* |
| pīhā | | *Spratelloides gracilis* |
| po'o-nui | bigeye tuna | *Thunnus obesus* |
| po'o-pa'a | hawkfish | *Cirrhitus alternatus* |
| pō'ou | wrasse | *Cheilinus rhodochrous* |
| pualua | surgeonfish | *Acanthurus xanthopterus* |
| puhi | moray eel | numerous species of the family Muraenidae |
| pū-loa | octopus ("night squid") | *Polypus* sp. |
| roi (Tahitian) | spotted grouper | *Cephalopholis argus* |
| ta'ape (Tahitian) | striped snapper or blue-lined snapper | *Lutjanus kasmira* |
| tako (Japanese) | octopus | *Polypus* sp. |
| tilapia (from genus name) | tilapia | *Tilapia* sp. |
| to'au (Tahitian) | black-tailed snapper | *Lutjanus fulvus* |
| 'ūkīkiki | gindai (snapper) | *Rooseveltia brighami* |
| uhu | parrotfish | *Scarus perspicillatus* |
| uku | gray snapper | *Aprion virescens* |
| ulae | lizardfish | numerous spp. of the family Synodontidae |
| 'ula'ula | red snapper | *Etelis marshi* |
| 'ula'ula koa'e | onaga | *Etelis carbunculus* |
| ulua | jack | *Caranx* spp. (over 10 pounds) |
| ulua kihikihi | long-finned jack | *Alectis ciliaris* or *A. indica* |
| uouoa | mullet (ocean) | *Neomyxus chaptali* |
| 'ū'ū | red squirrelfish (menpachi) | several species of the genus *Myripristis* |
| weke | goatfish | *Mulloidichthys flavolineatus* |
| weke-pueo | goatfish | *Upeneus arge* |
| weke-'ula | goatfish | *Mulloidichthys vanicolensis* or *M. pflugeri* |

*More Words from a Hawaiian Fisherman's Vocabulary*

| | |
|---|---|
| akamai | clever |
| ali'i | chief |
| 'a'ole (tide) | none; to be without |
| 'aumākua | family gods |
| hukilau | seine; to fish with a seine |
| i'a maka | raw fish |
| 'inamona | salted roasted kukui nuts |
| kahuna | native priest |
| kama'āina | native-born |
| kapu | taboo |
| ko'a | fishing grounds |
| ku'ula | fish god image |
| limu-kohu | a kind of seaweed |
| limu līpoa | a kind of seaweed |
| limu līpe'epe'e | a kind of seaweed |
| malihini | newcomer |
| pā | mother-of-pearl shell; lure made from this shell |
| palu | fish bait |
| pilikia | trouble |
| poke | raw salted fish |
| pūpū | hors d'oeuvre |
| sashimi | raw fish |
| shoyu | soy sauce |
| suji | nylon fishing line |

# Selected Bibliography

Beckley, Emma M. *Hawaiian Fishing Implements and Methods of Fishing*. Bulletin, U.S. Fish Commission, 6 (1886):245–246.

Brooks, Joe. *Salt Water Gamefishing*. New York: Harper & Row, 1968.

Buck, Peter H. (Te Rangi Hiroa). *Arts and Crafts of Hawaii*. B. P. Bishop Museum Special Publication 45. Honolulu, 1957.

Clemens, Dale. *Fiberglass Rod Making*. New York: Winchester Press, 1974.

Earp, Samuel A., and William J. Wildeman. *The Blue Water Bait Book*. Boston: Little, Brown and Co., 1974.

Evanoff, Vlad. *Natural Salt Water Fishing Baits*. Cranbury, N.J.: Barnes, 1953.

Farrington, S. Kip, Jr. *Pacific Gamefishing*. New York: Coward-McCann, 1942.

────── *Fishing the Pacific*. New York: Coward-McCann, 1953.

Goadby, Peter. *Big Fish and Blue Water*. Cremorne Junction, N.S.W.: Angus and Robertson, 1970.

Goodson, Gar. *Fishes of Hawaii*. Palos Verdes Estates, California: Marquest Colorguide Books, 1973.

Gosline, William A., and Vernon E. Brock. *Handbook of Hawaiian Fishes*. Honolulu: University of Hawaii Press, 1960.

Grey, Zane. *Adventures in Fishing*. Edited by Ed Zern. New York: Harper & Brothers, 1952.

Heilner, Van Campen. *Salt Water Fishing*. New York: Alfred A. Knopf, 1953.

Hobson, Edmund, and E. H. Chave. *Hawaiian Reef Animals*. Honolulu: The University Press of Hawaii, 1972.

Hosaka, Edward Y. *Sport Fishing in Hawaii*. Honolulu: Bond's, 1944.

Kamakau, Samuel. *The Works of the People of Old*. Bernice P. Bishop Museum Special Publication 61. 1976.

McClane, A. J. *McClane's Standard Fishing Encyclopedia.* New York: Holt, Rinehart & Winston, 1965.

Major, Harlan. *Salt Water Fishing Tackle.* New York: Funk & Wagnalls, 1939.

Mundus, Frank, and Bill Wisner. *Sportfishing for Sharks.* New York: Macmillan, 1971.

Reiger, George. *Profiles in Saltwater Angling.* Englewood Cliffs, N.J.: Prentice-Hall, 1973.

Samson, Jack. *Line Down!* New York: Winchester Press, 1973.

Sosin, Mark, and John Clark. *Through the Fish's Eye.* New York: Harper & Row, 1974.

Thomas, George C., Jr., and George C. Thomas III. *Gamefish of the Pacific.* Philadelphia: Lippincott, 1930.

Titcomb, Margaret. *Native Use of Fish in Hawaii.* Honolulu: The University Press of Hawaii, 1972.

Walford, Lionel A. *Marine Gamefishes of the Pacific Coast from Alaska to the Equator.* Berkeley: University of California Press, 1937.

Woolner, Frank. *Modern Saltwater Sport Fishing.* New York: Crown Publishers, 1972.

Wylie, Philip. *Denizens of the Deep, True Tales of Deep-Sea Fishing.* New York: Rinehart, 1953.

Yuen, Heeney. "Desired Characteristics of a Bait for Skipjack Tuna." Manuscript, 1974.

# Index

# ⅄ *Production Notes*

The text of this book has been designed by Roger J. Eggers and typeset on the Unified Composing System by the design & production staff of the University Press of Hawaii.

The text typeface is Garamond No. 49 and display matter is set in Garamond Extrabold Italics No. 49.

Offset presswork and binding is the work of The Maple Press Company. Text paper is Glatfelter P & S Hi-Opaque basis 60.